Abortion

Abortion

A Christian Understanding and Response

Edited by
James K. Hoffmeier

BAKER BOOK HOUSE
Grand Rapids, Michigan 49516

Copyright 1987 by
Baker Book House Company

ISBN: 0-8010-4317-4

Printed in the United States of America

Contents

15 After the Abortion   253

Herbert K. Jacobsen

Illustrations

Foreword

Abortion. As with the Holocaust, the word itself evokes feelings of such magnitude and intimacy that it cannot be considered without emotional undertones. Carnage and the disruption of life assault our convictions regarding the very meaning of life.

We need not completely set aside our emotions when we develop our convictions and determine a course of action on a highly charged issue. In fact, Christians could not suppress their feelings on the abortion issue if they tried. But emotion alone is not enough. Responsible thought and action also require reasoned arguments. Those who oppose abortion are unlikely to influence others without intellectually and morally persuasive reasons for their position.

This collection of essays is designed to increase a reader's understanding of the facts, issues, principles, and values that should be part of any discussion regarding abortion. It is no accident that Wheaton College professors have authored the essays. After all, disseminating information is one of the tasks of a college. But academic institutions must do far more than provide information. Along with the family, the media, and the church, they play a major role in conveying or changing the values that shape our decisions and therefore determine the nature of society itself.

The Christian college has an obligation to equip students to reason wisely on moral and social issues. Although a college can and should require conformity to certain regulations and standards within its do-

11

main, it cannot mandate belief and self-motivated action. The college
serves best when it helps students formulate a biblically derived world-
view and assists them in improving their own decision-making ability.
A college undercuts its very reason for existence when it attempts to
settle social issues by proclamation.

Wheaton College is rooted in the premise that the Bible is a reliable
guide to Christian thinking. Even where it does not offer direct commands on an issue, Scripture provides the foundational principles that
can be applied to moral and social issues.

These essays are the independent work and thought of Wheaton College faculty members. Though diverse in methodology and perspective,
they share a common commitment to discovering biblical principles as a
foundation for conviction and action. Furthermore, they clearly oppose
the pro-choice practice that now governs abortion in the United States.

Careful reflective thought is one of the distinguishing attributes of
people created in the image of God. The essays in this book are for
readers who want the benefit of competent Christian thinking on one of
the most pressing moral issues of our time. Such readers will have as
their traveling companions scholars whose underlying premise for all of
life is that God communicates authoritatively and accurately through
the Bible.

J. Richard Chase
President, Wheaton College

Acknowledgments

This book would not have been possible without the support and encouragement of many Wheaton associates. President Chase has encouraged the project from the outset, and to this Dr. Hudson Armerding, President Emeritus, has added his encouragement. The Academic Affairs Office, headed by Drs. Ward Kriegbaum and Patricia Ward, has provided financial support to assist us with publication costs. To these and to the many students and colleagues who have cheered us on, we give our heartfelt thanks.

Introduction

The past decade has witnessed the appearance of a plethora of books addressing the abortion problem. Why should this book be written—and why now?

This book will take its place in the long Wheaton College tradition of involvement in social action that is traceable to its first president, Jonathan Blanchard, an outspoken critic of and activist against slavery. This tradition of social concern continues among our faculty in a wide range of areas. We are avid "pro-lifers," a term we would extend to cover a wide range of "life" issues not restricted to abortion. But abortion is an outrageous social problem that has not gone away and is showing too few signs of doing so. Further, if one has no concern for the life of the unborn, what basis can there be to defend human or civil rights in other areas?

Much of the recent pro-life literature has been written by individuals who have expertise in one area related to the issue but not necessarily in others. Abortion is a complicated matter that touches on biological, psychological, legal, ethical, and theological considerations, to name but a few. Since no one person is qualified to deal with all of these areas, several symposia-type books have tried to tackle the issue from a number of angles. One evangelical attempt at a multi-disciplined effort was the publication of papers from a joint conference of the Christian Medical Association and the Evangelical Theological Society. This book, entitled *Birth Control and the Christian* (eds. W. A. Spitzer and C. Saylor: Tyndale, 1969), touched on the abortion issue, but the emphasis was on birth control, as the title suggests, and the work has been out of print for many years now. More recently, Americans United for Life sponsored the publication of *New Perspectives on Human Abortion* (eds. T. W. Hilgers, D. J. Horan, and D. Mall: University Publications of America, Inc., 1981). This volume, containing thirty-one essays, is quite technical and deals largely with medical concerns, although it also addresses ethical, philosophical, and legal questions. However, it lacks a biblical and theological foundation. Since we believe the interdisciplinary approach used in these two works is essential, we will embrace this model in our book, along with a biblical and theological emphasis.

As evangelicals, we maintain that the Bible is central for establishing our theological and ethical views. This will naturally affect our approach to the abortion issue, regardless of the academic discipline we represent as individuals.

When Supreme Court Justice Blackmun delivered his majority opinion in the now-infamous *Roe* v. *Wade* case of 1973, he said:

> We [the court] need not resolve the difficult question of when life begins.
> When those trained in the respective disciplines of medicine, philosophy,
> and theology are unable to arrive at a consensus, the judiciary, at this
> point in the development of man's knowledge, is not in a position to specu-
> late as to the answer.

It is our hope that our interdisciplinary approach, which will cover the areas mentioned by Justice Blackmun, will help the Christian community come to a consensus. As faculty of a Christian liberal-arts college, we believe that we are well suited to undertake this task.

In our dealings with hundreds of students over the years, we have come to realize that, while students may have already taken a position on the abortion issue, they are not usually certain why. In fact, the idea for this book grew out of questions students were raising in campus publications in 1985. In the foreword to this book, Dr. J. Richard Chase, president of Wheaton College, has rightly observed that those of us who oppose abortion "are unlikely to influence others without intellectually and morally persuasive reasons for their position."

The authors represented here want to help Christians be able to articulate their position with conviction and in a convincing manner, although the statistics presented in chapter 12 suggest that we are failing to do so. We want not only to persuade our own community; we wish to influence our lawmakers and the judiciary as well.

Justice Blackmun's statement quoted above indicates that the Supreme Court has not received a consensus that would compel it to protect fetal life. In fact, the justice in the same ruling said, "If the suggestion of personhood is established, the appellant's case, of course, collapses, for the fetus' right to life is then guaranteed specifically by the Amendment [the 14th]." These statements stand as a challenge to those of us who regard abortion-on-demand (or abortions of "convenience") as a heinous crime against God and man, who is made in his image.

Part One of this book begins with a survey of the legal and medical background to the practice of birth control and abortion from the ancient Near East, the world of the Bible (chapter 1). This not only helps establish the context for our approach, but it demonstrates that long before the early church's view of fetal life was established, most ancient civilizations sought to protect the unborn, even calling for the death penalty for those causing abortions. And these laws came from "pagan" societies!

We then proceed into the Old and New Testaments themselves (chapters 2 through 4), to examine key texts that relate (usually indirectly) to the abortion issue. This lays the necessary biblical foundation for a discussion of general theological concerns (chapter 5). The first five chapters were written by members of Wheaton's Biblical and Theological Studies faculty.

Part Two speaks from an ethical perspective and views abortion in light of the value systems derived from the biblical principles discussed in the first five chapters. In light of the relative silence of the Bible on abortion *per se*, Dr. Arthur Holmes, chairman of Wheaton's philosophy department, shares his thoughts on contemporary questions, including the conflict between various moral responsibilities (chapter 6). He also suggests some avenues for social change that are available to the Christian in a pluralistic society.

At least 95 percent of the abortions that occur in the United States are for reasons of convenience, and we have stated our abhorrence of this. But we also recognize that the remaining 5 percent involve complicated issues that are not so black and white and must nevertheless be dealt with. Dr. David Fletcher, a philosopher and ethicist, teams up with Dr. Albert Smith, a biologist, to address some of the complicated bioethical concerns (chapter 7). They review the views current in the expanding field of bioethics and critique them, offering Christian alternatives. The contributors to this book might not agree with each other on every point in the abortion debate. But we firmly believe that abortions of convenience, which represent the overwhelming majority of cases, cannot be justified and must become illegal. Furthermore, the "exceptional" cases should never be used to justify abortion.

The impact one person can have on his or her community, for good or for ill, can be great. Consider the efforts of Candy Lightner, whose daughter was killed by an intoxicated driver. Lightner founded Mothers Against Drunk Drivers (MADD) to combat the injustice of light sentences being given to drunk drivers, even repeated offenders. Her personal lobbying with Governor Jerry Brown of California led to the formation of a task force to study the problem. MADD grew both in size and influence and has been responsible for the stiffening of penalties in many states and the federal law that would cut off federal highway grants to states that do not raise their drinking age to twenty-one.

If one person, such as Candy Lightner, can so influence the nation, how much more can the Christian? And since there is strength in numbers, the Christian community should be able to wield even more influence! This raises the question of how churches respond to current issues. Theologian Dr. Morris Inch approaches this problem from historical, theoretical and practical angles, focusing largely on how a church (or *the* church) comes to a consensus (chapter 8).

We believe that abortions of convenience are biblically and theologically unjustifiable. But we live in a society where it is both a legal and a generally accepted practice. What can we do to change this? We need first to be aware of the forces within our society that shape its values. Dr. James Lower, Professor of Education, points out that our society's views of man are largely shaped within the schools (chapter 9). This realization urges us to be involved in education; as teachers and parents of students, we can help shape values towards a Christian world-view.

The third section of the book deals with some practical concerns that emerge when abortion is considered. Anti-abortion laws existed in many states as early as the end of the nineteenth century, their concern being chiefly for the safety of the mother. But medical advances of the last half-century led the pro-abortion lobby to argue that the danger to the mother was now no greater than the dangers surrounding childbirth. This position was argued by appellants in the *Roe* v. *Wade* decision, and Justice Blackmun concurred. However, more recent studies have shown numerous dangers for the woman having an abortion, and this issue, as well as other biological concerns, are treated by Dr. Dorothy Chappell (chapter 10).

Similarly, it has been argued, as reflected in Justice Blackmun's decision, that the psychological harm a mother might suffer as a result of having an unwanted child and/or the social stigma of having a child out of wedlock constituted grounds for having an abortion. Quite a few of the theologically liberal Protestant denominations have, unfortunately, cited the mental well-being of the mother as justification for aborting (cf. Nelson, in *New Perspectives on Human Abortion*, 394ff.). But the voices of many women who have had abortions now proclaim the fearful psychological consequences of abortion, despite assurances to the contrary. Women Exploited by Abortion (WEBA), with more than 30,000 members, is now working to inform women who are contemplating abortion about the physical and psychological side effects of abortion. A number of surveys and psychological studies of women who have had abortions often give the impression that there are few, if any, negative psychological effects on a woman after an abortion. But scrutiny of these studies (the focus of chapter 11) reveals that they are often methodologically flawed and even manipulated so as to attain the desired results! Psychologist Dr. James Rogers shows that the best scientifically controlled studies suggest, as we might expect, that women do suffer psychological ill effects.

For many, the solution to the abortion problem is a legal and/or political one. Dr. Lyman Kellstedt, a political scientist, outlines the options before us, showing where and under what conditions we are most likely to realize a change in current abortion laws (chapter 12). But we caution that while legislative change may eliminate many (if not most) abortions—a very good thing—it is not enough. We also need to reshape the values of our society. We need a bipartite strategy. The efforts of the pro-life lobby to change present law is imperative, and we applaud the efforts of the Christian Action Council, National Association of Evangelicals, and other political-action committees who are lobbying to change the laws. Individually we can support such groups, and some of the contributors to this book are active in these efforts. Local churches can work with them, too. Candy Lightner and MADD have demonstrated the effectiveness of such a strategy, pushing for and obtaining legislative change, while educating and molding the nation's conscience. She puts it this way:

> We are changing the way people think about drinking and driving. But more than that, we have caused people to change their behavior, and that is saving lives. I believe in the rights of victims. And I do feel that if you believe in something badly enough, you can make a difference [*Time,* January 7, 1985, p. 41].

We believe this dual approach is necessary because of the possibility of failure in the political and/or legislative process. We cannot put all our hopes in a single tactic.

Sociologist Dr. Ivan Fahs appeals to the church to work towards the Christianizing of our society's values, addressing, for example, the social complexities that lead to teenage pregnancies, which represent a third of the abortions performed each year (chapter 13). We would further urge local churches to be involved in aiding single mothers in rearing the children they decide to have. We may be encouraged that this is beginning to happen, but much more support is needed. The Roman Catholic Church has long advocated the adoption option for women faced with unwanted pregnancies. As one practical step, churches can certainly assist families within its membership who are willing to adopt but are financially pinched. Many lives could be saved if churches were willing to make small financial sacrifices.

One area where significant work is being done to deal with the problem of unwanted pregnancies is crisis-pregnancy counseling. Dr. Jeffrey Greenberg and his wife, Diane, have done considerable work in such counseling and draw on their expertise and vast experience to inform the Christian community about this strategic ministry (chapter 14). Their adoption of four children, two of whom are handicapped by disorders that many regard as grounds for aborting a fetus, is a glowing testimony to how their involvement has led to the preservation of life in very practical ways.

Finally, we recognize that women who have had abortions rightfully come to the church for help and counsel. How should the church respond? What counsel do we offer? Dr. Herbert Jacobsen, professor of theology and a respected counselor, offers some guidance that is biblically and theologically based (chapter 15).

The second question asked at the outset of this introduction was, "Why now?" The pro-life and pro-abortion forces have been locked in mortal combat for many years now, yet there has been no change in current law. We have obviously failed to convince many Christians of the severity of the problem, and we have not succeeded in significantly reducing the number of abortions. We therefore maintain that the Christian community needs to take a clear biblical and theological position. We need to adopt the suggested bipartite strategy of change through the political process as well as moral persuasion through the many available avenues—church, education, and media. It has been said that the Vietnam War was not lost on the rice fields and jungles of southeast Asia, but in the minds and consciences of Americans through the power of the media. Ultimately, the struggle we support will only be won as we work together with other like-minded people (including the Catholic and Jewish communities, and so on) to mold a new national perspective on human life.

Dr. C. Everett Koop, now the Surgeon General, addressed the 1973 graduating class at Wheaton. Earlier that year, the Supreme Court had handed down its decision in the *Roe* v. *Wade* case. Dr. Koop was gravely concerned about the abortion problem and the negative impact it would have on our nation. He made ten predictions that he believed would be a consequence of this decision. As a member of that graduating class, I shook my head in disbelief at his estimate that there would be more than a million abortions a year. But he was right. He also urged us "not to be apathetic but committed and to have a valid basis for what you believe." We take this challenge seriously. I join with my colleagues who have contributed to this book in urging the reader not to be apathetic. We hope that this offering will go a long way toward helping to develop "a valid basis for what you believe."

Abbreviations

ANET	*Ancient Near Eastern Texts Relating to the Old Testament*
BDB	Brown, Driver, and Briggs, *A Hebrew-English Lexicon*
CAD	*Chicago Assyrian Dictionary of the Oriental Institute of the University of Chicago*
CH	Codex Hammurapi
ISBE	*International Standard Bible Encyclopedia*
MAL	Middle Assyrian Laws
TDNT	*Theological Dictionary of the New Testament*
TDOT	*Theological Dictionary of the Old Testament*

Contributors

C. *Hassell Bullock,* professor of Old Testament and Hebrew at Wheaton College, is the author of *An Introduction to the Old Testament Poetic Books* and *An Introduction to the Old Testament Prophetic Books.* He received his Ph.D. degree from Hebrew Union College and has served at Wheaton since 1973.

Dorothy F. Chappell is associate professor of biology and chair of the biology department at Wheaton College. Her Ph.D. degree is from Miami University (Ohio). She has been active with campus and area pro-life groups since coming to Wheaton in 1977.

Ivan J. Fahs chairs Wheaton's sociology department and specializes in medical sociology. He holds a Ph.D. degree from Cornell University and is the author of numerous articles in such periodicals as the *American Journal of Public Health, Journal of Medical Education,* and *Public Health Reports.* Before coming to Wheaton in 1981, he taught at Harvard Medical School.

David B. Fletcher has team-taught bioethics at Wheaton for several years with Albert J. Smith. Fletcher, a philosopher and ethicist, received his Ph.D. degree from the University of Illinois. He has had articles in the *Evangelical Dictionary of Theology* and in the journals *Faith and Philosophy* and *Christian Scholar's Review.* Fletcher is the author of *Social and Political Perspectives in the Thought of Soren Kierkegaard.* An associate professor, he has taught at Wheaton since 1981.

Victor R. Gordon is the chaplain and assistant professor of New Testament at Wheaton College. His Ph.D. degree is from Fuller Theological Seminary. He has contributed to the revised edition of the *International Standard Bible Encyclopedia* and to the journal *Theology: News and Notes.* He regularly reviews books for *Eternity.*

Diane S. Greenberg has a B.Sc. degree in medical technology and has worked in cancer and immunology research. She has also worked in a family-practice clinic and directed a crisis-pregnancy center. She is married to Jeffrey K. Greenberg, who was vice-president of the board of directors of this center.

Jeffrey K. Greenberg, who joined the faculty of Wheaton College in 1986 as associate professor of geology, has a Ph.D. degree from the University of North Carolina. He was previously associate professor of geology at the University of Wisconsin, Madison. He has chaired a coalition of pro-life organizations in Madison and worked with his wife, Diane, in crisis-pregnancy counseling.

Andrew E. Hill received his Ph.D. degree from the University of Michigan. At Wheaton College he is an assistant professor of Old Testament studies and teaches courses on Mesopotamia and Old Testament ethics. He is the author of *Handbook of Bible Lists* and has had articles in *Journal of Biblical Literature* and *Vetus Testamentum.*

James K. Hoffmeier is associate professor of archaeology and Old Testament studies at Wheaton College. He received his Ph.D. degree from the University of Toronto and has been at Wheaton since 1980. He is the editor of *Egyptological Miscellanies* and *Scripta Mediterranea* (vols. 1–4). He has contributed to the revised *International Standard Bible Encyclopedia, Major Cities of the Biblical World,* and the forthcoming *Evangelical Bible Commentary.* His articles have appeared in *Biblica, Journal of the American Research Center in Egypt,* and *Journal of the Ancient Near East.* His book *"Sacred" in the Vocabulary of Ancient Egypt* was published in the monograph series *Orbis biblicus et orientalis.*

Arthur F. Holmes chairs the philosophy department at Wheaton College, where he has taught since 1951. He has authored many books, including *All Truth Is God's Truth, Contours of a World View,* and *Ethics: Approaching Moral Decisions.*

Morris A. Inch served for more than twenty years as chairman of the biblical, theological, and archaeological studies department at Wheaton College. In 1986 he became director of the Institute for Holy Land Studies in Jerusalem. He is a well-known author, some of whose recent works are *The Evangelical Challenge, Doing Theology Across Cultures,* and *Saga of the Spirit.* He received his Ph.D. degree from Boston University.

Herbert K. Jacobsen has been at Wheaton College since 1967 and is professor of theology. He has contributed to the *Baker Dictionary of*

Christian Ethics and is completing a textbook on systematic theology. His Ph.D. degree is from New York University.

Lyman A. Kellstedt came to Wheaton College in 1979, after teaching for many years at the University of Illinois, Chicago. He is now professor of political science and has written many articles and reviews in scholarly journals, including *Public Opinion Quarterly, Public Administration Review,* and the *Journal of the American Political Science Association.* He regularly presents papers at the national meetings of the societies that publish these periodicals. His Ph.D. degree is from the University of Illinois, Urbana.

Donald M. Lake received his Ph.D. degree from the University of Iowa. He is associate professor of theology and has taught at Wheaton since 1970. He has contributed articles and reviews to the *Journal of the Evangelical Theological Society, Journal of Religion, Zondervan Pictorial Encyclopedia of the Bible,* and the *New International Dictionary of the Christian Church.*

James M. Lower was professor of education at Wheaton College from 1965 to 1986 and is now professor emeritus. Having received his Ed.D. degree from Northern Illinois University, he specializes in educational psychology. Based on his more than twenty years of work with student teachers and public-school teachers at every level, his insights into the educational system and its impact on students are widely accepted as authoritative.

James L. Rogers is associate professor of psychology at Wheaton College. He came to Wheaton in 1976, after receiving his Ph.D. degree from Northwestern University. For several years he has studied psychological research on women who have had abortions. The chapter presented in this book represents a portion of a more technical study that he presented to the American Psychological Association and the American Public Health Association.

Albert J. Smith has a degree in theology from Northern Baptist Theological Seminary and a Ph.D. degree in biology from the University of Chicago. He is professor of biology at Wheaton, where he has taught since 1967. He contributes regularly to the *Yearbook of Science and the Future (Encyclopedia Britannica)* and to *Ecology.* He also wrote for the *Evangelical Dictionary of Theology.*

PART ONE

Historical, Biblical, and Theological Foundations

by ancient Near East societies. Included among these other methods were sterilization, continence, contraception, coitus withdrawal, alternative intercourse, and infanticide. In our overview of the historical background of the Old Testament, it is important to keep in mind that there was no standardization of birth-control practices in the ancient Near East. Rather, the several forms cited above were implemented by specific population groups within localized geographical settings and during a wide range of time periods. Further, while these multiple forms of reproduction control may have been known to the ancients, it is likely that most societies employed only one or two predominant methods of birth control at any certain time, given the characteristic socioeconomic and religious dynamics of a community.

As a prelude to the discussion of miscarriage and abortion, an overview of birth-control methods utilized in the ancient Near East is in order. This survey, while by no means an exhaustive study, is designed to acquaint the reader with the range of birth-control options available in the ancient world. The biblical response (if any) to these modes of birth control is included in the documentation. The profound biblical silence on the specific question of abortion becomes meaningful only when we take into consideration the general pattern of biblical response to the broader issue of reproduction control in the ancient Near East.

Sterilization. While artificial sterilization is usually included in any listing of birth-control measures in the ancient Near East, the actual implementation of medical procedures for the express purpose of preventing impregnation remains uncertain. Driver and Miles (1939, 67) claim that artificial sterilization of the female was beyond the scope of ancient surgery (cf. Saggs 1962, 330). Sterilization of the male could be accomplished surgically by amputating the penis or by crushing and/or removal of the testicles. Though castrated males, or eunuchs, are traceable to Near East antiquity as early as the second millennium B.C., exactly where and why human castration began is still obscure. However, as Cerling (1971, 50, n. 43) cogently recognizes, "there is a great deal of difference between castration and sterilization." The Middle Assyrian Laws (*ANET* 1969, 181, #s 15, 18, 19, 20; cf. 2 Kings 20:18) included castration as a punishment for adultery and homosexuality. However, what is known about the role of the eunuch in that cultural setting implies that the purpose of castration was other than a birth-control measure. The eunuch served as a bodyguard to the king, a palace official and courtier, statesman, and military general (cf. Borger 1963, *Lesestücke* I, lxxvi). The Greek historian Xenophon (*Cyropaedia* vii.5.60–65) reported that Cyrus the Great believed emasculation yielded more docile and easily controllable slaves who would be characterized by singlehearted loyalty since they were undistracted by family concerns.

Certainly the domestic use of eunuchs as attendants to the royal harem ensured fidelity, and in that sense could be understood as a preventive measure against possible impregnation if not sexual violation of the women in the harem (cf. Esther 2:3, 14, 15, etc.). While it is known that male attendants, including male prostitutes, were employed in the temple cultus in the ancient Near East, it is unclear as to whether these male attendants were also eunuchs. (According to the *Chicago Assyrian Dictionary,* there is little evidence that the *assinnu* [*CAD* 1968, 1/II: 341] or the *kurgarru* [*CAD* 1971, 8:558–559] were eunuchs or homosexuals. Likewise, the castration of male prostitutes is unlikely, given the accompanying sexual dysfunction within two years.)

The only mutilation that excommunicated an Israelite male from participation in the covenant community was castration, whether congenital, accidental, or self-willed: "He whose testicles are crushed or whose male member is cut off shall not enter the assembly of the LORD" (Deut. 23:1). The rationale for this exclusion is presumably multifaceted, and despite the modification of this statute later (Isa. 56:3–5; cf. Matt. 19:12), human castration for the purposes of sterilization and/or criminal punishment was not a custom appropriated by ancient Hebrew culture (cf. Burke 1982, *ISBE Revised* II:200–202).

Continence. An old Sumerian proverb states that "conceiving is nice, being pregnant is irksome" (Saggs 1962, 407). It would seem that continence might have been a logical solution to this dilemma, at least for the woman in the ancient Near East. Waltke (1969, 15) presumptuously argues this was indeed the case, on the basis of another Sumerian proverb that mentions a proud husband's boast that his wife had borne him eight sons and was still ready to lie down and accept his nuptial embrace (cf. Saggs 1962, 187). The inference here is that evidently some women would not respond so felicitously. Although it must be admitted that sexual abstinence has always remained an alternative to pregnancy, normal human behavior militates against any consistent and widespread popular support of this method of birth control. This seems especially true of the ancient Near East, where common and ritual prostitution, polygamy, and concubinage prevailed, making the ideal of sexual restraint much more the exception than the rule.

The Old Testament prohibits intercourse for females during their time of ceremonial uncleanness occasioned by menstruation (Lev. 15:19–28; 18:19; 20:18) and childbirth (Lev. 12:1–8). The Hebrew male might abstain from intercourse for religious (Exod. 19:15; 1 Sam. 21:4–5) or military reasons (2 Sam. 11:8–11). Elsewhere the Mosaic Code mandates that a man who takes another woman (as a wife) may not reduce her food, clothing, or conjugal rights (Exod. 21:10). Other factors usually cited as an indication that continence had little place in Hebrew marriage include the lack of any Old Testament sanction of celibacy (even among the Nazarites; cf. Num. 6:1–21), the premium placed on rearing children (Ps. 127:3–5; 128:3–4), and the exhortation to find sexual satisfaction in the wife of one's youth (e.g., Prov. 5:15–23). The New Testament also confirms this basic rejection of continence in normal marital relationships (cf. 1 Cor. 7:1–5; Heb. 13:4).

Mechanical Contraception. This method of birth control was known to and practiced by the ancients, particularly the Egyptians (cf. von Deines et al. 1958, 277–278). These devices included exotic potions applied as an anti-spermicidal douche (e.g., a willow-bark potion mixed with the burned testicles of a castrated ass) and simple instruments similar to present-day shields and sponges (e.g., a swab of wool coated with honey and inserted into the vagina [cf. Bardis 1967, 305–307; Noonan 1965, 9–10; and related articles in Kamal 1967]).

Although the Old Testament is completely silent on the utilization of these forms of contraception, ancient Israel was certainly aware of the existence of such contrivances, given four centuries of life in Egypt. One might therefore assume that either contraception of this type was never an issue with Israel because of their high regard for children (cf. Gen. 1:28; Ps. 127:3–5; 128:3–4; Prov. 18:6; etc.) or that the practice was accepted as normal and not considered worth mentioning. As with the issue of abortion, biblical silence has prompted differences of opinion on interpretation of passages relating to birth control (e.g., Gen. 38:1–11) and open controversy in respect to the use of mechanical contraceptive devices within the larger contemporary Christian community. The purpose here is simply to note patterns of biblical response to abortion-related topics. Anyone interested in a more complete discussion of the subject should read Cerling (1971); Noonan (1965); Waltke (1969, 1976), and follow up the bibliographies cited therein.

Coitus Withdrawal. It is generally assumed that *coitus interruptus,* or withdrawal, was the most commonly employed method of averting conception in the ancient Near East. Evidence for this supposition stems largely from logic, as written documentation is sadly wanting. The strongest support for the argument comes from Astour's (1966, 189) understanding of the etmyology of *nadītu* and *kulmašītu,* classes of Babylonian temple prostitutes. According to his study of the germane literature, these women were sexually active but were "pure of semen." Astour concludes that the phrase *kulmašītu ša qerebša ma'd[a]* should be translated "a *kulmašītu* whose womb is many" (i.e., who has intercourse with many men [p. 190, n. 32]). He then deduces that this expression points to a more normal way of intercourse (in contrast to the anal intercourse practiced by the *ēntu,* the *ugbabtu* priestesses [p. 187]) and hints of *coitus interruptus.*

The Old Testament provides one clear example of withdrawal with contraceptive intentions in the story of Onan (Gen. 38:8–10). The text reads,

> Then Judah said to Onan, "Go in to your brother's wife, and perform the duty of a brother-in-law to her, and raise up offspring for your brother." But Onan knew that the offspring would not be his; so when he went in to his brother's wife he spilled the semen on the ground, lest he should give offspring to his brother. And what he did was displeasing in the sight of the LORD, and he slew him also.

Though not a specific issue for this study, it should be noted that biblical context explicitly indicates that Onan's sin lay in his selfish denial to perform his levirate duty (Deut. 25:5–6), not in his practice of withdrawal (cf. Lev. 15:18). If *coitus interruptus* is meant in Leviticus 15:18, then the verse further substantiates the biblical acceptability of ejaculation without procreative intent. However, Cerling (1971, 148) correctly reminds us that *škb* can mean either "sleep" or "intercourse," so the verse may refer to nocturnal emissions (as in 15:15–17) or even semen that either runs from the vagina after intercourse or does not fully enter the vagina during intercourse (cf. Harrison 1980, 163). Later Jewish tradition also approved of withdrawal to avoid pregnancy, instructing that "a man must thresh inside and winnow outside" during the two-year period in which a child is nursed (*Talmud Yebamot*, 34b).

Alternative Intercourse. The proverbs and omen literature of Sumerian Mesopotamia provide enough details of lovemaking to reveal that both normal sexual behavior and the typical perversions were familiar to these ancient societies. The list of aberrations compiled by Saggs (1962, 187) includes such sexual maladjustments known to modern civilization as sodomy, lesbianism, prostitution, transvestism, cunnilinctus, and even bestiality. Alternative intercourse was especially important to the cult prostitutes of Sumerian and Babylonian religion. The *ēntu* priestesses were prostitutes consecrated to the service of the deities and as such were not allowed to bear children (Astour 1966, 188). One text indicates that these priestesses were sexually active but in a way unnatural for women. The *Chicago Assyrian Dictionary* translates, "the high priestess will permit intercourse per anum in order to avoid pregnancy" (*CAD* 1958, 4:325). Bestiality was also part of Mesopotamian culture (cf. Saggs 1962, 193, 309; *ANET*, 73–99, where Enkidu has intercourse with a wild beast), although it was regarded a crime in Anatolia by the Hittites except with a horse or mule (*ANET*, 34–35, #s 187–188, 199, 200). According to van Selms (1954, 82), there is

. . . no reason to doubt that bestiality occurred in Ugarit, as it occurs up to
the present day everywhere in the world. We do have reason to assume that
this abomination was not condemned by law as custom among the Uga-
ritians, as it was among the Hittites and in a far stricter way, in biblical
literature.

In addition to polygamy and concubinage, both sacral and secular prostitution remained engrained in the ancient culture of the Near East,
despite the fact that adultery was already punishable in the law codes of
Eshnunna (ca. 1900 B.C.) and Hammurapi (e.g., *ANET,* 162, #28 and
171, #129) and later in Middle Assyrian Laws (*ANET,* 181, #s 12–16; cf.
Hauck & Schulz 1968, *TDNT* VI:579–595).

This discussion of alternative intercourse assumes heterosexual relationships, since homosexuality was generally considered a criminal act
in Near East antiquity (cf. *ANET,* 34–35, A20, B27; 181, #s 19–20) and
expressly prohibited in the biblical legislation (Lev. 18:22; 20:13; cf.
Harrison 1980, 191–205). Likewise, the Old Testament includes bestiality in the catalog of sexual taboos for the Israelites (Lev. 18:23) and
deems it a capital offense (Exod. 22:19; cf. Harrison 1980, 193–195).
Whether a response to Canaanite fertility cult customs (Selvidge 1984,
621; cf. Ezek. 18:6; 22:10, where the admonition against menstrual sex
occurs in the context of sins associated with the pagan high places [see
also Zimmerli 1979, I:380] or to increase fertility [since abstinence
during menses means the couple will rejoin when the wife is most likely
to conceive—the exact opposite of the rhythm system of birth control—so
Wouk 1959, 156]) or simply to ensure the sexual integrity of the female
(cf. Harrison 1980, 163–164), the Old Testament restricts intercourse
for Israelite women during their ritual uncleanness due to menstruation and childbirth (Lev. 12:1–8; 15:19–28; 18:19; 20:18). Concerning
sacral and secular prostitution, Old Testament law shows a predilection
to restrict or eliminate the practice among the Israelites. For example, a
priest may not marry a common harlot (Lev. 21:7); a priest's daughter
who became a harlot was to be burned (Lev. 21:9); Israelites in general
were commanded not to allow their daughters to become harlots (Lev.
19:29); a woman found guilty of harlotry was to be stoned (Deut. 22:21);
and cult prostitutes (both male and female) were banned from Israelite
society (Deut. 23:17; cf. 1 Kings 15:12; 22:46; Jer. 3:2; Ezek. 8:14; Hos.
4:12–13). Finally, the Old Testament (and the New) is largely silent on
intercourse variations between consenting married couples (i.e., oral
and anal sex), although certain biblical principles are still to guide the
Christian's behavior (cf. Harrison 1980, 250–252; Smedes 1976,
76–106, 225–250).

Infanticide. Alberto Green's (1975, 201) thorough research indicates that human sacrifice for political and religious purposes, including ritual infanticide, continued intermittently in Mesopotamia, Egypt, and Syro-Palestine from the Early Bronze Age well into the Iron Age. This practice included foundation sacrifices of children for the protection of buildings and their occupants, expiatory sacrifices to various gods in times of national emergency, and other propitiatory, dedicatory, and expiatory rites on special occasions. In addition, exposure as a form of infanticide was apparently known to Mesopotamia, although evidence demonstrating the extent of the practice is meager (cf. Astour 1966, 193: n. 49, n. 50).

The Old Testament forbade the Hebrews from participating in rites of child sacrifice because it profaned the name of God (Lev. 18:21; although Ezek. 16:5 seems to indicate the Hebrews were aware of the exposure of infants, cf. Greensberg 1983, 275). Those found guilty of the crime were to be stoned, as it was a capital offense (Lev. 20:2–5). The biblical injunction is mentioned specifically in connection with the pagan custom of child sacrifice to the Ammonite god Molech (cf. Albright [1968, 152], who says that human sacrifice lasted much longer among the Canaanites, with the same holding true for sexual abuses in the services of religion). Despite the warnings against such Canaanite indulgences (Deut. 12:31; 18:10), Israel and Judah fell prey to this abomination on more than one occasion (cf. Judg. 11:29–40; 1 Kings 11:7; 2 Kings 16:3; 17:31; 21:6; Jer. 2:23; 3:24; 7:31; 19:5; 32:35; Ezek. 16:21; 20:31; 23:37).

Abortion. Abortifacient potions or herbal recipes of one sort or another for inducing miscarriages or expelling the afterbirth were known to Mesopotamia (cf. *CAD* 1980, 11/I:79) and Egypt (cf. Bryan 1974, 82–87; Noonan 1965, 9–10) as early as the second millennium B.C. These drugs continued to be part of ancient Near Eastern medical lore and legal tradition well into the Persian period (cf. Müller 1895, IV:179). Generally speaking, the application or ingestion of these abortifacient recipes and potions was the most common way to procure an abortion in the ancient world. This is not to deny the possibility that various "surgical" techniques were also employed to accomplish the abortion of the human fetus. Rudimentary developments in obstetrical surgery are attested as early as 1900 B.C., according to the publication of a cuneiform tablet by L. Oppenheim (1960), describing a caesarean section. While acknowledging that this kind of operation may have been in use in very early times, "at the stage of the development of obstetrics that one is allowed to presume for Mesopotamia in the second millennium B.C., forceps could have been used only at the cost of the child's life to save the mother, and the caesarean section to save the child" (Oppenheim 1960, 293). The question remains, however, as to what extent abortifacient drugs were prescribed by ancient medical practitioners and utilized by the public at large. At the present time, extant documentation would suggest that drug-induced abortion in Egypt and Mesopotamia was the exceptional rather than the routine experience in the ancient Near East.

Much to the consternation of biblical exegetes, the Old Testament—and the New Testament, for that matter—provides precious little material speaking directly to the subject of abortion (although some contend that the practice was known and perhaps resorted to by the Hebrews on the basis of Jer. 20:17–18 and Job 3:11–19; cf. Lundbom [1985, 596], who states that abortion of any sort at any time during the ancient Israelite period is highly questionable). The frequently cited biblical principles that implicitly argue against abortion as a normative element of Hebrew culture are framed in the chapters following this essay.

Miscarriage and Abortion
in Ancient Near Eastern Legal Texts

Our difficulties in understanding the ancient Near Eastern legal materials pertinent to the issue of miscarriage and abortion are compounded by questions related to the exact nature and purpose of those laws, their application to the various social strata of an individual society, and the dearth of legal codices from Egypt and Syro-Palestine (see "The Middle Assyrian Laws" below).

Recent scholarly opinion understands the ancient law codes to be related to a particular type of literature, namely scientific treatises (Westbrook 1985, 252). By analogy to the omen series, compiled by the diviners for the practical purpose of serving as reference works to determine the meaning of future events, the law codes were probably lists of judicial decisions compiled for similar reasons. In other words, they were a catalog of legal precedents to aid the king and/or judges of the royal courts when hearing difficult cases (Westbrook 1985, 254). The addition of prologues and epilogues to the central legal corpus gave rise to another literary genre, the royal *apologia* (e.g., Codex Ur-Nammu, Codex Lipit-Ishtar, and Codex Hammurapi). The primary purpose of the royal *apologia* was to exhibit, before the public, posterity, future kings, and the gods, evidence of the king's execution of his divine mandate: to have been a Faithful Shepherd and the *šar mīšarim,* or King of Justice (Westbrook 1985, 249). Though not law codes in the prescriptive or comprehensive sense, these laws were apparently representative of current legal philosophy and reflected normative legal tradition in the societies from which they originated (cf. Westbrook 1985, 258–264). The designation "law code" is retained here for convenience.

The specific application of ancient Near Eastern law to the citizens of the respective societies is a second major barrier to attempts to contextualize principles gleaned from these legal documents treating miscarriage/abortion and apply them in the contemporary abortion debate. Complicating factors include the developmental nature of *lex talionis* or the notion of "an eye for an eye" in ancient law (cf. Frymer-Kensky 1980, 231–232) and the inconsistent application of that concept because of the class structure of the society (e.g., *ANET*, 166, #39, #44). An illustration of this occurs in Codex Ur-Nammu, where the penalty for one accused of sorcery is the river ordeal, while the accuser is only fined if the charge proves false (*ANET*, 524, #10). On the other hand, in Codex Hammurapi the accused is subject to the river ordeal and so, too, the accuser, if the charge proves false (*ANET*, 166, #3). Likewise, what is determined a crime against one class of the citizenry may be judged merely a tort if committed against a lesser class of that society's constituency (e.g., assault against an *awīlum* versus assault against a *miškēnum* [*ANET*, 166, #8]; the same is true in biblical legislation with respect to slaves [cf. Exod. 21:18–20]). Any observations made or conclusions drawn about the practice of abortion and the value of human (and fetal) life from ancient legal materials of the Near East—and applications to Old Testament law and teaching and the current abortion debate—must be tempered by these considerations.

A digest of the Mesopotamian legal materials treating the topics of miscarriage and abortion are included below for the sake of completeness and clarity in understanding and evaluating the conclusion that follows.

The Sumerian Laws (YBC [Yale Babylonian Collection] 2177) are probably student exercises included on a practice tablet from one of the scribal schools of Sumer during the Old Babylonian period (ca. 1800 B.C.) and not a "law code" of some unknown pre-Hammurapi ruler. The so-called Sumerian Laws make no mention of abortion but do contain two laws pertaining to miscarriage (*ANET*, 525):

1. If (a man accidentally) buffeted a woman of the free-citizen class and caused her to have a miscarriage, he must pay 10 shekels of silver.
2. If (a man deliberately) struck a woman of the free-citizen class and caused her to have a miscarriage, he must pay one-third mina of silver.

Here the victim is singled out as a member of the free-citizen class, and the loss of the fetus is compensated by the payment of a fine. According to the interpretation of the translator, the fine is to be doubled if the blow to the woman was determined to be deliberate. However, the utilitarian value of these and related miscarriage laws is questionable since, medically speaking, a blow precipitating miscarriage in a pregnant woman is unlikely.

The Codex Hammurapi (CH) was promulgated during the second year of this king's long reign (ca. 1728–1686 B.C.), although information contained in the code's prologue and epilogue about certain military victories indicates that the laws took their final form late in his reign. It is the most complete of the ancient legal texts. According to the prologue, Hammurapi was commissioned by Shamash, the god of justice, "to guide the people aright, to direct the land, and establish law and justice in the language of the land, thereby promoting the welfare of the people" (*ANET*, 165).

The CH contains a section of six laws addressing miscarriage, but none directly related to the performing of abortions. The laws read as follows (*ANET*, 175):

209. If a seignior struck a(nother) seignior's daughter and caused her to have a miscarriage, he shall pay ten shekels of silver for her fetus.
210. If that woman has died they shall put his daughter to death.
211. If by a blow he has caused a commoner's daughter to have a miscarriage, he shall pay five shekels of silver.
212. If that woman has died, he shall pay one-half mina of silver.
213. If he struck a seignior's female slave and has caused her to have a miscarriage, he shall pay two shekels of silver.
214. If that female slave has died, he shall pay one-third mina of silver.

Unlike the Sumerian Laws, the CH prescribes the penalties incurred for inflicting damage (whether intentional or unintentional) sufficient to cause a miscarriage in three specific classes of females: upper class, middle class, and slave. In each case the penalty levied in compensation for the fetus is a fine, ranging from two to ten shekels and depending upon the social status of the female. Should the pregnant female die from her injuries, *lex talionis* applies only in the case of the upper-class female.

The Middle Assyrian Laws (MAL) date to the time of Tiglath-pileser I (ca. 1115–1077 B.C.) but are thought to reflect the ideology of Assyrian legal tradition as far back as the fifteenth century B.C. There are four MAL that discuss miscarriage caused by an injury and one that deals with self-inflicted abortion. The miscarriage laws are outlined first (*ANET*, 181, 184–185):

21. If a seignior struck a(nother) seignior's daughter and has caused her to have a miscarriage, when they have prosecuted him (and) convicted him, he shall pay two talents thirty minas of lead; they shall flog him fifty (times) with staves (and) he shall do the work of the king for one full month.

50. [If a seignior] struck a(nother) seignior's [wife] and caused her to have [a miscarriage], they shall treat [the wife of the seignior], who caused the (other) seignior's wife to have a miscarriage, as he treated her; he shall compensate for her fetus with a life. However, if that woman died, they shall put the seignior to death; he shall compensate for her fetus with a life. But, when that woman's husband has no son, if someone struck her so that she had a miscarriage, they shall put the striker to death; even if the fetus is a girl, he shall compensate with a life.

51. If a seignior struck a(nother) seignior's wife who does not rear her children and caused her to have a miscarriage, this punishment (shall hold): he shall pay two talents of lead.

52. If a seignior struck a harlot and caused her to have a miscarriage, they shall inflict blow for blow upon him; he shall compensate with a life.

While no strict class distinctions are drawn in the MAL, differentiation is made between a daughter, a wife, and a harlot who miscarry due to injury. Here the MAL differ from the CH, in that in the case of the wife (#50) and the harlot (#52) the fetus is considered a life, and *lex talionis* demands compensation with a life. A daughter who miscarries as a result of an assault (#21) has a lesser standing before the law, in that the loss of her fetus is recompensed by a fine and the guilty party incurs an additional penalty of a flogging and one month's forced labor. The law concerning the wife who does not rear her children (#51) proves more difficult, since it appears inconsistent with the application of talion to the fetus of an independent adult woman (#50 and #52). According to Driver and Miles (1935, 114–115), the negative description of a mother who fails to raise her children when born *(la murabita)* most probably implies some physical disability preventing the woman from carrying out her familial responsibilities. Hence her special status under this law, as seen in the reduction of the penalty for assault leading to miscarriage: a fine only.

MAL #53 is one of the few ancient Near Eastern laws dealing exclusively with abortion, specifically self-inflicted abortion (cf. *CAD* 1962, 16, 71, 1d). The law reads (*ANET,* 185):

53. If a woman has had a miscarriage by her own act, when they have prosecuted her (and) convicted her, they shall impale her on

stakes without burying her. If she died in having the miscarriage, they shall impale her on stakes without burying her. If someone hid that woman when she had the miscarriage [without] informing [the king]. . . .

The term used for "woman" in this text is a general one and suggests "any woman," not necessarily a wife. The Akkadian verb ṣalā'u in this context means literally "to drop an unborn child" and the *CAD* translates "if a woman aborts through her own doing." It also appears that anyone who would seek to cover up an abortion of this type is an accomplice to a criminal act, although the penalty prescribed remains unknown, as the tablet is damaged and the text breaks off at this point. Although the application of talion is consistent with that in laws #50 and #52—a life for a life—scholars have questioned the logic of such a harsh punishment for self-inflicted abortion, since Assyrian society tolerated the death of a child by exposure. Driver and Miles (1935, 166–117) make this observation:

> The explanation of this apparent inconsistency then may be that the law is passed not to protect infants whether legitimate or illegitimate, but to prevent an offence against religion. Indeed, from the savagery of the punishment, namely impalement, and from the refusal of burial it seems certain that the act is regarded as a most heinous and presumably sacrilegious offence. . . . The woman is to be impaled alive if she survives the abortion, or her dead body is to be so treated if she dies in consequence of it; and in either case her body is to be left unburied. Since impalement is prescribed in the Babylonian code only for the most heinous crime that can be committed by a wife against a husband, namely to procure his death on account of a paramour, it may be inferred that in the Assyrian law it is prescribed for the worst offence that a mother can commit, namely to procure the death of the unborn child in her womb. The reason may be here, as in the case of suicide, that the woman by her offence has caused the sacred blood of the family to flow and has thereby called down the wrath of heaven not only on herself but also on the whole community.

The Neo-Babylonian Laws are fragmentary and contain no reference to miscarriage or abortion.

Persian Law, as reflected in the Old Persian *Zend-Avesta* (or *Vendidad*), does make reference to miscarriage, abortion, and even prenatal neglect. The *Zend-Avesta* dates to about the sixth or fifth century B.C. and is the book of Persian law or, better, the code of purification for the devotees of Zoroastrianism. The pertinent sections of Persian law on the subject of miscarriage and abortion (Müller 1895, IV:177–179) are:

8. It is the fifth of these sins when a man has intercourse with a woman quick with child, whether the milk has already come to her breasts or has not yet come: she may come to grief thereby; if she come to grief thereby, the man who has done the deed becomes a Peshôtanu.

9. If a man come near unto a damsel, either dependent on the chief of the family or not dependent, either delivered [unto a husband] or not delivered, and she conceives by him, let her not, being ashamed of the people, produce in herself the menses, against the course of nature, by means of water and plants, it is a fresh sin as heavy [as the first].

11. If a man come near unto a damsel, either dependent on the chief of the family or not dependent, either delivered [unto a husband] or not delivered, and she conceives by him, let her not, being ashamed of the people, destroy the fruit in her womb.

12. And if the damsel, being ashamed of the people, shall destroy the fruit in her womb, the sin is on both the father and herself, the murder is on both the father and herself; both the father and herself shall pay the penalty for wilful murder.

13. If a man has come near unto a damsel, either dependent on the chief of the family or not dependent, either delivered [unto a husband] or not delivered, and she conceives by him, and she says, "I have conceived by thee"; and he replies, "Go then to the old woman and apply to her for one of her drugs, that she may procure thee miscarriage";

14. And the damsel goes to the old woman and applies to her for one of her drugs, that she may procure her miscarriage; and the old woman brings her some Banga, or Shaeta, a drug that kills in the womb or one that expels out of the womb, or some other of the drugs that produce miscarriage and [the man says], "Cause thy fruit to perish!" and she cause her fruit to perish; the sin is on the head of all three, the man, the damsel, and the old woman.

15. If a man come near unto a damsel, either dependent on the chief of the family or not dependent, either delivered [unto a husband] or not delivered, and she conceives by him, so long shall he support her, until the child be born.

16. If he shall not support her, so that the child comes to grief, for want of proper support, he shall pay for it the penalty of wilful murder.

According to these Persian laws, the man has an obligation to support his pregnant woman until the child is born. The loss of the fetus due to failure in performing these duties is considered "wilful murder"

(#s 15–16). Inducing abortion with drugs concocted from herbal recipes (for any reason[?]) is considered a criminal act. The woman, anyone party to her decision, and the nurse administering the abortifacient are guilty of willful murder (#s 13–14). A daughter pregnant out of wedlock is not to resort to a drug-induced abortion to avoid public scandal. If she does, the penalty for "wilful murder" rests upon her and her father (#s 9, 11, 12). Finally, a man engaging in sexual intercourse with a pregnant woman that results in the loss of her fetus is guilty of assault, and his sin makes him a *peshôtanu* (i.e., guilty of death, or a murderer[?]).

There is some question as to the meaning of *peshôtanu* (i.e., *margarzan*), as some suggest "subject to death" and others "subject to a flogging." Elsewhere, Persian law calls for capital punishment only in the case of the "false" or "unqualified cleanser" and the "carrier alone." The confusion is intensified when one examines the strange inequality of the punishments meted out for the corresponding crimes. For example, a murderer gets off with 90 stripes, whereas the man who serves bad food to a shepherd's dog receives 200 stripes, and the person who kills a stray dog is to be flogged 600 times! Those who argue that *margarzan* connotes "guilty of death" expand the list of capital offenses to include burning the dead, burying the dead, eating dead matter, unnatural sin, and self-pollution. While considered willful murder, the miscarriage, abortion, and negligence crimes are apparently not considered capital offenses.

The Persian understanding of "quick with child" in Persian laws is worth noting (*Zend-Avesta,* Fargard XV #8). According to the ancient commentators on the *Zend-Avesta,* this is when the soul has been joined to the body, and it occurs when the child has been in the womb four months and ten days. It is unclear whether the Persian laws on miscarriage, abortion, and neglect should be read with this fact in mind.

Hittite Laws. The legal standing of the human fetus in Anatolia appears to be much the same as that in the Codex Hammurapi and early Mesopotamia, if the Hittite laws are any indication. These laws were promulgated during the Old Hittite Kingdom, perhaps during the reign of King Telipinu (ca. 1550 B.C.). The laws in question, along with their later variations, address only miscarriage (presumably by assault). Two definite classes of females are cited, the free woman and the slave, and in each case fines were levied to compensate for the loss of the fetus (*ANET,* 190):

17. If anyone causes a free woman to miscarry—if (it is) the 10th month, he shall give 10 shekels of silver, if (it is) the fifth month, he shall give 5 shekels of silver and pledge his estate as security.

Later version of 17: if anyone causes a free woman to miscarry, he shall give 20 shekels of silver.

18. If anyone causes a slave-woman to miscarry, if (it is) the 10th month, he shall give 5 shekels of silver. Later version of 18: If anyone causes a slave-girl to miscarry, he shall give 10 shekels of silver.

The law pertaining to the free woman (#17) does attempt to prorate the fine on the basis of the age of the fetus, with the fifth month and the tenth month apparently referring to half-term versus full-term. It seems the slave-woman gains compensation under law only when she is in the second half of her term of pregnancy. The variations simplify the fines to a single fee, irrespective of the length of pregnancy, with the slave-woman receiving half of what the free woman receives.

Egyptian/Canaanite Laws. Although certain Egyptian mortuary texts contain so-called negative confessions (e.g., "The Protest of Guiltlessness," *ANET,* 34–36) that reflect Egyptian social law, strictly speaking there are no extant Egyptian or Canaanite legal texts from which to draw inferences as to how those societies may or may not have legislated against assault leading to miscarriage and/or the abortion of the human fetus (but see "Reproduction Control in the Ancient Near East" above; for a perspective of the Egyptian view of prenatal life, see chapter 2).

Conclusions

The ancient Near Eastern legal codices that predate 1400 B.C., namely the Sumerian Laws, Codex Hammurapi, and the Hittite Laws, do not specifically address the topic of abortion. Laws within these corpora that relate to assault leading to miscarriage in a pregnant woman do indicate that the human fetus was not granted the legal status of "person" or "human being" in respect to talion law. In every case, loss of the human fetus due to assault was compensated by imposing a fine on the perpetrator of the crime. The predetermined monetary figure awarded the victim was usually prorated with respect to her social standing.

Legal philosophy in Mesopotamia apparently underwent a shift in respect to the value placed on the human fetus with the promulgation of the Middle Assyrian Laws (somewhere between 1400 and 1200 B.C.), at least in respect to the principle of *lex talionis.* The application of talion in these laws accords the human fetus recognized "person" or "human being" status, with two exceptions: the fetus of the presumably unmarried daughter, and the fetus of *la murabita,* the woman who does not raise her own children because of physical disability. In addition, self-inflicted abortion among women in general is outlawed in the Assyrian codex, punishable as a capital offense by impalement.

Later Persian law affirms this basic Mesopotamian understanding of the fetus as a person or human being, in that abortion is considered willful murder, though seemingly not a capital crime. Also included are specific prohibitions against the use of abortifacient drugs by pregnant females, whether married or unmarried. Furthermore, those who conspire to counsel a woman to seek an abortion and/or administer abortion-inducing potions are likewise guilty under law of willful murder.

The culling of the data related to reproduction control in the ancient Near East yields a fairly consistent pattern of Hebrew response to the sex mores characteristic of the population groups within their immediate environs. With the exception of the Old Testament rejection of sterilization by castration and continence, which were a general part of Near Eastern experience, Old Testament response to the other categories of reproduction control has a clear focus: the Baal cult of the Canaanites. The biblical injunctions forbidding sex with animals, engaging in intercourse with women during menstruation, common and ritual prostitution, and ritual infanticide were directed at singular customs deeply engrained in the Canaanite fertility cults (cf. Lev. 18:30; 20:1–27; Deut. 7:1–7; 2 Kings 17:7–18; 21:1–9).

The foregoing summaries prompt three basic conclusions about abortion in the ancient Near East and the Hebrew response—or better, non-response!—to the issue. First, in view of such explicit prohibitions against abortion in Mesopotamian law after about 1400 B.C., biblical silence on abortion should not be deemed consent. Rather, it is more probable that the Hebrews accepted and assumed this kind of anti-abortion legislation to be the norm in the cultural milieu, especially since the actual practice of abortion appears to have been an exceptional activity in the ancient world. Hence, they saw no need to condemn such an obvious criminal act, although admittedly the "argument from silence," due to the lack of written witness germane to the subject from Egypt and Syro-Palestine, could be used either for or against any anti-abortion norm for *all* of the ancient Near East. It must be remembered that Israel was not living in a cultural vacuum. The Old Testament is replete with well-documented examples of Israelite adoption of other cultures' social customs, language(s) and literary features, legal precedent, political structure, and at times (unfortunately) religious ideology. This same kind of carryover with respect to legal prescription is even seen in the New Testament, where there is no specific prohibition against bestiality, as it is assumed on the basis of Old Testament teaching.

Second, in moving the biblical writers to warn Israel of the snare of pagan cult and culture, God placed a premium on moral issues that would directly affect Israel as they penetrated, subdued, and settled the land of Canaan (cf. Exod. 23:17–33; Lev. 18:1–4, 26–30; 20:1–24; Deut. 7:1–17, 25–26; 12:1–14, 29–32; Josh. 23:5–13; Judg. 2:1–19). Given this thoroughgoing censure of Canaanite religion and its attendant sexual perversions, it would have been highly irregular for God to have overlooked something as significant as abortion, if it indeed had been part of Syro-Palestinian culture.

Finally, God's design for Israel, as mandated by the precepts within Old Testament covenant structure, delineated a unique people, a special possession, a chosen nation set apart from the pollutions of pagan social, political, and religious influences (Exod. 19:3–6; Lev. 20:7; Deut. 4:23–31; 7:6–16; 26:16–19; 29:10–13, etc.). Again, the lack of biblical instruction regarding abortion would seem strikingly out of character, in light of the covenant obligation incumbent upon Israel to be holy even as God is holy (Lev. 11:44–45), unless abortion was a non-issue in Canaan—and all the evidence points to this being exactly the case.

Far from avowing approval of the practice of abortion, biblical silence on the issue, when evaluated from this vantage, may well register an overwhelming indictment against abortion, in that abortion was apparently so unthinkable to the Hebrew mind—given ancient Near Eastern legal norms and divinely revealed covenant stipulations pertaining to life and godliness—that it did not even warrant treatment in the Old Testament legal corpora!

References and Further Reading

Albright, W. F. 1968. *Yahweh and the gods of Canaan*. London: London Univ.

[*ANET*] *Ancient Near Eastern texts relating to the Old Testament*. 1969. J. B. Pritchard, ed. Princeton: Princeton Univ.

Astour, M. C. 1966. Tamar the Hierodule. *Journal of Biblical Literature* 85:185–196.

Bardis, P. D. 1967. Contraception in ancient Egypt. *Centarus* 12:305–307.

Borger, R. 1963. *Babylonisch-Asyrische Lesestücke*. Rome: Pontifical Biblical Institute, Vol. I, lxxvi, s.v. šūt rēšī.

Bryan, C. P. 1974. *Ancient Egyptian medicine: The papyrus ebers*. Reprint. Chicago: Ares.

Burke, D. G. 1982. Eunuch. In *International Standard Bible Encyclopedia* (Revised), G. W. Bromiley, ed. Grand Rapids: Eerdmans (II:200–202).

Cerling, C. E. 1971. Abortion and contraception in Scripture. *Christian Scholar's Review* I:42–58.

[*CAD*] *Chicago Assyrian dictionary of the Oriental Institute of the University of Chicago,* 1958–1980. I. G. Gelb et al., eds. Chicago: Oriental Institute (Vol. 1/ II, 1968; Vol. 4, 1958; Vol. 8, 1971; Vol. 2/I, 1980; Vol. 16, 1962).

von Deines, H.; Grapow, H.; & Westerndorf, W. 1958. *Ubersetzung der Medizinischen Texts (Grundiss der Midizin der alten Aegytpen* IV) Berlin: Akademie-Verlag.

Driver, G. R., & Miles, J. C. 1935. *The Assyrian laws.* Oxford: Clarendon Press.

Frymer-Kensky, T. 1980. Tit for tat: The principle of equal retribution in Near Eastern and biblical law. *Biblical Archaeologist* 43:230–234.

Green, A.R.W. 1975. *The role of human sacrifice in the ancient Near East* (ASOR Dissertation Series 1). Missoula: Scholars Press.

Greenberg, M. *Ezekiel 1–20.* In *Anchor Bible* 22. Garden City, New York: Doubleday.

Harrison, R. K. 1980. Leviticus. In *Tyndale Old Testament Commentaries.* Downers Grove: IVP.

Hauck, F., & Schulz, S. 1968. *porne,* etc. In *Theological Dictionary of the New Testament* [*TDNT*]. G. W. Bromiley, trans. Grand Rapids: Eerdmans (VI: 579–595).

Kamal, H. 1967. *A dictionary of Pharonic medicine.* The National Publication House.

Lundbom, J. R. 1985. The double curse in Jeremiah 20:14–18. *Journal of Biblical Literature* 104:589–600.

Müller, F. M. 1895. *The sacred books of the East* IV. Oxford: Clarendon Press.

Noonan, J. T. 1965. *Contraception: A history of its testament by the Catholic theologians and canonists.* Cambridge: Belknap Press of Harvard Univ.

Oppenheim, A. L. 1960. A caesarean section in the second millennium B.C. *Journal of the History of Medicine and Allied Sciences* 15:292–294.

Saggs, H.W.F. 1962. *The greatness that was Babylon.* New York: Hawthorn.

van Selms, A. 1954. *Marriage and family life in Ugaritic literature.* London: Luzac.

Selvidge, M. J. 1984. Mark 5:25–34 and Leviticus 15:19–20. *Journal of Biblical Literature* 103:619–623.

Smedes, L. B. 1976. *Sex for Christians.* Grand Rapids: Eerdmans.

Waltke, B. K. 1969. Old Testament texts bearing on the problem of the control of human reproduction. In *Birth control and the Christian* (7–23), W. O. Spitzer & C. L. Saylor, eds. Wheaton: Tyndale.

———. 1976. Reflections from the Old Testament on Abortion. *Journal of the Evangelical Theological Society* 19:3–13.

Westbrook, R. 1985. Biblical and cuneiform law codes. *Revue Biblique* 92: 247–264.

Wouk, H. 1959. *This is my God.* Garden City: Doubleday.

Zimmerli, W. 1979. *Ezekiel I (Hermeneia),* R. E. Clements, trans. Philadelphia: Fortress.

2

Abortion and the Old Testament Law

James K. Hoffmeier

The Problem: No References to Abortion

Despite a thorough search of the Old Testament, a text that clearly prohibits abortion is not to be found. This silence has led some to conclude that since no prohibition is present, then abortion—which was certainly known in parts of the ancient Near East—was both practiced and permissible (Waltke 1969, 9–10; Scott 1974, 33–34). Others think abortion simply was not an issue for the Israelites, since having children was an important illustration of God's blessing (Ps. 127:4–5) and was necessary for reasons of inheritance (cf. Kantzer 1969, 553; Cerling 1971, 51; Scott 1974, 51). On this latter point, recall the steps to which Abraham went to ensure that he had a male heir. First, he adopted Eliezer (Gen. 15:2), a practice that is attested in the ancient Near East (Harrison 1970, 77–78); second, he had a child (Ishmael) by a surrogate mother (Hagar). The provision of a surrogate mother for a barren wife was also a known practice and was legally required, and in some cases was specified in marriage contracts (Harrison 1970, 76). Finally, from Abraham and Sarah's union, Isaac was born (Gen. 21:1–2).

This sequence of events in the life of Abraham and Sarah well illustrates the point that the birth of children, especially boys, was extremely important in that culture, as it still is in the Middle East. But this emphasis on children alone does not explain the silence of Old Testament law on the matter of abortion.

Infant Sacrifice: The Real Issue for Israel

The traditional view concerning the writing of the Law (i.e., the Books of Exodus through Deuteronomy) is that it was authored by Moses during the forty-year period in the wilderness. Exodus would have accompanied the theophany and covenant at Mount Sinai, while Deuteronomy was the covenant renewal that took place prior to the death of Moses and the entrance into Canaan. One would naturally expect the prohibitions in the Mosaic legislation to relate to matters that would impact Israel in Canaan. The most critical obstacle to Israel's faith in their new home would be the syncretistic religion of the Canaanites. It was for this reason that God ordered the Hebrews not to marry the inhabitants of the land, for this would lead to Israel's faith being undermined by the introduction of pagan practices that were loathsome to God (cf. Deut. 7:1–4; 12:29–32). Furthermore, God commanded the destruction of the Canaanite worship centers (Deut. 7:5) and repeated the injunction of Exodus 20:3–4 in Deuteronomy 5:7–8: "You shall have no other gods before me. You shall not make for yourself a graven image. . . .." It is noteworthy that these two commands stand at the beginning of the Decalogue. God certainly knew how easy it would be for the Israelites to succumb to the fertility-oriented religion of Canaan. His fear was not unfounded because, before the generation that had entered Canaan had died off and before Joshua's death, they were already experimenting with local deities (Josh. 24:14).

To the best of our knowledge, abortion was not practiced in Canaan, as it apparently was in Egypt and Mesopotamia (see chapter 1). While we do have abortafacient prescriptions from ancient Egypt,[1] there is no surviving evidence to suggest under what circumstances an abortion would be performed. That the Egyptians did have a very high view of prenatal life is evidenced by the practice of mummifying miscarried fetuses and stillborn babies.[2] This practice indicates the belief that the fetus could live in the next life.

---

[1]There is a prescription in Papyrus Ebers for inducing abortion. It consisted of "Dates, Onions and the Fruit-of-the Acanthus" being ground "in a vessel with honey, sprinkled on a cloth and applied to the vulva." Cf. C. P. Bryan, *Ancient Egyptian medicine, the papyrus ebers* (1930), p. 83. Bryan goes on to say "It (the recipe) ensured abortion either in the first, second or third period."

[2]Two mummified stillborn babies were discovered in Tutankhamun's tomb, complete with miniature gold mummy cases. In a display case at the Field Museum of Natural History (Chicago), one can see a mummified fetus that was about four months old.

An issue somewhat related to abortion that faced the Israelites in Canaan was human sacrifice, specifically infant sacrifice (Scott 1974, 34). A thorough study of the practice of human sacrifice has been made by Green (1975). While human sacrifice was practiced in several Near Eastern regions, usually in earlier periods, child sacrifice in the second millennium B.C. appears to be restricted to Canaan (Spalinger 1978, 53).

The evidence for child sacrifice in Canaan is now considerable. In addition to the references in the Old Testament, there is pictorial evidence from fourteenth and thirteenth century (B.C.) Egyptian temples. These illustrations, most recently studied by Spalinger (1978) and discussed by Hoffmeier (1987, 60–61), reveal one and sometimes two children being sacrificed on the wall of a Canaanite city that was under siege by Pharaoh's troops. The sacrifice is apparently being made to Baal so that he might intervene and deliver the city (Spalinger 1978, 48). This is precisely what the king of Moab did when he was about to be defeated by the Edomites (2 Kings 3:26–27). In Egyptian scenes showing the king attacking the Bedouin encampments of the Negev and northern Sinai, child sacrifice is not shown (Spalinger 1978, 52). And the Israelites, it must be recalled, came out of this nomadic tradition into Canaan.

Child sacrifice of this sort was obviously not practiced on a regular basis, but only in times of national danger. The more common rationale for sacrificing infants was in fulfillment of a vow (nzr), just as in the case of Jephthah (Judg. 11:30–40). The most ghastly evidence for the practice of infant sacrifice came with the discovery of the cemetery of infant-sacrifice victims (called a Tophet) in Carthage (modern Tunis).

Beginning in 1921 and again in the mid to late 1970s, archaeologists uncovered a vast burial area that spanned the period from about 750 to 146 B.C. (Stager & Wolff 1984, 35). The exact size of the Tophet has not yet been determined, since part of the area is covered by present-day occupation. However, for the period 400 to 200 B.C., an estimated 20,000 urns were interred, containing the bones of children and animals, never adults. The infants' ages range from neonates (newborn) to age three or four (Stager & Wolff 1984, 39), and the bones are charred from burning.

Carthage was a Phoenician/Canaanite colony founded in North Africa at the end of the ninth century B.C. The Phoenicians, in addition to bringing the Phoenician culture and Semitic language, called Punic in North Africa, continued in the old Canaanite practice of infant sacrifice—in this case to the goddess Tanit/Tinnit, the Carthaginian equivalent of Canaanite Astarte (Ringgren 1973, 143) and consort of Baal. The burial stones (stelae) that accompany the urns frequently contain Punic inscriptions; the words nzr and mlk appear. Nzr has been mentioned above. Mlk appears now to mean sacrifice or offering, not the god Molech as translated in the Old Testament (e.g., Lev. 18:21; 1 Kings 11:7; Jer. 32:35; cf. Stager & Wolff 1984, 44–47).

This lengthy discussion provides us with essential information on the issue that faced the Israelites as they settled in their new home. The Law has much to say about child sacrifice; it is condemned in the strongest language. Leviticus 18:1–5 instructs Israel not to walk in the practices of the Canaanites, but after God's ordinances, and then specifies, "You shall not give any of your children to devote them by fire to Molech [or "as a sacrifice"] and so profane the name of your God . . ." (v. 21). According to Leviticus 20:2, the person who did this should be stoned to death. Deuteronomy 12:31 and 18:9–10 label the practice as *toěbah*, "an abomination" to God. This means that child sacrifice is repugnant to God, completely the opposite of what he wanted (*ISBE* I, 13–14). Again it should be underscored that this injunction comes on the eve of Israel's entrance into Canaan.

When the prophets saw that children were being sacrificed, we find them outraged and outspoken (cf. Jer. 7:30–34; Ezek. 16:21, 36; 20:31; 36–39). Furthermore, the atrocities at "Topheth" (same word as found in connection with the Carthage burials) of Jerusalem are condemned (2 Kings 23:10; Jer. 7:31–32; 19:6, 11–14). Jeremiah 15:4 explicitly attributes the forthcoming destruction of Jerusalem to the sins of Manasseh, which are enumerated in 2 Kings 21:2–6 and 2 Chronicles 33:2–9, and include the burning of his son as an offering.

But what does child sacrifice have to do with abortion? One might think that child sacrifice is simply a vulgar religious act. The information now emerging from the Tophet at Carthage suggests that more was involved.

Along with the human remains, the charred bones of sheep and goats are frequently found. The presence of the animal bones is thought to be for substitutionary purposes (Stager & Wolff 1984, 39–40). On this point we recall Abraham's near sacrifice of Isaac in Genesis 22 and how God provided a ram to substitute. (This account also illustrates that Abraham must have been aware of the practice of infant sacrifice, for he offered no protest or sign of revulsion at the suggestion.)

The burial urns from the early phases of the Carthage Tophet (which parallels the beginnings of the colony) are more frequently filled with animal remains than human (Stager & Wolff 1984, 40–41). At this preliminary stage, when the population was relatively small, life was considered less expendable. But as time went on, the Tophet reveals an increase in the number of infant burials and a decrease in animal remains. This development parallels the growth of the city. By the fourth through third centuries B.C., when the city attained its greatest population—estimates go from 250,000 to Strabo's suggested 700,000 (Stager & Wolff 1984, 42)—the accompanying phase of the Tophet contains the greatest number of infant burials. Human sacrifices increased as time went on. This of course goes directly against the theory of cultural evolution, which would see man initially engaging in barbaric human sacrifice and then advancing to the stage where animal substitutes were used (Stager & Wolff 1984, 41–42).

Why should these people from a highly sophisticated culture be going from bad to worse, from our moral perspective? At Carthage it appears that the sacrifices were seldom made in times of crisis. And, since multiple burials are found within a single urn, they cannot be regarded as a dedication of the firstborn to the deity (Stager & Wolff 1984, 47). The fact that most of the remains are neonates argues against their being sacrificed in a crisis situation.

Sociologists believe that ritual infanticide, as in the case of Carthage, was used to regulate the population. In some cultures this was achieved by the abandonment of children, often baby girls (recall Ezek. 16:1ff.) The Canaanites, it appears, opted for sacrificing their children, in the name of "religion." Stager and Wolff suggest that population control in Carthage would have been important for all levels of society. The upper class would want to consolidate and maintain family wealth, while the common people would have a "hedge against poverty." They conclude their article with a profound statement on ritual infanticide (Stager & Wolff 1984, 51):

> Of course, it had the overt support of the state. We feel discomfort with the ostentation of the Carthaginian cult—its special precinct, the painted urns, the inscribed monuments. It is repulsive, but then too is the way so many children in our tradition have perished in less obvious ways. Perhaps the Carthaginians would have gotten better press in the West had they concealed their practices more subtly.

The implication of the foregoing discussion is that infant sacrifice that we read about in the Old Testament was practiced not only for religious reasons. Abortion of a fetus, even in the most sophisticated of ancient societies, was a health risk for the mother. It was certainly safer to sacrifice a newborn than perform an abortion, and one could do it with the blessing of "the church and state" in Canaan (and later in Carthage). For this reason, this author believes that the Old Testament is concerned with the practice of infant sacrifice, which might be considered the Canaanite counterpart to abortion. This may explain the silence of the Law and Prophets on abortion.

A Theology of Man Rooted in Creation

Even if one were to reject the above argument—that the Old Testament indirectly condemns abortion when child sacrifice is prohibited—

a case against abortion can be made when based on a biblical view of man that is rooted in creation.

Many appeal to the statement in Genesis 1:26–27—since man is made in the image of God, life is sacred and cannot be destroyed. From the writings of the church fathers to the present day, theologians have debated the meaning of "Let us make man in our image after our likeness. . . ." Unfortunately, there has been more "theologizing" of this phrase, leading often to unfounded conclusions, than sound exegetical interpretations. The interpretative history of this expression is traced in such works as *ISBE* (II:803–805) and *Dictionary of New Testament Theology* (II:286–288). Suggested meanings range from physical and spiritual to intellectual, creative, moral, and relational aspects of man. Jewish commentators and rabbis were more occupied with the issue of the plurality of God in the text than with the "image" question (Cassuto 1961, 54–57). This could simply imply that they had a pretty good idea what it meant. The Hebrew text of Genesis offers no explanation either, suggesting that the meaning was clear to ancient readers (von Rad 1961, 144). So we must place ourselves in an ancient Near Eastern context as much as possible, if we are to get any closer to the meaning.

It is clear that the words render "image" *(ṣelem)* and "likeness" *(demoth)* are synonyms (BDB, 198 & 853), although some think the latter may qualify the first, i.e., "something like the image of God" or "a copy" (von Rad 1961, 144–45; Eichrodt 1967, II:122; *TDOT* III: 257–60). *Ṣelem* literally means "something carved," i.e., a statue (*TDOT* III:259; BDB, 853). On the one hand, we would not want to understand this too literally, for that would lead to obvious heresy with respect to the nature of God (*ISBE* II: 803). But, on the other hand, to depart too hastily from a good Hebrew or Near Eastern understanding of "image" has led to a plethora of interpretations. And this, too, is undesirable.

Two good contextual extrapolations can be made. H. W. Wolff (1974, 159–60) has observed that ancient kings were accustomed to leaving their statues or stelae (which would have included a relief of the king) in areas that they had conquered. The presence of the statue would symbolize the sovereignty of that king over his new territory. Man's creation in God's image comes at the end of God's creative activity, thus making man God's Vice Regent or deputy on earth (Wolff 1974, 160; Eichrodt 1967, II:127). This view finds support in the concluding part of the same verse: "and let him have dominion . . . over every creeping thing that creeps upon the earth" (Gen. 1:26b).

Second, "images" or statues were primarily used in a cultic context in the ancient world, they were not simply *objets d'art*. Rather, a statue was considered the abode of a deity, which spiritually occupied the carved or molded object (Morenz 1973, 150–153). This concept is readily applicable to Genesis 1:26, for God blew his breath or *nephesh* into man. Along with the *nephesh,* which can be rendered "soul" or "being" (Cassuto 1961, 106; Wolff 1974, 17–18), the other vital life forces that make man a "living being" *(nephesh ḥayîm)* are blood (Wolff 1974, 59–62; cf. Gen. 9:4–7) and breath, *ruaḥ or nĕshāmâ* (Wolff 1974, 33–35). If a person were deprived of any of these, he would die.

We conclude, then, that "image of God" means that God placed his *nephesh* in man, and man is given charge of God's new creation. From these two interpretations emerge profound theological implications for the abortion issue, which will be discussed below.

Genesis 2:7 refers to God's "forming" *(yāṣar)* man out of the "dust" *('āphār)* of the ground. *Yāṣar* is a technical term that is used to describe the activity of a potter (cf. Jer. 18:1–6), and in the context of creation is applied to all of God's creation, including animals (Gen. 2:19; Amos 7:1) and land forms (Amos 4:13). God is portrayed as the Master Craftsman creating the cosmos and everything in it. This picture is reminiscent of the Egyptian creator god, Khnum, who is shown in temple scenes forming man on the potter's wheel. A connection with this imagery and Genesis 2:7 has been posited by some Old Testament scholars.[3]

Two points emerge from this image of God as a potter. First, he is the Master Craftsman who exercises his creativity in his work. This is reflected throughout the Bible. In 2 Corinthians 4:7 Paul reminds us that we are "earthen vessels" and in Ephesians 2:10 that "we are his workmanship." Second, the Potter is in absolute control over the clay; he is sovereign. Isaiah 29:16 and 45:9 are cited by Paul in Romans 9:20–21 to demonstrate God's sovereignty over man:

> But who are you, a man, to answer back to God? Will what is molded say to its molder, "Why have you made me thus?" Has the potter no right over the clay, to make out of the same lump one vessel for beauty and another for menial use?

These two principles have a direct bearing on the abortion issue because the Bible makes it clear that human creation was not something that just took place in the past; rather, it continues. Eve is quoted as saying "I have created [*qānāh*] a man with the Lord" (Gen. 4:16, author's translation). She was certainly not implying that Adam had nothing to

---

[3]As early as 1920, J. S. Forester-Brow saw a possible connection in his book *The two creation stories in Genesis* (pp. 119–120). More recently, R. Davidson in *Genesis 1–11* (Cambridge: 1973) 14; C. Gordon, "Khnum & El," *Scripta Hiersolymitana* XXVIII (1982), 203–214; and this writer in "Some Thoughts on Genesis 1 & 2 and Egyptian Cosmology," *Journal of the Ancient Near Eastern Society of Columbia University* 15 (1983), have argued for a literary connection between the two motifs.

do with Cain's birth; Genesis 4:1a makes that clear: "Now Adam knew Eve his wife, and she conceived. . . ." Sarah's barrenness is attributed to God's prevention (Gen. 16:2). Concerning Isaac's birth (Gen. 21:1–2a) the text states: "The LORD visited Sarah as he had said, and the LORD did to Sarah as he had promised. And Sarah conceived, and bore Abraham a son. . . ." God's activity in conception is further seen in the cases of Leah (Gen. 29:31), Rachel (Gen. 30:2, 22), Hannah (1 Sam. 1:5), and Ruth (Ruth 4:13).

These examples sufficiently demonstrate that birth is considered a co-creative process involving man, woman, and God. God's ongoing work in the creation of new life is further illustrated in statements where God reminds Israel that he "formed" them (Isa. 43:1, 7; 44:21) and declares, "I formed [you] for myself . . ." (Isa. 43:21). In these passages from Isaiah, the word rendered "formed" is *yāṣar*, as it is in the oft-quoted Jeremiah 1:5: "Before I formed you in the womb, I knew you intimately."[4] The choice of *yāṣar* in these texts is deliberate, for it connects the creating of individuals to God's "forming" activity witnessed in Genesis 2:7. Instead of using clay, God uses human instruments to continue the process of creation that he set in motion by his creative activity and then by his command to "be fruitful and multiply" (Gen. 1:28; 9:7). On this note, Babbage (1963, 15) aptly says, "God permits man to share in the joyous task of creation."

Ultimately the creation of new life in the Old Testament is attributed to God the Creator, who is both Designer and Artist. What would a human artist think if he was working on a masterpiece and someone destroyed his work? Even though not complete, the expected reaction would no doubt be anger and rage. If this is the reaction of the earthly artist, how much more intense would be God's revulsion at the destruction of a fetus, his masterpiece that is being formed!

Some might suggest that "the deformed" (physically and mentally) could not be considered God's handiwork and therefore attempt to justify abortion in such cases. But here, too, caution needs to be taken. As hard as it might be to understand, God claims that he alone makes humans with deformities. In Exodus 4:11 God says to Moses, "Who has made man's mouth? Who makes him dumb, or deaf, or seeing, or blind? Is it not I, the LORD?" Jesus observes that the blindness of the man he healed was not due to sin, rather that God might demonstrate his

---

4This translation is from J. A. Thompson's *The Book of Jeremiah* (1980), 143. Although the word he renders "knew intimately" is only *yādaᶜ*, his translation hits the mark because this word is used in this context where sexual knowledge is understood (e.g., Adam *knew* Eve, Gen. 4:1a), hence the idea of intimacy.

"works" (John 9:1–4). Therefore, we must allow the sovereignty of God to extend to the weak and handicapped, for they too are his creation!

The reality of an artist's hurt and anguish over the willful destruction of his handiwork became apparent to me during an exhibition of an art student at Wheaton College in the early 1970s. Someone took a can of spray paint to a couple of canvases that met with that person's disapproval. The artist was understandably crushed. This deliberate destruction of an art object expressed a lack of respect for both the artist and the art. So, too, the indiscriminate destruction of human fetuses declares precisely the same attitude toward God and man.

The matter of child sacrifice and principle that human life belongs to God come together in a stinging denunciation of Judah by God in Ezekiel 16:20–21:

> And you took your sons and daughters, whom you had borne to me, and these you sacrificed to them [pagan deities] to be devoured. Were your harlotries so small a matter that you slaughtered my children and delivered them up as an offering by fire to them?

Note especially God's claim, "you slaughtered *my* children." They were his because he was their creator and is figuratively Israel's husband, whom he had married by virtue of the Sinaitic covenant (Ezek. 16:8). Therefore, the children of Israel were his. In this connection, reconsider the passages from Isaiah that were cited above, especially Isaiah 43:20–21: ". . . my chosen people, the people who I formed for myself. . . ."

Analysis of Exodus 21:22–25

In order to resolve the perplexing question as to whether the Old Testament regards the fetus as a "person" who has the "image of God," we must now turn to Exodus 21:22–25.

This passage has received much treatment in the past fifteen years or so. But, even before the abortion issue was the reason for such attention, it was discussed in detail by Jewish rabbis because of several ambiguities and the implication for juridical procedure. The text of Exodus 21:22–25 reads as follows:

> When men strive together, and hurt a woman with child, so that there is a miscarriage, and yet no harm follows, the one who hurt her shall be fined according as the woman's husband shall lay upon him; and he shall pay as the judges determine. If any harm follows, then you shall give life

for life, eye for eye, tooth for tooth, hand for hand, foot for foot, burn for burn, wound for wound, stripe for stripe.

Debate in recent years has particularly centered upon the expression rendered "miscarriage" and the identity of the recipient of the injury. An article by House (1978) contains an excellent exegetical analysis of the text as well as a history of the debate beginning with B. K. Waltke's influential 1969 article and those that followed for the next ten years. Waltke (1969, 11) had concluded that since this law was concerned with the injury to the mother and only demanded the life of the attacker in the event of the mother's death, "clearly, then, in contrast to the mother, the fetus is not reckoned as a soul *(nephesh)*." Waltke's observations seem to have influenced people like Jewett (1969, 60) and Hardesty (1971, 70). Montgomery (1969, 86–89) reacted strongly against this view, arguing that the injury applied to the fetus. He appealed to the authoritative works of Cassuto (1961) and Keil for support. Cotrell (1973) in *Christianity Today*, carefully exegeted the text and concluded, contra Waltke, that "the weight of scholarly opinion (i.e. that the concern is for the mother) . . . is outweighed by the text itself." Three years later, Waltke (1976) published an article in which he modified his stance, more of which will be discussed below.

Other scholars writing in the early 1970s, such as Paul (1970), Cole (1973, 169) and Hyatt (1971, 233–34), continued to maintain that "injury" in the Exodus text refers to the mother, not the fetus. However, Cole is firm in saying that this passage cannot be appealed to by proponents of abortion, for that simply is not the issue being dealt with. Hyatt feels that since ancient Near Eastern laws dealt so regularly with the matter of an injury to a pregnant woman leading to miscarriage that "causing a miscarriage . . . was considered almost equivalent to murder" (Hyatt 1971, 234).

It seems that Paul, Hyatt, and others have been more influenced by the manner in which Mesopotamian codes handle this problem than in what the Hebrew text actually states. (On the comparison between biblical and Near Eastern law on this matter, see chapter 1.) The translation "miscarriage" in Exodus 21:22 by many well-known English Bible translations (e.g., Revised Standard, Jerusalem, New American Standard, New English, Berkeley, Amplified) is misleading, if not incorrect. The Hebrew literally reads "so that her child(ren)[5] come out." Now this

---

[5]Why this word should be pluralized is perplexing and a number of good suggestions have been proffered. Keil (135) suggests that the plural allows for the possibility of multiple births. The generic plural, which allows for the child to be male or female, is proposed by Cassuto (275). Meanwhile, Kline (198–199) postulates that plurality is meant to apply to either contingency; live birth or stillbirth.

expression is used in connection with stillbirths when some form of the word *mwt* ("dead") occurs (Jackson 1973, 292). Since the Exodus passage is not qualified in this way, premature birth must be envisioned. It has also been observed that the Hebrew word for miscarriage, *shākal*, is not used here (House 1978, 111; Kaiser 1983, 170). Therefore, we assume that the blow to the pregnant woman led to a premature birth. Nothing in the text requires us to understand that the fetus is born dead. This conclusion is significant because it affects how the following verses are understood.

Another related point is that the Hebrew language lacked a word for "fetus" or "embryo." The word *zera*ᶜ means "seed," i.e., "semen" as well as "offspring" (BDB, 282). A second word is *yeled,* (used in Exod. 21:22), which means "child" (BDB, 408). This indicates that in Hebrew thought there was no distinction between a fetus and a baby (House 1978, 113–114). Therefore, what would happen to the mother or fetus would be of equal concern to God (and to Exod. 21:22–25).

The next phrase of verse 22 reads, "and yet no harm follows." Here is where there could be some ambiguity. This statement does not specify whose injury or possible injury was in mind. The problem lies more in the English translations than in the Hebrew. The grammatical antecedent of this phrase in the Revised Standard Version is "miscarriage." But in Hebrew it is "her child(ren)." On grammatical grounds, "harm" should apply primarily to the prematurely born child. This interpretation is supported by the Septuagint's translation:

> And if two men strive and smite a woman with child, and her child be born imperfectly formed, he shall be forced to pay a penalty: as the woman's husband may lay upon him, he shall pay the valuation. But if it be perfectly formed, he shall give life for life. . . .

While making certain that the law is concerned with the consequences to the child, this introduces a Hellenistic Jewish concept on the viability of the fetus (Jackson 1973, 302). This of course is *not* justified by the Hebrew textual tradition.

As mentioned above, scholars have differed as to whether the text is expressing concern for the child or for the mother's injury. The evidence presented here demonstrates that the child was most certainly in mind. However, the statements "and yet no harm follows" (v. 22) and "if harm follows" (v. 23) could have been constructed so that one might know for sure which was meant. Exodus 21:23b–25 contains the longest formulation of the *lex talionis,* the law of retaliation: "life for life, eye for eye" and so on. Since this passage contains both the longest talionic statement, and the only law to deal with an injury to a pregnant woman, it could be purposefully detailed to allow for any possible damage to both parties.

The two parts of this law imply that if there was no harm—which seems to mean serious or life-threatening injury (Jackson 1973, 274–75; House 1978, 117–120)—then a fine was imposed. The reason for the fine, even if there was no injury to either party, was because of the prospective danger to the fetus (presumably a bump from two fighting men would not be life-threatening to a woman who was not pregnant). Jackson (1973, 296) refers to the "horror" of stillbirth to the Hebrews as being the major reason for a fine, even if no hurt was caused.

In the event that there was a laceration to the one party, let us say, while the other died, the death penalty would be exacted and the fine dropped according to the Midrash and Talmudic law (Loewenstamm 1977, 359).

Implications of Exodus 21:22–25

The interpretation of Exodus 21:22–25 presented here is vitally significant to the life of the unborn. First of all, this passage is situated in a section that deals with personal injury resulting from someone's striking of another (Exod. 21:18–27), which might be considered a minor crime for which the death penalty was not required. However, if the attack was premeditated and the wound sustained leads to death, the guilty person was to be put to death (cf. Exod. 21:12–14; Paul 1970, 67–68). If the attack was not premeditated or was accidental, then the person was to receive the protection of one of the cities of refuge (Exod. 21:13; Num. 35:9–15; Deut. 19:4–10).

In Exodus 21:22, however, the men who were brawling accidentally strike a pregnant woman (see Cassuto 1961, 275). Some have suggested that she may have been trying to break up the fight (Hyatt 1971, 233; Cole 1973, 169), but this may be reading the context of Deuteronomy 25:11–12 into the passage, which would be unwarranted. One might be inclined to think that since the brawlers had no intention or plan to hit the woman, they would have the protection of a refuge city should a death occur. But this is not the case. Why? The only difference here is that the injured person is a pregnant woman, and this would open up a whole range of potential damage to both mother and child. So the talion is introduced, and the severity of punishment corresponds to the degree of damage, including the death penalty if mother or child dies.

The fact that the life of a man is demanded in this case of involuntary manslaughter places extremely high value on the life of the mother and the developing child. It also illustrates that the Law sought to protect both (House 1978, 122).

The reasons given for the application of capital punishment is that man is made in "the image of God" (Gen. 9:6), and/or that one man has taken the *nephesh* of another (Lev. 24:17–18). The implications for the unborn are clear. First, the fetus is given "image of God" status. Second, it must be a "soul" or "life," since it is considered a *nephesh*. An animal is a *nephesh* (Gen. 1:2–2:19), but only man is made in the image of God; herein lies his uniqueness. Leviticus 24:17–18 specifies that it is "*nephesh* for *nephesh*" for man and animals. But only in the case of man is the guilty party's life taken, whereas if man kills an animal, restitution is made.

Mention has already been made of Waltke's two important articles (1969; 1976). In the first he argued that the human fetus was not regarded as being a *nephesh* (Waltke 1969, 11). Subsequently he reversed this position, stating "the image of God is already present in the fetus. . . . We conclude then, on both theological and exegetical grounds, that the body, the life and the moral faculty of man originate simultaneously at conception" (Waltke 1976, 13).

That the fetus is regarded as being a *nephesh* is important, because much of the debate surrounding abortion concerns whether or not the fetus is a "person," and *nephesh*, as well as meaning "life" and "soul," also means "person" (Wolff 1974, 21–22). Furthermore, the fetus cannot simply be considered a "potential person," as many argue. From the perspective of Deuteronomy 25:11 and Hebrews 7:11, "potential life" is in the loins of the father.

Since the Hebrews did not distinguish between an unborn or born child (House 1978, 14), and because the fetus was considered a *nephesh* that had the image of God, we need go no further than the sixth commandment ("Thou shalt not kill") to find the biblical prohibition against abortion. It is hard to believe that God, who orders the protection of a bird's eggs in a nest (Deut. 22:6), should not do the same for man, his special creation. We are reminded that Jesus said:

"Are not two sparrows sold for a penny? And not one of them will fall to the ground without your Father's will. . . . Fear not, therefore; you are of more value than many sparrows." [Matt. 10:29, 31].

Conclusions

We have suggested that the silence of the Old Testament on the abortion problem is not because abortion was unknown in the ancient world, but rather because it was not really an issue that faced the Israelites as they entered Canaan. The biblical and archaeological evidence suggests that the real problem that confronted Israel was the Canaanite practice of infant sacrifice, which was likely a method of population control and was probably the second millennium B.C. Canaanite counterpart to abortion. The Law and Prophets forbid and denounce that practice in the strongest language.

We have argued that a proper view of "man" as God's creation is an important consideration for the sanctity-of-life issue. Since God is the Creator of all human life, then mankind does not have the right to usurp the work of the divine Creator.

A thorough investigation of Exodus 21:22–25 leads to the conclusion that God is concerned for the life of mother and fetus in a case where damage might be done. We suggest that this is the most critical passage in the Old Testament for the life of the unborn, for it makes it clear that God regards the unborn as having great value. We conclude that this passage clears up the question concerning the personhood of the fetus. It is considered a *nephesh* that has the "image of God."

Looking at Old Testament law from a proper cultural and historical context, it is evident that the life of the unborn is put on the same par as a person outside of the womb. For the evangelical, then, this biblically based discussion should be foundational to theological and ethical considerations regarding the abortion issue that so plagues our world today.

References and Further Reading

Babbage, S. 1963. *Christianity and sex.* Downers Grove: IVP.

Cassuto, U. 1961. *A commentary on the book of Genesis I.* Jerusalem: Magnus Press.

Cerling, C. E. 1971. Abortion and contraception in Scripture. *Christian Scholar's Review* II:42–55.

Cole, R. Alan. 1973. *Exodus, an introduction and commentary.* Downers Grove:IVP.

Cotrell, J. W. 1973. Abortion and the Mosaic law. *Christianity Today* XVII, 13 (March 16):6–9.

Dictionary of New Testament theology, C. Brown, ed. 1976. Grand Rapids: Zondervan.

Eichrodt, W. 1951. *Man in the Old Testament.* London: SCM Press.

_____. 1967. *Theology of the Old Testament* II. Philadelphia: Westminster.

Green, A.R.W. 1975. *The role of human sacrifice in the ancient Near East* (ASOR Dissertation Series 1). Missoula: Scholars Press

Hardesty, N. 1971. *Eternity.* 22, No. 2, February: 70.

Harrison, R. K. 1970. *Old Testament times.* Grand Rapids: Eerdmans.

Hoffmeier, J. K., 1987. Further evidence for infant sacrifice in the ancient Near East. *Biblical Archaeology Review* XIII, No. 2, (March/April):60–61.

House, H. W. 1978. Miscarriage or premature birth: Additional thoughts on Exodus 21:22–25. *Westminster Theological Journal* 41:108–123.

Hyatt, J. P. 1971. Exodus. In *The New Century Bible Commentary*. Grand Rapids: Eerdmans.

[ISBE] International Standard Bible Encyclopedia I–II. 1979 & 1982. G. W. Bromiley, ed. Grand Rapids: Eerdmans.

Jackson, B. S. 1973. The problem of Exodus XXI 22–5 (IUS TALIONIS). *Vetus Testamentum* 23:273–304.

Jewett, P. K. 1969. The relationship of the soul to the fetus. In *Birth control and the Christian*, W. O. Spitzer & C. L. Saylor, eds. Wheaton: Tyndale.

Kaiser, W. C. 1983. *Toward Old Testament ethics*. Grand Rapids: Zondervan.

Kantzer, K. 1969. The origin of the soul as related to the abortion question. In *Birth control and the Christian* (551–558), W. O. Spitzer & C. L. Saylor, eds. Wheaton: Tyndale.

Keil, C. F., & Delitzsch, F. 1869–70. *Commentary on the Old Testament I (The Pentateuch)*. Grand Rapids: Eerdmans (reprint, 1983).

Kline, M. 1977. Lex talionis and the human fetus. *Journal of the Evangelical Theological Society* 20:193–201.

Loewenstamm, S.E. 1977. Exodus XXI 22–25. *Vetus Testamentum* 27:352–360.

Montgomery, J. W. 1969. The Christian view of the fetus. In *Birth control and the Christian* (67–89), W. O. Spitzer & C. L. Saylor, eds. Wheaton: Tyndale.

Morenz, S. 1973. *Egyptian religion*. Ithaca: Cornell Univ. Press.

Paul, S. M. 1970. Studies in the book of the covenant in the light of cuneiform & biblical law. *Vetus Testamentum Supplement* 18.

von Rad, G. 1961. *Old Testament theology* I. New York: Harper & Row.

Ringgren, H. 1973. *Religions of the ancient Near East*. London: SPCK.

Scott, G.A.D. 1974. Abortion and the incarnation. *Journal of the Evangelical Theological Society* 17.1:29–44.

Spalinger, A. 1978. A Canaanite ritual found in Egyptian reliefs. *Journal of the Society for the Study of Egyptian Antiquities* VIII, No. 2:47–60.

Stager, L. E., & Wolff, S. R. 1984. Child sacrifice at Carthage—religious rite or population control? *Biblical Archaeology Review* X:31–51.

[TNDT] Theological Dictionary of the New Testament. 1964. G. Kittel, ed. Grand Rapids: Eerdmans.

Waltke, B. K. 1968. The Old Testament and birth control. *Christianity Today* XIII, No. 3, November 8:3–5.

_____. 1969. Old Testament texts bearing on the problem of the control of human reproduction. In *Birth control and the Christian*, W. O. Spitzer & C. L. Saylor, eds. Wheaton: Tyndale.

_____. 1976. Reflections from the Old Testament on abortion. *Journal of the Evangelical Theological Society* 19:3–13.

Wolff, H. W. 1974. *Anthropology of the Old Testament*. Philadelphia: Fortress.

3

Abortion and Old Testament Prophetic and Poetic Literature

C. Hassell Bullock

This chapter, while rounding out an examination of the Old Testament on the subject of abortion, will deal mainly with a hermeneutical issue. Hermeneutics, or the discipline of interpretation, is a task we all engage in, whether we are interpreting the Word of God or the daily weather report. If the meteorologist reported that there was a 40 percent chance of rain in the afternoon, it is not quite accurate to say, "The weatherman said it is going to rain this afternoon." In fact, he only described the prospects for rain, which are less than fifty/fifty. Applying this caution to Scripture, it would be a gross misinterpretation to say that when Jeremiah cursed the day of his birth and wished he had died in the womb (Jer. 20:14–18), he made legitimate allowance for abortion. (Fee & Stuart's book [1982] provides some helpful guidelines for interpreting different types or genres of literature.)

When we interpret Scripture, the way we handle it is of great importance. Rather than looking for the proverbial "needle in the haystack" (in this case, abortion) and perhaps forcing selected passages to say things they do not intend, we shall take the following approach. First, we shall consider the question of how to interpret those passages that seem to have relevance for the issue at hand. Second, we shall look at the texts themselves in light of our hermeneutical discussion and listen for any germane word on the subject of abortion.

Scripture speaks to us in basically two ways. It *prescribes* and *describes*. L. Ryken (1984, 25–32), from a literary perspective, uses the expressions "expository writing" and "literary writing" respectively for what we call *prescriptive* and *descriptive*. The legal materials of the Pentateuch, for example, contain many prescriptive words. As a rule, they are imperatives (e.g., "Thou shalt love the Lord thy God with all thine heart"; "thou shalt not commit adultery"). They *prescribe* a mode of behavior or an attitude. Such behavioral patterns or attitudes become "normative" for Israel, which means that the lives of all Israelites are regulated by these prescriptive words. In contradistinction, the *descriptive* function of Scripture is to draw a picture of certain circumstances without encumbering the reader with the conditions of those circumstances. When the psalmist spewed out his hateful words against the Babylonians, "Happy shall he be who takes your little ones and dashes them against the rock!" (Ps. 137:9), he was *describing* his and his countrymen's vehemence against an enemy who had perpetrated unimaginable atrocities against Judah. He was not *prescribing* an attitude toward one's enemies that should be normative.

It should be noted at this point that any relevant references in the Old Testament's poetic literature (Job, Psalms, Proverbs, Ecclesiastes, and the Song of Songs) and prophetic books that impinge upon the abortion issue are largely descriptive. In other words, we do not find any prescriptive words on this subject in this material. That does not mean, however, that only prescriptive words are relevant. The descriptive portions of Scripture are instructive and are just as important a part of God's Word as the prescriptive. Even when the prescriptive element is absent, the descriptive can provide guidelines that shape our attitudes toward a particular subject.

We shall examine selected texts in the poetic and prophetic books under two rubrics: (1) those texts that elevate the value of life; and (2) those texts that despair of life and speak of physical extinction.

Elevation of Life

This literature is replete with texts that elevate human life. In fact, the poetic and prophetic books may be the greatest Old Testament witness against abortion as it is practiced in the modern world. W. Kaiser (1983, 152–172) has recently drawn attention to the elevated status of humanity within the stipulations of the Sinaitic covenant (cf. Exod. 22:21–24; Deut. 10:18–20). Here is expressed concern for and protection of individuals, regardless of social status, but especially the poor, widows, and orphans. These concerns are further seen in the prophetic books (e.g., Isa. 10:1–2; Amos 2:6–7; 4:1) and poetic literature (Prov. 22:22–23; 23:10). Similarly, Kaiser sees the status of the family (1983, 153–158) and the unborn (1983, 168–172) described in the same manner, and he discusses some of the texts under consideration here.

Scripture, then, affirms that human life is a precious gift from God. To abuse it is to abuse the Creator. That principle was articulated very early in the biblical record: "Whoever sheds the blood of a man, by man shall his blood be shed; for God made man in his own image" (Gen. 9:6).

At the apex of this category of texts stands Psalm 139. While the entire psalm is relevant, verses 13–18 are particularly germane to our concern:

> For thou didst form my inward parts,
>   thou didst knit me together in my mother's womb.
> I praise thee, for thou art fearful and wonderful.
>   Wonderful are thy works!
> Thou knowest me right well;
>   my frame was not hidden from thee,
> when I was being made in secret,
>   intricately wrought in the depths of the earth.
> Thy eyes beheld my unformed substance;
>   in thy book were written, every one of them,
> the days that were formed for me,
>   when as yet there was none of them.
> How precious to me are thy thoughts, O God!
>   How vast is the sum of them!
> If I would count them, they are more than the sand.
>   When I awake, I am still with thee.

The psalmist had begun by solemnizing his inability to hide from God in his daily life. The terms of the first stanza (vv. 1–6) show how comprehensive God's scrutiny of the psalmist's life was (italics are added to emphasize the psalmist's personal activities):

> Thou knowest when I *sit down* and when I *rise up;*
>   thou discernest *my thoughts* from afar.
> Thou searchest out *my path* and *my lying down,*
>   and art acquainted with *all my ways.*
> Even before a word is on *my tongue,*
>   lo, O LORD, thou knowest it altogether [vv. 2–4].

Then the poet enunciates the spatial implications of the truth that he cannot hide from God:

> If I ascend to heaven, thou art there!
> If I make my bed in Sheol, thou art there!
> If I take the wings of the morning
>   and dwell in the uttermost parts of the sea,
> even there thy hand shall lead me,
>   and thy right hand shall hold me [vv. 8–10].

Next the psalmist extends the intimacy of God's knowledge of him even to the prenatal stage (vv. 13–16). He was thoroughly convinced that God conducted, regulated, and observed his prenatal development. In short, God was his creator (Allen 1983, 162).

Admittedly this psalm does not address the subject of abortion directly. It is *descriptive* of the psalmist's inability to hide from God, and of God's constant scrutiny and care of him. Should that God who knew him so intimately not also deliver him from his enemies? (vv. 19–24). The stanza that describes God's prenatal care of David does not prescriptively prohibit abortion. Yet the profound respect for life in the prenatal stage is a strong descriptive word in favor of life and its preservation. While the *prescriptive* element is absent from the psalm, the *descriptive* nature of the psalm so strongly favors respect for life that one would be hard put indeed to allow for anything less in the psalmist's theology.

One might object, however, that David himself in the final stanza verbalized his disdain for life by attesting to his hatred for those who hate God (v. 21). Yet we must observe that the situation was one of war. That puts the question—whether it is permissible to kill—in quite a different category. Scripture clearly distinguishes between murder and killing in war (cf. 1 Kings 2:5). The unborn child has of his own accord encroached upon no one and earned no one's hostility. If enmity is directed against him, he is entirely innocent of it.

While this psalm offers no prescriptive word on the subject of abortion, it does provide us with certain descriptive elements on which we can make life's decisions. A respect for life that is rooted in God's creative role and providential involvement ought to influence our decisions in favor of life. Moreover, it can hardly be said that this psalm justifies elevating the *quality-of-life* ethic above the *quantity-of-life*. In fact, the psalmist had no intention of facing off one category against the other.

This psalm and other passages like it have to be interpreted in the context of Old Testament theology, which affirms God's creative activity and continuing providence in the world (Kaiser 1978, 72–75; Westermann 1984). Within that range of theological presuppositions, certain behavioral patterns and attitudes, as we have already observed, are laid out for Israel and for us. However, there is another category of texts, which are based on the assumption that all nations share a universal human ethic (or natural law) that governs society. This subsidiary category may be illustrated by the Lord's condemnation of the Ammonites who "ripped up women with child in Gilead, that they might enlarge their border" (Amos 1:13b). We cannot assume that the Ammonites had the same legal code as Israel, thus stipulating the same behavioral and attitudinal patterns toward human life, born or unborn. However, the assumption of this indictment is that the Ammonite greed for territorial expansion could not take precedence over the welfare of pregnant women and their unborn children. The only way the indictment can be fair is that it be based upon some ethical standard that the Ammonites understood and accepted. It would make no sense to condemn them for an atrocity that was permissible by their own code of ethics. The inference to be drawn is that Amos drew upon a code of ethics that demanded respect for pregnant women and their unborn children, even during a state of war.

Again we encounter a descriptive statement in this oracle of Amos, but underlying it is a code that regulated life, including respect for the unborn.

Despair of Life

By far the most troubling passages in the prophetic and poetic books are those whose authors despair of life and wish they had never been born or that they had been stillborn. In so doing, the speakers frequently use a type of literature called a "lament." Laments of a personal or community-wide nature are often found in the Old Testament as well as in ancient Near Eastern literature in general (B. Anderson 1983, 65–82). Laments arise out of one's agony. They contain the cries of the brokenhearted to God. From the standpoint of interpretation, one needs to bear this in mind, for clearly "normative" attitudes or behaviors are not being described. The speaker of a lament *describes* his or her despair. Therefore, a lament should not be the basis for guiding in ethical decisions or extracting theological principles.

Job's lament after his loss of family, property, and health is a classic statement of despair (F. I. Anderson 1976, 101):

> Let the day perish wherein I was born,
>   and the night which said,
> "A man-child is conceived."
> Let that day be darkness!
>   May God above not seek it.
>   nor light shine upon it.
> Let gloom and deep darkness claim it,

> Let clouds dwell upon it;
> let the blackness of the day terrify it [Job 3:3–5].

After his affirming statements of faith in 1:21 and 2:10, Job drops off the edge into the abyss of despair. Life had become so bitter that he wished it had never begun. However, this is a descriptive statement; given Job's terrible tragedies, it is understandable why he should say such things. Statements of despair can never be taken as normative (F. I. Anderson 1976, 99–101). It should be observed that contrary to his wife's challenge that he "curse God and die," Job refused that drastic option (2:9–10) and cursed only the day of his birth (F. I. Anderson 1976, 93).

Jeremiah was privately a morose prophet (cf. Thompson 1980, 94 ff.). In public he was a tower of strength and courage, but when he was alone he sometimes was overcome with despair. In one of his personal prayers (20:14–18) he exclaimed:

> Cursed be the day
> on which I was born!
> The day when my mother bore me,
> let it not be blessed!
> Cursed be the man
> who brought the news to my father,
> "A son is born to you,"
> making him very glad.
> Let that man be like the cities
> which the LORD overthrew without pity;
> let him hear a cry in the morning
> and an alarm at noon,
> because he did not kill me in the womb;
> so my mother would have been my grave,
> and her womb for ever great.
> Why did I come forth from the womb
> to see toil and sorrow,
> and spend my days in shame?

Jeremiah's life had become so painful that he wished he had never been born, or that he had died in his mother's uterus. It has been suggested that in his emotional state, Jeremiah was neither rational nor coherent (Lundbom 1985, 593). His words are *descriptive* of the anguished life he had endured. Only by the grossest hermeneutical distortions could one see the faintest allowance for abortion. The text is descriptive in the strictest sense of the word. It does *not* prescribe a view of life that would allow for extinction in the womb or for abortion. In a recent and very thorough study of this passage, Lundbom (1985, 596) doubts that abortion was in Jeremiah's mind, because there is simply no evidence to suggest that medical abortion was practiced at any time in Israel's history.

Conclusions

Essentially we have observed that the prophetic and poetic books offer no *prescriptive* word on the subject of abortion. *Descriptively,* however, they say much about the supreme value of life. Those statements, viewed in the wider context of Old Testament theology, build a firm foundation for respect for human life in all its states, pre- and post-natal. Next to God, human life is the most valuable entity in the world. According to this hermeneutical principle, while the statements of despair that we have reviewed offer a sharp contrast, they only describe the depths of dejection to which their proponents had plunged. They neither commend this state of mind as a normative psychological disposition nor give space for the evil of abortion.

References and Further Reading

Allen, L. 1983. Psalms 101–150. *Word Biblical Commentary 21*. Waco: Word.

Anderson, A. A. 1972. Psalms (73–150). In *The New Century Bible Commentary*. Grand Rapids: Eerdmans.

Anderson, B. 1983. *Out of the depths: The Psalms speak for us today*. Philadelphia: Fortress.

Anderson, F. I. 1976. Job: An introduction and commentary. In *Tyndale Old Testament Commentaries*. Downers Grove: IVP.

Fee, G., & Stuart, D. 1982. *How to read the Bible for all its worth*. Grand Rapids: Zondervan.

Kaiser, W. 1978. *Toward an Old Testament theology*. Grand Rapids: Zondervan.

———. 1983. *Toward Old Testament ethics*. Grand Rapids: Zondervan.

Lundbom, J. R. 1985. The double curse in Jeremiah 20:14–18. *Journal of Biblical Literature* 104:589–600.

Ryken, L. 1984. *How to read the Bible as literature*. Grand Rapids: Zondervan.

Thompson, J. 1980. Jeremiah. In *New International Commentary on the Old Testament*. Grand Rapids: Eerdmans.

Westermann, C. 1984. Biblical reflection on Creator-Creation. In *Creation in the Old Testament* (90–101), B. W. Anderson, ed. Philadelphia: Fortress.

4

Abortion and the New Testament
Victor R. Gordon

The New Testament makes no mention of abortion, a fact that makes the task of writing on the New Testament's perspective on abortion obviously difficult. Neither has there been extensive scholarship exploring New Testament teaching on abortion. This New Testament silence must continually be kept in mind while addressing this subject. Indeed, each of the four sections of this chapter is built around a question related to this silence:

1. Is the New Testament silent on abortion because abortion was unknown in the first-century world of early Christianity?
2. Does the New Testament touch on abortion in any indirect way? Do any of the New Testament writers allude to abortion or related issues?
3. Does the broader theological and ethical perspective of the New Testament have anything to contribute to the abortion debate? Does any of the New Testament teaching have direct implications regarding abortion?
4. Can the failure of the New Testament to address abortion directly be explained?

Certainly such questions are appropriate to ask of the New Testament. Every Christian should be concerned that his or her world-view is informed by Scripture. Even if the Bible does not directly address a particular issue that is pressing in our day, we must still inquire into how its teaching may inform our thinking on such an issue.

Was Abortion Known in the New Testament World?

A quick guess as to the reason for the New Testament's silence on abortion may be that the practice of abortion was not known in the first-century world. If so, the New Testament writers cannot be expected to address a "modern" issue that was completely unknown to them. However, historical investigation refutes such a theory. The evidence clearly shows that the Greco-Roman and Jewish cultures of the first century A.D. were familiar with the practice of abortion (see, for a start, Noonan 1965, 1970; Gorman 1982).

One can find numerous pagan thinkers in the Greco-Roman world who condemned abortion as evil. There was a clear promise in the fifth century B.C. Hippocratic Oath that the doctor would not help a woman get an abortion. Soranos, the leading Greco-Roman gynecologist (ca. A.D. 98–138) in the days of the early church, allowed for abortions only when the mother's life was endangered. Earlier, both Plato and Aristotle had seen abortion as permissible as a device for population control, but with great restrictions (especially by Aristotle). Abortion was, however, a fairly common practice in the Greco-Roman culture in which the early church quickly spread. As Noonan (1970, 6) says,

> Abortion, indeed, according to contemporary observers, was practiced very generally in the Greco-Roman world. The divided opinions of a few sages scarcely checked the powerful personal motives which made it attractive.

For our purposes, the details of the differing views and perspectives on abortion are not pertinent. The point is that the New Testament's silence on abortion is not because the practice was unknown. Our explanation must come from elsewhere.

While the Jewish people lived in the midst of a culture where abortion was known and practiced, there is comparatively little said about it in Jewish writings. Abortion is mentioned only once in the Talmud. However, the reason that abortion is rarely mentioned in the Jewish writings is that "it never became a practice in Jewish society" (Grisez 1970, 127; cf. also Jakobovits 1975). The traditional Jewish position was, and still is, strongly against abortion. The first-century Jews Philo and Josephus both considered abortion murder and deserving of the death penalty:

The Law orders all the offspring to be brought up, and forbids women either to cause abortion or to make away with the fetus; a woman convicted of this is regarded as an infanticide, because she destroys a soul and diminishes the race [Josephus, *Against Apion,* II, 202, Loeb trans.]

Does the New Testament Address Abortion Indirectly?

While the New Testament does not explicitly mention abortion, some have identified passages referring to abortion or related issues. Our concern in this section is to listen carefully to statements of the New Testament in which some have seen allusions or references to abortion. Are there texts that, while not mentioning abortion, speak clearly and unambiguously to the issue? My reading of the literature on the New Testament's perspective on abortion has led me to conclude that there are both exaggerated and understated views of what the New Testament offers. This imbalanced interpretation is often due to a bias in the interpreter in one direction or the other. I am not claiming an unbiased interpretation in these pages. Although my bias *is* against abortion, I have listened carefully to the texts and have attempted not to read more into them than is there nor to reject their possible implications. The reader will have to judge the success of this interpretive effort.

In 1 Corinthians 15:8, Paul, in describing Christ's resurrection appearances, says that "last of all, as to one untimely born [*ektrōmati*], he appeared also to me." *Ektrōma* is a word that always has reference to a premature birth and can mean "untimely birth," "miscarriage," or "abortion." Paul's exact meaning for *ektrōma* in this context is difficult and debated, but he clearly is not referring to abortion. Many scholars regard *ektrōma* as a derogatory term applied to Paul by his opponents at Corinth to cast doubt on his apostleship. If this is so, Paul acknowledges this but still argues strongly for his apostleship. The most prevalent interpretations recognize that Paul became an apostle in an abnormal way. Hence, *ektrōma* is probably to be understood in one of two ways: (1) Paul's call to apostleship was untimely, i.e., it was too late, in that he did not follow the earthly Jesus as a disciple as all the others had; or (2) Paul's call to discipleship was premature in comparison to the other disciples, in that the abrupt Damascus Road experience did not allow him a normal "gestation" period (cf. Peter's experience in Mark 8:27–30; Mark 14:66–72; Acts 2:14ff.). The use of this term, therefore, has nothing at all to do with literal abortion.

Three related words are sometimes viewed as having a reference to abortion: *pharmakeia* (Gal. 5:20; Rev. 18:23—"sorcery, magic, medicine"), *pharmakon* (Rev. 9:21—"poison, magic potion, medicine, drug"), and *pharmakos* (Rev. 21:8; 22:15—"magician, poisoner"). In the ancient Greco-Roman world, drugs were often used to induce abortions. These words are used of abortion-inducing drugs by pagan writers of the times (e.g., Plutarch; Soranos) and also by later Christian writers. Some interpreters have seen these passages as indirect references to abortion. They all occur in negative contexts and are condemned. The question is whether the condemnation of occult magic and medicine practice includes or refers specifically to abortion-inducing drugs. John T. Noonan, one of the leading scholars of the history of abortion, concluded that this possibility exists, but there is little evidence to support such a position (Noonan, 1965, 44–45). Five years later, Noonan shifted his position to a more positive attitude, based on similar statements in *Didache* (2:1–3) and *The Epistle of Barnabas* (19:5). The evidence of these latter documents is itself not clear and, to my mind, is not convincing. The major commentators do not even mention a reference to abortion as a possibility in these passages. Most commentators see these words as referring to the general sin of sorcery. While it remains a remote possibility, it is highly unlikely that Paul in Galatians or John in Revelation had abortion in mind when they penned these words.

There are several passages in the New Testament that express condemnation of infanticide (Matt. 2, esp. vv. 16–18; Acts 7:17–19). But it is going beyond the evidence to argue that these passages also prohibit abortion. The babies killed in these passages had already been born. Abortion is not in view here. The same kind of logic also applies to the positive picture the New Testament paints of the value of babies and children (Matt. 11:25 and par.; 19:13–15 and par.; 21:16). These passages are speaking of already-born babies or children, not fetuses. While both of these sets of passages may caution us with regard to taking a low view of fetal life, neither can be seen as a clear and unambiguous prohibition of abortion.

A more helpful teaching is the New Testament perspective on conception and barrenness. Conception is seen as a blessing and a gift of God (Matt. 1:20; Luke 1:24–25, 30, 31; John 16:21; 1 Tim. 2:15; 5:14) and barrenness a curse (Luke 1:24–25, 36). Several cautions are in order here. First, this teaching is not found frequently in the New Testament, especially the teaching of barrenness as a curse. Indeed, the passage cited in Luke only says that Elizabeth was held in reproach by humans, not by God. Second, since the conceptions of Jesus and John the Baptist are admittedly not normal, one must be careful in making exegetical deductions from them. But, despite these cautions, this teaching does raise questions about the appropriateness of the termination of a pregnancy when pregnancy is viewed in such a positive light. Again, however, the implications for abortion remain clouded.

The most often cited passage in the New Testament to argue the value of the life of the fetus and against abortion is Luke 1:41–44. Mary had just arrived at the home of Zechariah and Elizabeth. As Mary greeted Elizabeth, "the babe [John the Baptist] leaped in her womb . . ." (v. 41, *eskirtāsen to brephos en tā koilia autās*). Elizabeth explains that when she heard Mary's voice, "the babe in my womb leaped for joy" (v. 44; cf. Gen. 25:22). Ellis (1974, 7b) comments, "As Luke the physician perhaps knew, an emotional experience of the mother can cause a movement of the fetus." Meye (1969, 41) says that this is a "manner of speaking." However, Marshall (1978, 80) is closer to the mark when he argues that "it is more likely that a miraculous expression of the emotion of the unborn child is meant." The key is in understanding the ministry of John the Baptist. He is to be "filled with the Holy Spirit, even from his mother's womb" (Luke 1:15) and have a prophetic ministry announcing the coming of the Messiah, which ministry begins with this announcement to Elizabeth regarding Mary's baby. Elizabeth now knows not only that Mary is pregnant, but that she is carrying the Messiah. The prophetic ministry of John the Baptist has begun: "Now John the Baptist begins to prophesy in the womb by jumping with gladness . . . a gladness that hails the advent of the messianic age" (R. Brown 1977, 341; cf. Fitzmyer 1981, 357f., 363–67). The leaping of the fetus is intended by Luke to be understood by the reader as a prophetic action, inaugurating the ministry of John the Baptist. (For an excellent exposition of this view, see R. Brown 1977, 341–46.)

The question remains whether such an interpretation leads one to conclude that the fetus is a human person and that abortion is therefore wrong. My conclusion is that there is something to Meye's argument that this is "a manner of speaking." To be sure, we do not have here a medical statement by Dr. Luke on the status of the fetus. Although there remains ambiguity regarding the fetus, certainly Meye (1969, 41) goes too far when he says that this text "must not be understood as anything but a manner of speaking" and has nothing at all to say about the value of fetal life. It *is* "a manner of speaking," not scientific language, but it is clearly intended by Luke to involve a fetus in prophetic activity. While we cannot say that this teaching unmistakably prohibits abortion, neither can we affirm that it offers nothing whatsoever to the debate. A text such as this, while not giving final answers, points us in the direction of valuing the life of the fetus as something very significant in God's created order. Early in the Christian tradition, this passage was used to argue that the fetus was a living person (e.g., by Clement of Alexandria).

We thus conclude our survey of New Testament passages often held up as offering a view of abortion. We have drawn three conclusions:

1. Most of the texts used to present a New Testament view of abortion clearly or most likely do not have abortion in view. There is an abundance of reading things into the texts that solid exegesis will not allow.
2. There is no clear and unambiguous teaching on abortion in these passages. In short, these New Testament texts do not provide us with a New Testament position on abortion.
3. There is to be found, however, in several of these texts, an emerging perspective that would call the reader to take seriously the value of the fetus and to be cautious and reticent about abortion.

What Are the Implications of the Broader New Testament Teaching?

In this section we will examine the implications of the wider New Testament theological and ethical perspective on the issue of abortion. I am convinced that while the New Testament does not directly address the abortion issue, there are elements of its theological and ethical teaching that have implications for our view of abortion today.

The first group of New Testament ideas that I propose for inspection has to do with the question of the value of the fetus. This issue is central to the abortion debate. The key questions in formulating one's view of abortion are: "What do you think of the fetus? What value does the life of the fetus have? Is the human fetus a human person?" These comprise the central set of issues in the abortion debate, and we begin by addressing them from the overall theological and ethical perspective of the New Testament.

The Value of Human Life

There can be no doubt that the New Testament has a high view of human life. Paul's proclamation on Mars Hill in Athens that God "himself gives to all men life and breath and everything" (Acts 17:25b) sums up the position of the New Testament. God is the giver of life. Life is his good gift. The Old Testament prohibition of murder is reaffirmed (Matt. 5:21–22; 15:19; 19:17–18; Rom. 1:29; Rev. 22:15). This prohibition of the destruction of human life is strongly stressed because of the high value assigned to human persons in the image of God (James 3:9; cf. Rom. 8:29; 2 Cor. 3:18; Eph. 4:24; Col. 3:10; 2 Peter 1:4; 1 John 3:2). Not only are we humans in God's image, but God in Christ took on human flesh, which removes any doubt as to human dignity (John 1:14; Phil. 2:6–7). O'Donovan (1973, 3) asks, "Who is this child, who is this young woman, who is this senile old man, but one with whom the Son of God shared human flesh?" Christ's sacrificial death on behalf of humanity stretches the human imagination beyond its limits to comprehend God's commitment to the human race.

The Unity of the Human Person

A dominant theme in recent New Testament (as well as Old Testament) theology has been the unity of the human person. Humans do not possess a body and a soul, nor are they a *combination* of body-soul-spirit. Rather, each human person is a body-soul in unity and wholeness. In short, there is no New Testament sanction for separating the human person into parts. Rather, there is consistent teaching that the human person is a psychosomatic unity. It must also be stated that while this wholistic view of the human person is much more accurate than the traditional dichotomistic/dualistic or trichotomistic view of the human person, some New Testament scholars have missed a strand of teaching that offers, in Evans's words, a "minimal dualism." These passages deal with life after death (Matt. 10:28; 2 Cor. 5:1–10; Rev. 6:9–11; 20:4). This is not the place to rehearse the New Testament evidence for the wholistic or minimal-dualist view. Montgomery (1969, 70–75) gives a well-balanced summary, and Evans's article (1981) is very helpful.

Meye, in an important and helpful article, affirms "the New Testament anthropology in which man is constantly viewed in terms of his wholeness as a person." However, he goes on to state that "there is no reason at all to relate this teaching to the unborn fetus" (Meye, 1969, 41). No reasons are given for this conclusion. Oliver O'Donovan, an evangelical ethicist at Oxford University who has not yet attracted the attention he deserves by American evangelicals, offers another view of the implications of this New Testament teaching:

> In a period when the most orthodox of current orthodoxies in theological anthropology has been that the Bible teaches 'body-soul unity', it is ironical that Christians should have allowed their view of the fetal soul to drift upon a sea of speculation without seeking anchorage in any account of the fetal body. What has happened as a result could easily have been predicted. The notion of individual humanity which ought to be a notion of something irreducible and given, something which claims us in the most unprepossessing and unsuccessful of our fellow-human beings, has become a notion of achievement. . . .
>
> If Christians should ever decide to throw themselves into opposition to this trend of thought and hunt for minimal criteria, it will be because of their belief that manhood is given by God and not won as a prize [O'Donovan 1973, 11].

O'Donovan (1973, 10–21) argues—on the basis of life's being the gift of God and the body-soul unity of the human person—that the fetus is a human person. If the soul and the body are basically inseparable for human beings, and if a fetus has a physical body, then is not a fetus a human person? This line of reasoning is intriguing, if not totally convincing. While one may or may not wish to follow O'Donovan all the way, I would argue that the New Testament's teaching on the wholeness of the human person must be reckoned with in determining a contemporary position on abortion. It at least points in the direction of the human fetus's identity as a human person.

Personal Continuity

Personal identity seems to begin in the New Testament with conception. The New Testament seems to teach personal continuity from the womb to the grave (and beyond, for the believer in Christ). I am concerned here only with the several indications of this personal continuity that extend to the womb, i.e., to the fetus.

The clearest example of this perspective is found in the Lukan birth narrative, where the continuity of prenatal and postnatal human life is assumed. Luke's choice of words indicates this personal continuity. The same Greek word, *brephos,* is used of the fetus in the womb (Luke 1:41, 44) and of the newborn child (Luke 2:12, 16; also Acts 7:19; cf. 1 Peter 2:2). The fetus is a "babe." The same word is also used later in the gospel of older children (Luke 18:15, 16; cf. 2 Tim. 2:2). This understanding fits well with Luke's perception that the prophetic ministry of John the Baptist began in his mother's womb (see above). It seems incontrovertible that "the ethos of the infancy narratives reflected a high interest in infant and fetal life" (Noonan 1970, 8; Luke 1:15, 24, 31, 35–36, 41–44; 2:5; Matt. 1:18; 2:1–18).

The Christology that developed from these and other New Testament texts also points to the humanity of the fetus. Adoptionist Christology says that at some point the man Jesus became God, but the creed affirms that God became man at the moment of conception. The eternal Son became incarnate in Mary's womb. This is a main point in the doctrine of the virgin birth and the confession that Jesus was conceived . . . born . . . suffered . . . died . . . raised . . . exalted . . . and is coming again. Each of these affirmations describes the same Jesus who has personal continuity as the incarnate Son of God. One may certainly argue that these were extraordinary circumstances and the eternal Son was already a person before conception. This is true (although there would be serious problems with this view [cf. O'Donovan 1973, 15f.; Scott 1974, 21ff.]), and the analogy cannot be pressed to present a conclusive argument that the fetus is a person. But neither is there proof that Jesus' existence as a person from conception is not one of the ways that he was fully human (cf. Darroch 1985). We find here another pointer to the humanity of the fetus.

"But when He who had set me apart, even from my mother's womb . . ." (Gal. 1:15, NASB; cf. Jer. 1:5; Isa. 49:1–6) is a text often pressed to defend the position that the fetus is a human person. Clearly, the main thrust of the text is not intending to affirm this. But can we really say, especially in light of the other biblical emphases on personal continuity, that such passages have absolutely nothing to say regarding abortion? I think not. All statements have implications beyond their original intended meaning. This is a prime concern for both the preacher and the theologian. It is the main way the Bible speaks to us today—indirectly. Paul is saying that God "set *me* apart while I was in my mother's womb." While he is not trying to instruct the Galatians on personal continuity, it seems, especially in view of other biblical teaching, that this may well be an implication of Galatians 1:15. It must be acknowledged that while *ek koilias mātros* probably means "from before birth" (cf. Jer. 1:5), it could also mean "from birth," which would eliminate any reference to the fetal state.

These indications of personal continuity in the New Testament again do not amount to a clear-cut basis for the rejection of abortion. They do, however, stand as a warning "against distinguishing with careless sharpness between fetal and infant life" (Frame 1978, 49; cf. O'Donovan 1973, 14–16).

The New Testament Love Ethic

Some base their rejection of abortion on the undeniable New Testament emphasis on agape love, which is unconditional (e.g., Matt. 5:43–48; 22:34–40; John 13:34–35; Rom. 13:8–10; 1 Cor. 13; Gal. 5:14, 22–23; 1 John 4). The condition, the argument goes, of "fetushood" is not adequate to keep the fetus from the sphere of love. The love ethic of the New Testament, according to this view, prohibits abortion. (Although there is no room to discuss it in this chapter, others argue similarly from Jesus' ethic of non-violence in Matthew 5:38ff.)

O'Donovan has an elaborate argument, based on the parable of the good Samaritan (Luke 10:25–37), that the only way the question "Who is a person?" can be answered is in a relationship of love. That is the Christian way of answering this important question:

> To discern my neighbor I have first to prove neighbor to him. To perceive a brother or sister, I have first to act in a brotherly way. To know a person, I have first to accept him as such in personal interaction [O'Donovan 1984, 60].

He goes on to argue that we can only know that fetuses are persons by loving and caring for them.

> Unless we approach new human beings, including those whose humanity is ambiguous and uncertain to us, with the expectancy and hope that we shall discern how God has called them out of nothing into personal being, then I do not see how we shall ever learn to love another human being at all [O'Donovan 1984, 66].

I find O'Donovan's perspective intriguing and challenging but exegetically unsubstantiated. His argumentation is not grounded in the New Testament texts the way they must be to proclaim a biblical position. But certainly the New Testament ethic of radical love calls us to pause when we face the issue of abortion. Noonan (1970, 7) is correct when he says that the theological context for New Testament thinking about abortion is this agape love. Can abortion ever be an act of love? Very early in the Christian church, this was answered in the negative. *The Epistle of Barnabas* (19:5; ca. A.D. 130) defined the fetus as a neighbor, and abortion is prohibited as an unloving act (cf. also *Didache* 2:2; ca. A.D. 140). Further reflection and exegetical work may yet substantiate O'Donovan's thesis as an accurate application of the New Testament love ethic.

Karl Barth argues somewhat similarly to O'Donovan, but on a different basis—the Christian gospel explicated in the New Testament. For Christians—who are redeemed by God's goodness, grace, and mercy— abortion seems inconsistent. For Karl Barth, the gospel (which, of course, is the main message of the New Testament) and the practice of abortion simply cannot coexist: "Those who live by mercy will always be disposed to practice mercy, especially to a human being which is so dependent on the mercy of others as the unborn child" (Barth 1961, 418). Maybe Barth is right, and while there are no New Testament prooftexts against abortion, the whole makes a clear proclamation.

Before concluding this section, I want to deal with one other specific issue in the abortion debate on the basis of a Pauline text: the rights of the mother over her own body. Smedes (1983, 135) states succinctly that "certainly we are on shaky grounds when we open the door to a mother's needs." Paul makes it clear that the Christian woman, at least, does not own or rule over her own body (1 Cor. 6:15–7:5). In this context Paul is dealing with matters physical and sexual. The claim that "I can do whatever I wish with my own body," so widely accepted in contemporary culture, is obviously wrong according to biblical standards. For the Christian, abortion can never be reduced to a woman's dealing with her body as she desires. The Christian woman does not claim the freedom or right of self-determination of her body. Sexual intercourse outside of marriage is a sin against one's own body (6:18). Abortion might also be such a sin.

Why Is the New Testament Silent?

There are no definitive answers to our final question. But there are several things we do know that, taken together, offer a reasonable explanation:

1. The New Testament is made up of twenty-seven *occasional* documents, each of which addresses a particular church or group of churches in a particular situation, place and time. The issues addressed in a New Testament document are those that are pressing in that particular situation.

2. Early Christianity was closely related to first-century Judaism. It is important to remember that although Judaism at this time was against abortion, the issue was rarely mentioned, because it was not a practice in which the Jews became involved. Indeed, "in biblical times, as in later ages, such operations with criminal intent were generally unknown [i.e., not practiced] among the Jews" (Jakobovits 1975, 171). Abortion was not addressed, because it was not an issue for the Jewish community.

3. There are reasons to believe that if abortion were being practiced by any of the churches to which the New Testament documents were addressed, the author(s) would have condemned it. This evidence is threefold. First, the early church saw itself in continuity with Israel and the Old Testament revelation, which had a negative outlook on abortion (see chapters 1–3). The Old Testament was the Scripture of the first-century church. Also, the close relationship early Christianity had with Judaism, although not the same kind of continuity it had with the Old Testament, was especially strong in the ethical realm. One can reasonably assume, unless stated otherwise, that the outlook of the early church on an issue such as abortion would be very similar to that of the Old Testament and even Judaism (see e.g., Meye 1969, 29, 31). Second, a main thrust of this chapter has been that while the New Testament does not have direct teaching on abortion, there are several important themes in New Testament teaching that point in the direction of opposition to abortion. Therefore, one would expect that if abortion were a problem for any of the churches the New Testament writers address, the author(s) would have discussed the subject and most likely in a very negative way. Finally, as the early church developed in the second century and became less influenced by Judaism and more and more impacted by Greek thought and the Greco-Roman culture (e.g., Justin

Martyr), the issue of abortion did come up. It was not until the second century that abortion became a serious temptation to Christians. Just as one would expect, these early Christian writers condemned abortion:

> Thou shalt not procure abortion, thou shalt not commit infanticide [*The Epistle of Barnabas* 19:5].
> Thou shalt not procure abortion, nor commit infanticide [*Didache* 2:2].

The rest of the early church tradition maintains this opposition to abortion. Bruce Metzger, a New Testament expert from Princeton, affirms "the opposition of the early church to contemporary practices of abortion. It is really remarkable how uniform and how pronounced was the early Christian opposition to abortion" (cited in Gorman 1982, 9).

Therefore, the most reasonable explanation for the New Testament silence on abortion is that the early Christian community, like its Jewish counterpart, was not faced with abortion as a pressing problem in the first century. Since the early Christians did not practice abortion, there was no reason urgent enough for the writers to condemn it.

Conclusions

In answer to whether the New Testament addresses abortion indirectly, the threefold conclusion at the end of that section stands. The implications of broader New Testament teaching presented in the next section make the New Testament posture against abortion even clearer. That the New Testament had no occasion to condemn abortion outright does not negate the fact that the implicit teaching of the New Testament calls the practice of abortion into question. O'Donovan (1973, 4) is correct when he says that "there is, too, among Biblical Christians the widespread and false impression that the Bible says nothing much to the point." I have tried in this study to steer a steady course between this error and the opposite error of reading too much about abortion into the texts of the New Testament. Certainly the New Testament offers no ground *for* the practice of abortion. We can say at the very least that abortion appears to go against the grain of the teaching of the New Testament, to say nothing of the tradition of the early church. Some may find in the New Testament teaching that has been presented as a clear and strong statement of caution regarding abortion. Others, based on the cumulative force of this teaching, may even argue for an implicit prohibition.

References and Further Reading

Barth, K. 1961. *Church dogmatics* (vol. 3, part 4). Edinburgh: T & T Clark.

Brown, H. O. J. 1977. *Death before birth*. Nashville: Thomas Nelson.

Brown, R. 1977. *The birth of the Messiah*. Garden City: Doubleday.

Darroch, M. 1985. The conception and unborn life of Christ as a theme for Christian worship. *Evangelical Review of Theology* January:60–69.

Ellis, E. E. 1974. *The Gospel of Luke*. Grand Rapids: Eerdmans.

Evans, S. 1981. Separable souls: A defense of 'minimal dualism.' *Southern Journal of Philosophy* 19:313–31.

Fitzmyer, J. A. 1981. *The Gospel according to Luke, I–IX*. Garden City: Doubleday.

Frame, J. 1978. Abortion from a biblical perspective. In R. L. Ganz, *Thou shalt not kill: The Christian case against abortion* (43–75). New Rochelle: Arlington House.

Gorman. M. J. 1982. *Abortion and the early church*. Downers Grove: IVP.

Grisez, G. G. 1970. *Abortion: The myths, the realities and the arguments* (esp. chapter 4). New York: Corpus Books.

Jakobovits, I. 1975. *Jewish medical ethics*. New York: Bloch.

Marshall, I. H. 1978. *The Gospel of Luke: A commentary on the Greek text*. Grand Rapids: Eerdmans.

Meye, R. 1969. New Testament texts bearing on the issues. In *Birth control and the Christian* (25–47), W. O. Spitzer & C. L. Saylor, eds. Wheaton: Tyndale.

Montgomery, J. W. 1969. The Christian view of the fetus. In *Birth control and the Christian* (67–89), W. O. Spitzer & C. L. Saylor, eds. Wheaton: Tyndale.

Noonan, J. T., Jr. 1965. *Contraception: A history of its treatment by the Catholic theologians and canonists*. Cambridge: Belknap Press of Harvard Univ.

———, ed. 1970. An almost absolute value in history. In *The morality of abortion; legal and historical perspectives*. Cambridge: Harvard Univ. Press.

O'Donovan, O. 1973. *The Christian and the unborn child*. Bramcote, Notts, England: Grove.

———. 1984. *Begotten or made?* New York: Oxford Univ. Press.

Scott, G.A.D. 1974. Abortion and the incarnation. *Journal of the Evangelical Theological Society* 17:29–44.

Smedes, L. B. 1983. *Mere morality*. Grand Rapids: Eerdmans.

Stott, J. R. 1985. *Involvement: Social and sexual relationships in the modern world* II. Old Tappan: Revell.

5

A Theological Perspective on Abortion
Donald M. Lake

Theological Dimensions to the Abortion Dilemma

The perplexing problem of abortion not only divides our society but is also a divisive issue within the Christian community. Among non-Christians, our only appeal is to a general moral sensitivity and to commonly shared rational purposes for man and society. Many non-Christians feel that abortion-on-demand is a poor solution to a very difficult problem. One only needs to read Dr. Bernard N. Nathanson's exposé of the development of the abortion crusade to see that morally sensitive people, even those without religious connections, reject abortion-on-demand as a solution to unwanted pregnancy. Nathanson, incidentally, is a "non-religious" Jewish obstetrician and gynecologist who got his college girlfriend pregnant and then helped to influence her to have an abortion. But his personal involvement in the abortion movement turned him against abortion-on-demand. He (Nathanson 1979, 227) states emphatically that

I find the philosophies that accept abortion under all circumstances to be inadequate because they fall so far short of the most profound tenet of human morality: "Do unto others as you would have them do unto you."

Because of ancient religious traditions, we have put an aura of sanctity around the Golden Rule, as though it were either a sectarian tenet or some impossible ideal that we must strive to meet.

On the contrary, it is simply a statement of innate human wisdom. Unless this principle is cherished by a society and widely honored by its individual members, the end result is anarchy and the violent dissolution of the society. This is why life is always an overriding value in the great ethical systems of world history. If we do not protect innocent, non-aggressive elements in the human community, the alternative is too horrible to contemplate. Looked at this way, the "sanctity of life" is not a theological but a secular concept, which should be perfectly acceptable to my fellow atheists.

Since Christians—even evangelical Christians—are not agreed on either a general opposition to abortion or the grounds for legitimate versus illegitimate abortions, the theological grounds for and against abortion must be examined. Even if one is convinced that one or more biblical texts directly or indirectly address the issue of abortion, it is the task of theology to provide the rational framework within which the issue of abortion can be discussed. This chapter is an attempt to lay out some of the theological issues that abortion raises and to show how these issues can help us formulate a more consistent theological position on abortion. This chapter is not a treatise in exegetical or biblical theology. And while it is too narrow an issue to be dealt with as a fundamental issue of systematic theology, the approach here is intended to be "systematic."

It may be helpful to distinguish systematic theology from three other approaches to theology: biblical or exegetical, historical, and tractarian. *Biblical* or *exegetical theology* is and should be an objective analysis of the biblical text, showing what the biblical authors believed and taught. Everything they believed and taught may not necessarily apply literally today. As an extreme example, God told the Israelites to literally "wipe out" the Canaanites, but very, very few Christians today would argue for a mass slaughter of non-Christians. *Historical theology* is methodologically identical with biblical theology, except that its scope is broadened to deal with the post-biblical period. Likewise, showing what Luther believed about the slaughter of peasants in 1525 may help our historical understanding of the sixteenth-century religious and economic situation, but that does not mean that Christians today ought necessarily to advocate the slaughter of any and every radical group in the United States. *Tractarian theology* is different. Anyone familiar with Luther's voluminous writings knows that most of what Luther wrote were tracts for the times. He took an issue and tried to find a Christian approach to it. He dealt with the marriage problem of Philip of Hesse as well as with the freedom of the Christian. He not only challenged his contemporary theologians to debate him on indulgences in his Ninety-five Theses, but he also attacked the humanist scholar Erasmus on free will. *Systematic theology,* on the other hand, is an attempt to set forth the Christian message in a coherent and consistent fashion—to show that the Christian faith is not simply a set of loosely held theological convictions but a "system." Analogously, tractarian theology takes the pieces of a puzzle and analyzes each piece as a separate and even unrelated part, whereas systematic theology wants to put the pieces of the puzzle together. Most attempts to deal with the issue of abortion come under the category of tractarian theology. My approach, on the other hand, is to set the issue of abortion within the context of the broader Christian world-view and to show how abortion in all but one circumstance violates the foundational principles of a consistent Christian philosophy of life.

To do this I will look at the abortion problem from four different perspectives: the *imago Dei,* reproduction, the "rights" of women, and the incarnation.

The *Imago Dei:* Key to Humanization

The biblical text (Gen. 1:26–27) clearly indicates man's uniqueness and superiority as a result of man's being created in the image of God. Scripture does not overly emphasize this fact of man's uniqueness. In fact, a careful study of both the Old and New Testaments will reveal that the importance of this concept cannot be determined by its frequency but rather by its place in crucial texts. What is also somewhat perplexing is the fact that the Bible does not seem to define exactly what this "image" is. We can explore philosophically and theologically the ways that man surpasses the rest of animal creation and then reflect upon man's distinctive traits, such as man's artistic and creative capacities. However, these are theological observations rather than exegetical. What is important for our discussion is not what the *imago Dei* is, but rather how the image of God is related to fetal development. Does the fetus possess the image of God from the moment of conception? Or is the image of God what a human being *becomes* at the conclusion of the birth process?

Many evangelicals (as argued in chapter 2) feel that the image of God is fully present at the moment of conception. Others argue that since the image of God deals more with man's function, such as "lording it over creation" (see Gen. 1:28 ". . . and have dominion over . . . every living thing"), than it does to an ontological dimension of human nature, the image is not present at the moment of conception. Harold O. J. Brown writes in *Death before Birth* that "according to the biblical view, then, man is made in God's image. He has stewardship dominion over the animals and may use them for meat" (Brown 1977, 121). In a somewhat unique way, my position combines both of these perspectives.

While I maintain that the image of God is present in the fetus (as is the *nephesh*), it is not something static. Rather, it is dynamic. It develops through one's life. The image of God refers to the total human being, shape and form as well as his role in creation. Consequently, the image of God is something that a human being grows into rather than simply is.

The juxtaposition of Genesis 1:27 (which indicates that God made man and woman in his image) and 1:28 (where he commands them "be fruitful and multiply . . .") suggests that God's image is most completely manifested when, through the marriage union, there is the creation of new life. In addition, by virtue of Genesis 1:27 and 2:15, it is clear that humanity has a God-given task to maintain God's creation. But the relational dimension between God and man, man and woman, and interpersonal relationships in general is where a fuller demonstration of the presence and outworking of the image of God is realized. On the matter of interpersonal relationships, consider James 3:9, where we are warned not even to curse our fellowman, because that person is "made in the likeness of God."

There is a Christological-moral analogy to this developmental idea when the New Testament speaks of our being "conformed" to the image of Christ (Rom. 8:29–30). This process begins with spiritual birth and continues to grow through one's lifetime. However, no Christian prior to the second-coming transformation will fully reflect the image or likeness of Christ (see Phil. 3:17–21; 1 John 3:1–3). Second, the *imago Dei* is not only those distinctive traits that distinguish man from the rest of the lower creation, nor is it simply man's role of ruling creation. The image of God is a part of the creative power that gives the fetus the spiritual power to develop the way it does.

For this reason, the image of God is tied to bisexuality (i.e., man and woman) in the Genesis account. With our naturalistic way of thinking, we suppose that the power of reproduction lies with the ovum and sperm and is controlled by the genetic code of the child being developed in the uterus. However, theologically speaking, the "image of God" causes the fetus to develop into a full human being. Philo, the first-century Jewish thinker, believed that the image of God was tied to man's physical development and that the actual punishment for causing the miscarriage of a well-developed fetus should result in capital punishment for the one causing the miscarriage (Grisez 1970, 130–31). We would agree with Clifford E. Bajema in his *Abortion and the Meaning of Personhood* that "the image of God (relative to man's status and nature) is not the end result of a process in which a nameless entity or product of conception acquires manness or humanness by degrees, until at birth it finally has sufficient manness or humanness to merit the protective diploma stating that it is now 'image of God'" (Bajema 1974, 39).

But, like most God-man relationships, the relationship between the fetus and the image of God is dynamic—God and man, the divine and the human, work together! Just as in the incarnation, God and man— the Holy Spirit and the Virgin Mary—cooperate in bringing the Savior into the world, so in the case of the child God and man cooperate. Although the genetic code does come from the biological mother and father, the fact that this genetic combination of ovum and sperm produces a "human being" results *not* from the genetic process but from the image of God *incarnate* in the genetics of conception! I am aware that many reading this interpretation may object, but I challenge the reader to discard his or her naturalism and to adopt a more thoroughly consistent biblical and theological perspective. From a philosophical point of view, the distinction I am making is analogous to the Aristotelian distinction between form and substance: the human parents provide the substance and the divine image provides the form of humanness. Both form and substance are present at conception, but both grow into the manifestation of the image of God.

Consequently, abortion is wrong not just because the killing of the fetus is destroying the image of God, but rather because abortion *prevents* the image of God from being fully manifest! Just as creation is a manifestation of God's glory, so human beings are manifestations *(epiphaneia)* of God's glory. Look at the text of 2 Corinthians 4:1–6 (esp. vv. 4–6) for a salvific–Christological analogy. When a fetus is destroyed, no matter at what point in the pregnancy, the abortion process prevents the image of God from being manifest. Analogies of growth and maturity further reenforce this interpretation.

We conclude, then, that abortion is a very serious sin against the purposes of God in creation and should be permitted only in those extremely rare cases where the life of the mother is at *real* risk! Then abortion is the lesser of two evils.

Reproduction: Human Creativity

The point we have just made about the image of God leads directly to the issue of human reproduction. I move now from the genetic-theological argument to the question of birth control and the popular use of abortion for the purposes of ending pregnancy or preventing childbirth. Ethically, what makes the abortion issue such a scandal is that we are living in the most knowledgeable age of man as far as sexual behavior is concerned. This is not to deny that there is still appalling ignorance on the part of many people about human sexuality. Nevertheless, contraceptives are more readily available today than at any previous period in history, and some devices may be purchased in many public rest rooms as well as the local drug stores. In spite of this, we have more illegitimate births and more teenage pregnancies than at any time in modern history. There is indeed a sexual revolution! We are more open on the subject, yet we exploit it in every conceivable manner. But, from a moral and a theological perspective, is birth control in any form permissible—and is abortion one of the ethically legitimate means of controlling reproduction?

In contrast to Roman Catholic moral theology, which forbids any form of controlling the birth of children technically, most Protestants have defended the moral right of legally married couples to try to control the conception of their offspring. Some may argue that the Roman Catholic Church permits the "rhythm method" of birth control, but this a common misunderstanding. What the Roman Catholic Church allows is that couples may engage in sexual relations when the wife *may* not be fertile, but a *deliberate* attempt to prevent conception while "enjoying" sex is still wrong. Married couples may legitimately express their love through sexual relations (i.e., have intercourse and "leave to God" the results), but to deliberately attempt to avoid pregnancy in any form is sin. The official Roman Catholic position is that sexual relations are for the primary purpose of procreation, and any attempt to distort that purpose—even calculating the wife's fertility—is sin. There are Protestant evangelicals, like Bill Gothard of the Institute for Basic Youth Conflicts seminars, who argue against married sexual relationships primarily for the joy of physical pleasure. (See also the earlier writings of John R. Rice—a well-known fundamentalist evangelist of three or four decades ago.) But probably most Protestants do not see marriage as primarily or exclusively for the purpose of producing children—especially if this means having as many children as possible!

In the previous section, I have connected the image of God with the development of the fetus into a "born human being" and then into mature and responsible adulthood, with the assumption that under normal circumstances human beings will marry and produce children. On the surface this may appear to support the Roman Catholic view that procreation is the primary purpose of marriage and sexual relations. The Catholic defense of this position on the grounds of "natural theology" raises very difficult questions. For one thing, what is "natural" for a man—a male human being? Most men have to fight to control their sexual desires and would probably become sexually involved with a wide variety of females, were it not for the higher moral principles that lead males to redirect their sexual desires in more constructive directions. (To see the effects of male sexuality upon welfare, economics, and the family, see George Gilder's best-selling *Wealth and Poverty,* pp. 83ff., and also his work *Sexual Suicide.*) Only higher principles or practical considerations lead human beings to want to avoid pregnancy, either temporarily or entirely, or to limit the number of children they want. Biblically and theologically, I would argue against a "natural" theology when it comes to human sexuality and would introduce a more responsible biblical and theological argument for marriage: the controllable family! Taking one's clue from the biblical account of creation: first, sexuality is a fundamental part of our humanness; second, repopulation of the earth is a responsible, rather than an irresponsible, mandate; and third, love, sex, and marriage are legitimate even where there are no children—especially where one or both spouses are incapable of either bearing or fathering a child.

In my judgment, the creation mandate to populate the earth has been fulfilled. I frankly believe we have too many human beings living on Planet Earth now! Although I have no personal intention of trying to get rid of any, I think responsible parenting involves *not* producing as many human beings as we can and/or more than our planet or society can responsibly care for. Sexual relations are enriching, legitimate, and wholesome ways of expressing our affection for our God-given spouses, and we should utilize whatever safe and healthy means are available to us to control reproduction. But abortion is not one of the legitimate means—nor, in my judgment, is the IUD or any other method that in effect destroys a *fertilized* ovum by preventing its normal implantation and gestation in the uterus. *Preventing conception* is fundamentally different from *destroying* what has already come into existence!

The healthy and responsible way to handle both illegitimate births and unwanted pregnancies is to adjust to the situation and accept full responsibility for one's actions or, in those cases where a woman cannot properly care for the child, to offer the child for adoption. Abortion cannot be equated to the removal of a malignant tumor! Nor can pregnancy honestly be considered a disease to be avoided. The human capacity to reproduce must be managed responsibly, but abortion is a clear violation of all that human sexuality implies. When Adam produced his son Seth (Gen. 5), and we are told that just as God had created man in his own image, Adam had now produced a child in his image, we see how intimately human reproduction is related to divine creativity and the image of God. This does not mean that the primary purpose of sex is procreative, nor does it deny humans the control of their desires or their capacity to reproduce. But once a child is conceived, its destruction at any point in the gestation process violates the procreative purposes of sexual love.

Human sexuality and the gift of reproducing another human being take on meaning within the Christian theology of creation, of which the family is a primary feature. Medical technology will continue to raise questions about genetic engineering and what we *can* do versus what we *should* do. However, I would argue that sterilization is fundamentally and qualitatively different from abortion. We can surgically alter many bodily functions without destroying life. A gallbladder operation certainly alters an important part of the body, but it may, in fact, enhance a person's life and improve one's health in so doing. Generally speaking, genetic engineering should be avoided when the purpose is to *control* persons or when it leads to a dehumanizing of the persons. Abortion may solve a pregnancy, but it destroys life and thereby defeats God's purposes.

Abortion and the "Rights" of Women

One of the major arguments advanced by feminist spokespersons for legally allowing abortion-on-demand is that abortion primarily reflects the "right" of a woman to have control over her body. On the surface this argument seems to have some plausibility, since people ought to have some rights with regard to the use or misuse of their bodies. But, in the case of abortion, the question of rights involves more than one person. Even if we assume for the moment that the fetus is not a complete human being (which is, I think, the correct way to think of the fetus: not *sub*human but certainly not a *complete* human being), this does not allow the woman carrying the child exclusive right to the developing human being now carried in her body. Unlike any other bodily function, pregnancy is a bisexual act. No matter how the conception occurs— whether by rape, through married love, or by artificial insemination— there has been only one truly virgin birth, and medical science has not as yet made auto-conception, self-impregnation, or homo-conception possible. What makes abortion completely unique is the fact that human life is a social reality. None of us came into this world single-handedly, none of us lives in isolation, and very few things we do are strictly personal and private. And certainly one of the most "public" things we all do is to be born and to participate in the ongoing life-giving process.

Biblically and theologically, life is a gift from God! Regardless of how we measure or evaluate the quality of life for human beings or qualify our humanness with such adjectives as "retarded" or "physically deformed" or "handicapped," the truth of the matter is that life—in whatever form—is life. I realize that any non-Christian reading this chapter will not be convinced by this argument, but the people to whom I am primarily writing are professing Christians—especially Christian women contemplating an abortion or the parents of a teenage daughter who is pregnant and considering an abortion. Their concern often seems to be more one of pride and public opinion than it is theology (the "word of God," not in the sense of the Bible, but in the sense of God's truth about life). That the fetus is alive is beyond doubt, medically, philosophically, and theologically. That the fetus can "survive" at some stage in the gestation process is beside the point, since no newborn infant could survive without some attention and care—not for very long, anyway!

Let us face head-on, then, the issue of "rights" with regard to abortion, particularly the rights of the woman having the abortion. Nowhere has the medical profession more hypocritically compromised the ethics of its profession than in the case of abortion. Medicine has no other purpose than to promote, save, and improve life. It is for this reason, and this reason alone, that I would only allow an abortion when the *physical life* of the mother is at stake. In my judgment, neither rape nor anticipated physical or neurological deformity are legitimate reasons for an abortion, and certainly not the lame excuse that "I do not want to have a child right now." Theologically speaking, mankind is called to emulate God in his creative work. Our rights—both female and male—are directly tied to the creation mandate to produce, to protect, and to promote life in all species of creation, and certainly among human beings. Even war, if ever justifiable, is theologically legitimate only when, in the end, the taking of life will actually promote life. This does not imply adopting some ill-defined "quality of life," so that a mother of four children is permitted to abort the fifth child because it would financially or culturally adversely affect the quality of life of the other four children.

One of the great ironies of the current abortion debate focuses on capital punishment. Many of the same people who strongly advocate abortion-on-demand oppose capital punishment. But capital punishment differs fundamentally from the issue of abortion and the so-called "rights" of a pregnant woman. Even capital punishment, which may or may not be a psychological deterrent to murder, is certainly a deterrent to the offender's killing a second or third or fourth victim if he or she were executed after having deliberately killed the first person. The taking of the life of a capital offender can only be justified as a witness to the sanctity of life in general and an actual deterrent to future offenses. But the issue of the "right to life" is the highest right of society and supersedes a woman's so-called "right" to treat a fetus as if it were a bowel movement or a malignant cancerous condition. The founding fathers of American society were theologically right when they argued that God had invested man with the right to life! That again is why if a mother's own life were at stake in the birthing process, it is the mother's life that must be guarded, even if the life of the fetus cannot be saved. The creation mandate calls us to produce, to protect and to promote LIFE! If abortion is defended on the grounds of a woman's right to her own body (man-made law), she may very well find this same argument turned against her when the man-made law is changed for some future scientific experiment—as in Nazi Germany—or as an expendable commodity—as with the thirty million "sacrificed" Chinese who died during Mao's attempts to communize China. The "right" to life derives from a higher source and should not be taken away by humans. "Rights" are fragile realities. No one has a right to do whatever he or she will with his or her own life, nor with the life of another, except in very rare and unusual circumstances. Pregnancy is not an "unusual" circumstance; it is rather one of the highest callings God gives to human beings: the privilege of participating in the life-creating process of bringing another human being into God's world. That is our *right*! Our *calling* is not to stop the process once it has begun!

Abortion and the Incarnation

Given the moral climate of the first century, if that society had had the knowledge we possess today with regard to conception, contraception, and abortion, I am convinced that Jesus of Nazareth would not have been born! That is indeed a shocking fact! We tend to idealize the gospel story, tend to play down the truly human drama of this life-and-death historical event. Consider the scandal! The public embarrassment of an unmarried pregnant teenager was probably worse in the first-century Jewish culture than it is today. And very few males would want to have been in the place of Joseph! One of my colleagues does a dramatic reading about Joseph's dilemma over Mary's pregnancy, and it brings home, as few sermons do, the internal struggle that Joseph faced. Any engaged man who has read the gospel narratives of Mary's virgin conception of Jesus the Christ must have wrestled with what he would have done had he been Joseph. The current use of abortion to handle an unexpected and unwanted pregnancy confronts us all with the reality of the incarnation event, since there are several aspects of the incarnation that have an indirect bearing on the abortion issue.

First, God is not afraid of scandal! In my work as a teaching theologian and as an active pastor, I have had several firsthand professional involvements with young women from evangelical Christian homes who came to me for counseling on how to handle an unwanted pregnancy. From my work in the church, I know of many who have either had an abortion or rejected it as a solution to an unwanted pregnancy. I am sorry to report that several I have counseled not to have an abortion had one anyway! Two cases here are worth citing. One was the case of a girl who claimed that she was drugged and sexually abused by several fellows at a party at the apartment of one of the young men. She awoke to find herself unclothed and in the bed of one of the fellows. Several weeks later she came to my office, aware that she was pregnant. This girl had naively gone to this apartment thinking that she was a guest at a large party, only to find herself a drugged rape victim. And pregnant! I encouraged her to have the baby and put it up for adoption, but *because of potential public scandal,* both she and her parents decided for an abortion. Another leading family in this same evangelical congregation, whose rebellious daughter became pregnant by her irresponsible and "worthless" boyfriend, also opted for an abortion against my pastoral advice, again for reasons of avoiding public embarrassment. Of course, it is theoretically possible that the incarnation might have occurred in some other manner than it did. However, it is insightful that God did not attempt to avoid public scandal. Admittedly, pregnancy out of wedlock is less and less the scandal it once was—it is far too common today! But in many evangelical circles, abortions are being performed primarily because the scandal of a professing Christian's having been sexually irresponsible and then becoming pregnant causes the Christian girl or her Christian parents to adopt the world's way, rather than the way of the incarnation: turning scandal into redemptive love!

Second, the incarnation illustrates how good may come from what appears to be evil. I do not advocate premarital sex, and no one should misunderstand the following statements as either an implied or explicit approval of sexual involvement without the bonds of marriage. I am convinced that intimacy prior to marital commitment is dangerous to the marriage and to the persons involved, no matter how well-intended. But the facts are that biblically and theologically speaking, marriage is not a church wedding nor an expensive ceremony! Although it is very unwise to engage in sexual intercourse before the legal and spiritual consummation of the marriage, we ought never to socially or morally pressure a couple to have an abortion simply because the wedding day is several weeks or months away. As Joseph took Mary to be his lawful wife both to protect her as well as the child, so two people who have behaved improperly and prematurely ought to consummate their marriage legally and spiritually, because *in God's sight the marriage union has already been accomplished,* although the marriage union will require a lifetime to fulfill!

There is, however, a third implication from the incarnation. Some evangelicals would allow for an abortion when the pregnancy is the result of rape or incest. What we face in the abortion issue is a clear-cut issue. Shall we handle human problems humanly or from a clearly Christian perspective? From a purely human perspective, there is no way that Joseph would have "bought" the story that Mary was pregnant by the Holy Spirit. How many young men or fathers reading this story would have believed it if their fiancée or daughter told them they were pregnant by the Holy Spirit? It is only because Joseph was the man of God he was that he was willing to lay aside his male (human) pride and to consider that Mary was being honest and faithful and that God might work in this highly unusual way. In cases of rape or incest, I would still counsel a young woman—as I did those mentioned above—to have the baby and let God work a miracle of love for some childless couple. The incarnation shows how God is always working good through the humanly irrational and publicly unacceptable. While I have witnessed the tragedy of unwanted pregnancy and abortion, I have also witnessed several young women who admitted their sin and went ahead with the pregnancy. I have seen wonderful congregations "adopt" both the mother and the baby—as well as the family. They shower them with love and bring great blessing out of what appeared to be a terrible tragedy. In one church where I served as the pulpit pastor, we dedicated the baby while several of the spiritual men in the church publicly stated their willingness to act as the mother and child's surrogate "fathers and grandfathers." This young woman's own father had died from cancer several years earlier. It was a moving ceremony that morning as the young unwed mother admitted her wrong, asked the congregation for forgiveness, and then the three "fathers" who stood on the platform promised to assist the mother and the child financially, emotionally, and spiritually until the young woman was married to a Christian husband. She has now moved to another state, but several months ago I received a wonderful letter from her, telling how God had brought a wonderful young man into her life and that they were married and her daughter now had a good father.

The Ultimate Theology of Abortion: Life and Forgiveness

Abortion is one of the greatest tragedies of the twentieth century—if not the greatest! Far more human beings have been killed through abortion than in all the wars of our century! The destruction of life in any form is the antithesis of God's primary purpose in creation. The biblical picture of evil and the devil is of a destroyer of life. Even war, a sometimes excusable exception, is no less a horror and an affront to the purposes of God. For this reason, if in the life-giving birthing process the *life* of the mother is at stake, a judgment must be made as to whether to save the mother's life or that of the child. Since we can never know whether the newborn child will be stillborn or survive, and since we do know that the mother is now living, the rational and theological approach suggests that we save the mother, even if we cannot also save the child. This situation is indeed medically very rare in our day of sophisticated techniques for treating problem pregnancies, but the provision must be there for those cases where the situation arises. At this point a value judgment must be made; weighing all factors, there can be little doubt that a living mother-wife's life is of greater social value than that of an unborn infant!

Professionally, I have had to counsel several young and not-so-young women who have had abortions. I know their scars from this secondhand perspective, and no one whom I have counseled now lives "at peace" with the reality of having had an abortion. But we cannot bring back the dead! Nor will we be able to remove the scar that an abortion causes physiologically, mentally, and morally. However, there are several things that any woman or man who has been involved in abortion can do. Like Dr. Bernard N. Nathanson—the reformed abortionist—one can speak about the evils and dangers of abortion-on-demand (the primary reason behind this book!). Until our entire society—not just the Supreme Court—becomes morally conscious of the horrible evil of abortion, no Christian can remain silent, and men who have encouraged an abortion, as well as women who have had one performed, are the best spokespersons we have in this crusade! Along with speaking out, we can be visibly active. Picketing and demonstrating at abortion clinics is a legitimate form of protest, as long as we do not injure the people we are trying to save or destroy property (all life and property belongs to God). We can counsel in hot-line programs or counseling centers. A woman who has been personally involved in the tragedy of abortion is a far more powerful voice than a theologian speaking theoretically.

A second aspect to be considered is that a victim of abortion needs to live with God's complete forgiveness. Carrying a heavy load of guilt will not correct the incorrectable. Guilt is a weight that no one needs to carry! If there is any feature of the Christian faith that puts it head and shoulders above all other religious systems, it is Christianity's concept of forgiveness. The one truly legitimate death is the death of God for our human failures! God knows how to forgive and yearns for every human being to find that complete release, not only from the power of sin but also from the guilt of sin. Guilt is one of the most debilitating psychological ailments to afflict the human race. If you have violated the sacred trust of co-creating, preserving, and protecting life, then confess that sin to God and accept his wonderful promise that "if we confess our sins, he

[God] is faithful and just, and will forgive our sins and cleanse us from *all* unrighteousness" (1 John 1:9, italics mine; cf. Isa. 1:18–19). If you have sinned through the act of aborting a potential human being, my prayer is that God will give to you the peace you desire through Jesus Christ, the One who died for *all* sin!

References and Further Reading

Bajema, C. E. 1974 (1977). *Abortion and the meaning of personhood.* Grand Rapids: Baker.

Brown, H. O. J. 1977. *Death before birth.* Nashville: Thomas Nelson.

Cohen, M.; Nagel, T.; & Scanlon, T., eds. 1974. *The rights and wrongs of abortion.* Princeton: Princeton Univ. Press.

Granfield, D. 1969. *The abortion decision.* Garden City: Doubleday.

Grisez, G. G. 1970. *Abortion: The myths, the realities, and the arguments.* New York: Corpus Books.

Hardin, G. 1973. *Stalking the wild taboo.* Los Altos: William Kaukmann.

Hilgers, T. W., & Horan, D. J., eds. 1972. *Abortion and social justice.* New York: Sheed & Ward.

Koop, C. E. 1984. *The right to live: The right to die.* Wheaton: Tyndale.

Lader, L. 1973. *Abortion II: Making the revolution.* Boston: Beacon.

Noonan, J. T, ed. 1970. *The morality of abortion.* Cambridge: Harvard Univ. Press.

Nathanson, B. N., & Ostling, R. N. 1979. *Aborting America.* Garden City: Doubleday.

Regan, T. 1980. *Matters of life and death.* Philadelphia: Temple University.

Sarvis, B., & Rodman, H. 1973. *The abortion controversy.* New York: Columbia Univ. Press.

Sumner, L. W. 1981. *Abortion and moral theory.* Princeton: Princeton Univ. Press.

Wennberg, R. N. 1985. *Life in the balance: Exploring the abortion controversy.* Grand Rapids: Eerdmans.

PART TWO

Ethical Perspectives and Value Systems

6

Some Ethical Questions
Arthur F. Holmes

While it seems to me quite clear that the value Scripture places on human fetal life as a trust from God stands against abortion-on-demand, abortion as a means of birth control, abortions of "convenience," and so forth, there are some questions that this Judeo-Christian view of life does not answer by itself. Additional premises are needed if we are to draw even tentative conclusions about such specific matters as life-threatening situations for the mother, the possibility of therapeutic abortion, the victim of rape or incest, and similar tangled problems. On these matters, as we have seen in part one, the Bible offers no explicit guidance or direct statements, and our attempts at drawing inferences are complicated by conflicting moral concerns that often point us in two different directions at once. Yet any consideration of abortion is superficial and insensitive if it fails to take such cases into account.

Nor are these the only unanswered ethical questions. In a pluralistic society, where the Judeo-Christian view of life no longer has the field to itself and abortions seem unrestrained, what can the Christian do that is consonant both with Judeo-Christian values and their coexistence with other viewpoints in a democratic setting? What paths are open to us? Is it ethical to try to legislate for everybody the morality of just one segment of society? What else can be done?

These are difficult issues, which in Christian integrity we dare not gloss over. The cases referred to above represent only a small minority of all the abortions performed, but minorities are still people for whom we are morally responsible. Moreover, the relation of law to morality in a pluralistic society is not that of a theocracy. But then the New Testament church did not live in a theocracy either. How should the relationship be conceived, and what other avenues than the law are available for social change?

For years evangelical scholars have found nothing in Scripture that directly addressed the abortion question, for even the somewhat ambiguous Exodus 21:22–23 passage discussed in chapter 2 is about injury to a pregnant woman, not about voluntary or therapeutic abortion.[1] More recent scholarly suggestions still need extended critical appraisal, but in any case the biblical material leaves us to draw inferences rather than simply to apply what is explicitly taught on the subject. Even my opening assumption about the Judeo-Christian view of life makes an inference concerning abortion, rather than reporting what is explicit. While I find that particular inference unavoidable, the Scripture seems even less clear on the other questions I raised. How are we to proceed?

I propose to sketch some approaches that ethicists have developed, largely in addressing other topics than abortion, and thereby to suggest procedures for thinking about abortion.

Lack of Explicit Biblical Teaching

Evangelicals accept Scripture as the final rule for both faith and practice, in the sense that it has the last and decisive word. This is not to say, however, that Scripture is to be our *only* source of knowledge or moral guidance, that no other input is ever available, or that it says everything we need to know on every topic. The Bible is in fact neither exclusive nor exhaustive.

In matters where the Bible is silent, inexplicit, or very generalized, we do have additional resources: inference, extra-biblical insights (including philosophical ethics), and the history of Christian ethics. Much of what Christians have written about abortion, in this volume and elsewhere, is by inference from Scripture rather than by direct application. Not all so-called inferences follow of necessity from their premises: some are simply consonant with those premises without being necessitated by them. The value of fetal life is itself an inference from a few biblical statements and the overall doctrine of creation. But more spe-

---

[1]See, for example, papers from a joint conference of the Evangelical Theological Society and the Christian Medical Society, *Birth control and the Christian*. W. O. Spitzer & C. L. Saylor (Tyndale, 1969); and R. F. R. Gardner, *Abortion: The personal dilemma* (Eerdmans, 1972).

cific inferences about the more difficult issues require more specific premises than something that generalized. Such premises involve what ethicists call "middle-level concepts."

Moral insight also comes from extra-biblical sources. The apostle Paul recognized natural moral knowledge (Rom. 1:19–32; 2:14–15), and Christian ethicists have historically often appealed to a natural moral law or to a moral sense or conscience grounded in the doctrine of creation. What natural law emphasizes, particularly in the tradition that comes to us from Thomas Aquinas, is that certain universal aspects of human life manifest natural ends that God intends we should seek. Our understanding of these ends provides us with the middle concepts we need.[2]

A third resource, the history of Christian ethics, provides reflection on virtually every aspect of our existence, an accumulation of wisdom from those steeped in Scripture and in the experience of Christ's church. This, too, focuses frequently on middle-level concepts.

What are these middle concepts? To cite one example, in addressing business ethics within the complexities of a modern corporation, we need a concept of work and its proper ends in God's creation. A biblical theology of work is the place to start, with notions of stewardship and servanthood grounded in biblical materials. Understanding the inherent nature and ends of work will help: its economic function, the disciplines and skills it requires, the creativity it might elicit, the sense of community it engenders, the service it renders. And the history of Christian ethics about economic matters of various sorts further shapes the concept: Luther's doctrine of vocation, the Franciscan emphasis on humble service, and so forth.

What middle-level concepts apply in regards to abortion? One is the human sexual relationship. Here, too, we have both biblical and natural indications, as well as the historical resources of Christian ethics. Biblically, sex is seen as both potentially reproductive and potentially unitive, and the same ends are indicated by the nature of human sexuality itself. The unitive element is evident in its capacity to develop, renew, and maintain devotion and loyalty throughout a couple's years together. But both these possibilities bring responsibility: voluntary sexual activity is a tacit acceptance of responsibility for its reproductive as well as its unitive outcomes. To selfishly shun either responsibility violates the God-given meaning and purpose of sex. This argues against abortion for the sexually active as a "way out" of either marriage or parenthood. On the other hand, the rape or incest victim is in a different situation, for

---

[2]For example, the Episcopal wedding service begins with a statement of God's *purposes* for marriage.

appeal cannot be made to responsibility for one's sexual activity when it is involuntary and against one's will. In such instances, the case against abortion, especially at a very early stage, is less clear, and with this the wisdom of Protestant sexual ethics has generally agreed.

Even more significant is the concept of human life. What is there about human life that is of such value? Initially I simply spoke of it as a trust from God, but other things of lesser value also come to us in trust from God. What is there about human life that bears on its value? How we answer this question will influence what we say about the value of fetal life and about abortion in "difficult" cases. First, a human life is a created thing, therefore not of absolute, unconditional value. Only God has absolute, unqualified value, unsurpassed by all others. "Thou shalt not kill" was not, in its Mosaic setting, an exceptionless command, since capital punishment was admissible for at least ten crimes, and there are other biblical contexts in which human life was forfeited. Yet both that commandment and the natural law of self-preservation that we see at work throughout creation tell us that human life is to be valued and preserved. But why the higher value on specifically human life than on other living things?

The human soul has been one point of emphasis. Medieval scholars surmised that since soul gives life to the body, it must be imparted to a fetus at the point of quickening when the mother first feels the baby move within her. By such reckoning, fetal life attains individual human value at that point, around ten weeks. But the time of ensoulment is, of course, really impossible to identify, and not all Christians regard the soul as an ingredient added. Others appeal to the *imago Dei,* which marks us off from other creatures: it is this capacity for God-likeness that is so valuable. Still others, pursuing that clue, appeal to the distinctiveness of being persons, self-conscious and responsible beings in relation to God and to other people. Each of these approaches, it should be noticed, distinguishes the *biological* life we have in common with other creatures from *more distinctively human* aspects of a life. A human embryo is valued because of what it not yet is but already has the biological potential to become.

This kind of approach has been vigorously criticized, since the naturalistic pro-choicer sees no value in the "mere potential" of a fetus. But that line of criticism misses the crucial role of presuppositions. The naturalist presupposes that physical things are themselves entirely value-free and that values only arise because we humans place value on things; these presuppositions, of course, imply that a fetus has no value unless those involved want to keep it. But Judeo-Christian presuppositions are different. God has created a world loaded with potential for ends he intended, some of which ends he calls us humans to help actualize. The fetus, then, has God-given purpose and value, and its life must be respected even though it still lacks developed personhood. To simply trumpet the value of early fetal life and refuse any distinction between biological and personal existence plays into the hands of naturalistic presuppositions—in addition to gutting the term "person" of any distinctive meaning. The middle-level concept of what distinguishes *human* life, namely the person, must be developed, or we have insufficient premises for addressing abortion questions.

One result of recognizing the developing potential of unborn human beings is that abortion becomes increasingly objectionable as a pregnancy proceeds. The genetic individuality established by fertilization of an ovum is a necessary precondition for the development of human personal qualities. It is a gift from God to be cherished; it is necessary but not sufficient for personal existence. But the necessary months of fetal development are divinely provided, too. Hence most people regard a stillborn child or a twenty-week abortion, even a ten-week miscarriage, far differently than they view the use of an IUD. One prefers early medical treatment for the rape victim over "waiting to see" if she is pregnant; and if a therapeutic abortion is ever justifiable at all, it should be undertaken as early as possible. Without a middle-level concept of human life that involves the fetal development of the person, one should make no such distinctions. The IUD, a twenty-week abortion, and assassinating the president would all carry the same moral condemnation on exactly the same grounds.

A further result of recognizing this middle-level concept has to do with the question of therapeutic abortion. This issue now focuses on the fetus's potential for personal human existence. A case of uncorrectable brain malformation that precludes any development of self-consciousness and of the capacity for relating to other persons seems to be nature's indication that the distinctively human potential has *already* been aborted. More agonizing still is the fact that such indications come in varying degrees, so that ambiguity accompanies any decision or even the withholding of one.

In many ways this is a paradigm of the larger problem of evil. God's creation is loaded with potentials that may or may not be actualized in the course of time—by nature, by human work, by science, or by art. As creation now stands, some potentials are actualized for good, some for evil, perhaps most with a mixture of the two. Some are truncated and others completely frustrated. How are we to respond to the potential for radical natural evil and what should we do about it? That is the larger question of which the question of therapeutic abortion is part. The evil lies in what has already happened to the potential for human personal existence.

Middle-level concepts give us something of a handle for moral reflection, but they need to be accompanied by a second point of reference, the overarching principles of biblical ethics, namely justice and love. I call them overarching principles since they apply to every area of moral responsibility, whereas the sixth and seventh commandments apply to two particular areas. That they are overarching ethical principles is frequently the claim of both philosophical ethics and the history of Christian ethics—the same resources we appealed to before. Even when the Bible is silent on particulars, when explicit biblical guidance is lacking, we are still obligated to practice justice and love.

Tying this into middle-level concepts, we can now ask how to pursue the proper purposes of an activity (a pregnancy, for instance) with justice and love. Under what conditions might abortion be the most just and loving course to follow, considering the unborn, as well as the mother and family? Ethicist Paul Ramsey argues on this basis for terminating pregnancy in situations that threaten the mother's life, for she has become the victim, as it were, of unjust attack. On the other hand, love may lead a couple to give of themselves in an uncertain future with their malformed child.

Questions about what is the just and loving thing to do in such cases can rarely be given unequivocal answers. Nor do middle-level concepts, however illumined by introducing justice and love, always yield ethically unambiguous answers. Life is too complicated, too twisted, too often laced with conflicting moral duties.

Conflict of Moral Responsibilities

If every moral decision were a clear-cut black-or-white distinction between unequivocal right and wrong, life would be a lot simpler. Unfortunately, the complexities of the human condition sometimes preclude such answers, and we are faced with moral dilemmas.

Consider punishment. We have a moral responsibility to respect another person's life, liberty, and property, but society also has a responsibility to punish criminal offenders. This poses a dilemma, for punishment may involve taking the offender's property (fines) or his liberty (imprisonment) or, in the most extreme case, his life—which normally we are to respect. One responsibility or the other must yield.

Consider civil disobedience. We have the moral duty of obedience to civil authorities, but we also have the duty of upholding just treatment for all: a moral dilemma. One responsibility or the other must yield.

The case of defensive war is similar. In the face of armed aggression, the duty of respecting all human life and property conflicts with the duty of protecting the innocent from unjust violence. We cannot fulfill both duties. Again, one must yield to the other.

Similar dilemmas give rise to the question of abortion, whether for the rape victim or the mother whose life is at risk or because of some extreme condition of the fetus. How may we decide in such conflicts of responsibility?

A purely consequentialist approach to ethics, such as utilitarianism, runs into problems here, for it resolves dilemmas by simply weighing one set of consequences against another. The difficulty is their incommensurability. It is like comparing peaches and pears; there is no common denominator. And at times our moral duties tell us to accept the consequences we most dread. The alternative to consequentialism is to recognize that not all our duties or responsibilities have equal priority, and so we rank them for their centrality to justice and love. Civil disobedience rests on the priority of seeking justice for all over obedience to unjust laws. The legitimacy of war depends on the prior duty of government to defend peace and justice. Similarly, I suggest, with difficult abortion cases. If an abortion is at all justifiable, it can only be because of some higher duty than protecting a fetal life.

The possibility of allowing exceptions to normal moral obligations poses the danger of things getting out of hand. For that reason, ethicists over the centuries have hedged exceptions to moral rules with rules to govern such exceptions. "Rule-governed exceptions" become the only ethically allowable ones. The paradigm comes from the "just war" theory, whose rules insist both on justice in going to war *(jus ad bellum)* and justice in the conduct of war *(jus in bello)*. There must be just cause (defense against unjust aggression), just intention (to restore a just peace for friends and foes alike), proportionate means, the immunity of innocent parties from intentional violence, and so forth. Analogously with civil disobedience, there must be just cause, just intention, proportionate means, and the immunity of innocent parties. The same with criminal punishment. Rules must govern the tragic exceptions.

We need the same kind of provision in regards to abortion. A blanket prohibition of all abortions for any reason whatsoever would be like calling fines "stealing" or prison sentences "kidnapping," or like forbidding civil disobedience under any circumstance. The Judeo-Christian objection to abortion is valid, but its detailed application needs much closer attention. Christian ethicists need to take further the kind of work that has previously been done in identifying typical cases that may or may not warrant abortion. What constitutes just cause? just intention? and so forth. Pastors, counseling centers and hospital ethics boards need such guidelines.

Conflict Between Contemporary Practice and Christian Ethics

We live in a highly litigious society that expects legislation and the courts to rectify every problem. Many of us have the same tendency as individuals. If current practices violate our own moral convictions, we want laws that will change things. To an extent this is appropriate, but vesting our hopes in legislation leads to two kinds of difficulty: other avenues for social change can be neglected; and the attempt to legislate our own moral convictions can conflict with the rights of other groups in a pluralistic society.

Legislation is, after all, only one way of effecting change. Following is a list of the non-violent means available, arranged in order of increasing moral complexity:

1. The life of a community that bears witness to a better way
2. The preaching and teaching of the church
3. Social work, for instance with unwed mothers and adoption agencies
4. Education
5. Publications and the use of the media
6. Engaging in ethical dialogue with those who do not agree
7. Campaigns to influence public opinion
8. Entering power structures (e.g., public service, hospital, or school boards) to change things from within
9. Political pressure groups affecting both legislation and government regulations
10. Boycotts
11. Strikes and sit-ins
12. Civil disobedience, leading to test cases in court

Within this listing, legislation and judicial decisions certainly have a place. The difficulty is the dilemma they can create: we fulfill one responsibility by securing morals legislation, but thereby we violate another responsibility to respect certain rights and liberties of others. On the other hand, if we respect those rights, then we violate the moral responsibility that the legislation was to satisfy. Moreover, whose morality is to be imposed on us all? Would we, to put the shoe on the other foot for a moment, want the Ayatollah Khomeni's moral beliefs imposed on everybody? How would we respond to some brave-new-world law, rooted in lifeboat ethics, that after having one child a woman must terminate every subsequent pregnancy?

A relationship exists between law and morality, but not necessarily the exact relationship we see in the early Israelite theocracy of the Old Testament, in which the law of God was in every specific the law of the land. Calvin's Geneva and the New England of Hawthorne's *Scarlet Letter* no longer exist, and we cannot force people willy-nilly into that form of government. Indeed, the relationship between law and morality in the New Testament is markedly more limited than in the Old. The churches to whom the apostles wrote lived under Roman law, in a religiously and ethically pluralistic society. The functions of government to which Paul refers, therefore, have to do with retributive justice and the civil order (Rom. 13:1–7), which are surpassed (but not abrogated) by biblical morality (Rom. 13:8–14). The history of Christian ethics recognizes this, too. Thomas Aquinas's *Treatise on Law* grounds civil and criminal law in the natural moral law, not in the divine law revealed in Scripture and entrusted to the church, which goes beyond what natural law alone requires.

Our own judicial system is influenced more by John Stuart Mill's libertarianism, with its insistence that an individual's liberties may only be restricted in order to prevent harm to other persons. He was particularly concerned to protect a minority group against a "tyranny of the majority." But he saw no relation between law and morality other than in terms of the human consequences of legislation. At the other extreme is the kind of legal moralism that views a main function of law as the enforcement of morality, in the tradition of ancient Israel and Calvin's Geneva. In between, paternalists want legislation that prevents individuals from harming themselves as well as others and perhaps forces them to do what benefits them. These alternatives need careful consideration whenever morals legislation is proposed, for the question of law and morality lies behind whatever legal action we do or do not pursue.[3]

One way of handling this in a pluralistic society is to try to develop a moral consensus, a less-than-ideal position, on which overall agreement could be reached. The Old Testament theocracy was established by God's covenanting with his people. On the basis of that consensus, the law was established. In regards to abortion in our society, this might mean working for a consensus that, for example, objects to late abortions and so proposing legislation to restrict abortions after the first trimester, with rule-governed exceptions only as approved by ethics boards. Both pro-life and pro-choice advocates should find this preferable to the others'

---

[3]For Christian treatments of this topic see J. N. D. Anderson, *Morality, law & grace* (IVP, 1972); B. Mitchell, *Law, morality and religion in a secular society* (Oxford Univ. Press, 1967); and A. F. Holmes, *Ethics: Approaching moral decisions* (IVP, 1984), ch. 11.

previous alternatives. Meantime, the educative and other processes are free to work still further.

The fact is, I believe, that law does and must enforce at least a minimal morality that is essential to the harmonious functioning of a society. In a pluralistic context with democratic concerns, some sort of moral consensus is necessary before legislation can go any further than that.

Where does this leave us? Plainly, not where we would like to be. Such is the moral condition of this fallen world. But working through those underlying ethical issues does shed light on some difficult questions. Ethical reflection on moral dilemmas, or where Scripture is less than explicit, is rarely conclusive. When decisions lack logical certainty (and even when they do not), they require wisdom and teachability. The last word on abortion, moreover, should not be about either moral law or governmental legislation, but rather about the grace of God that imparts a new life of forgiveness, freedom, and hope.[4]

References and Further Reading

Anderson, J. N. D. 1972. *Morality, law and grace.* Downers Grove: IVP.

———. 1976. *Issues of life and death.* Downers Grove: IVP.

Callahan, D. J. 1970. *Abortion: Law, Choice and Morality.* New York: Macmillan.

Gardner, R. F. R. 1972. *Abortion: The personal dilemma.* Grand Rapids: Eerdmans.

Grisez, G. G. 1970. *Abortion: The myths, realities and the arguments.* New York: Corpus Books.

Mitchell, B. 1967. *Law, morality and religion in a secular society.* Oxford: Oxford Univ. Press.

Noonan, J. T., ed. 1970. *The morality of abortion.* Cambridge: Harvard Univ. Press.

Ramsey, P. 1978. *Ethics at the edges of life.* New Haven: Yale Univ. Press.

Simons, P. D. 1983. *Birth and death: Bioethical decision making.* Philadelphia: Westminster.

---

[4]Roman Catholic writers on the subject include D. J. Callahan, *Abortion: Law, choice and morality* (Macmillan, 1970); G. G. Grisez, *Abortion: The myths, realities and the arguments* (Corpus Books, 1970); J. T. Noonan (ed.), *The morality of abortion* (Harvard Univ. Press, 1970). Protestant writers in addition to those in note 1 include J. N. D. Anderson, *Issues of life and death* (IVP, 1976); D. G. Jones, *Brave new people* (Eerdmans, 1985); Paul Ramsey, *Ethics at the edges of life* (Yale Univ. Press, 1978); P. D. Simons, *Birth and death: bioethical decision making* (Westminster, 1983); L. B. Smedes, *Mere morality* (Eerdmans, 1983), pp. 124–145; R. N. Wennberg, *Life in the balance* (Eerdmans, 1985).

Smedes, L. B. 1983. *Mere morality*. Grand Rapids: Eerdmans.

Spitzer, W. O., & Saylor, C. L., eds. 1969. *Birth control and the Christian*. Wheaton: Tyndale.

Wennberg, R. N. 1985. *Life in the balance: Exploring the abortion controversy*. Grand Rapids: Eerdmans.

7

Abortion, Bioethics, and the Evangelical

David B. Fletcher and Albert J. Smith

The ongoing abortion debate in our society is characterized by sloganeering, picketing, politicking, and editorializing, all of which make broad emotional appeals to our sympathies toward either fetuses or women. Amid the clatter is a less-publicized dialogue, a thoughtful and painstaking discussion in the field of bioethics. A relatively new interdisciplinary field, bioethics combines the efforts of philosophers, theologians, physicians and other health-care professionals, lawyers, social scientists, and others. The rise of contemporary bioethics dates to the pioneering efforts of Protestant theologians Joseph Fletcher and Paul Ramsey, along with others, in the 1950s and 1960s. Today its booming activity can be seen in the great number of articles on bioethics appearing in philosophical, theological, and medical journals, in specialized bioethics journals, and in organizations dedicated to research and discussion of bioethical issues, such as the Hastings Center, the Kennedy Institute for Ethics at Georgetown University, and the Park Ridge Center. Bioethics is now studied by presidential commissions; in workshops for ethicists, physicians, lawyers, and government officials; and in courses in colleges and medical schools.

Issues often addressed cursorily on the evening news and in the Sunday newspaper supplement are treated at a high level of intellectual sophistication by bioethicists. Alongside the classical issues of truthtelling and paternalism have arisen new concerns from such recent biotechnology as test-tube babies or the artificial heart. Each of the various disciplines brings to bioethics its unique contribution, and commitments of faith and ideology affect the ways these issues are addressed. Although few distinctively evangelical approaches have been offered, a genuine hearing is given to religious perspectives in the bioethical dialogue, from the secularism of H. Tristam Engelhardt to the Roman Catholicism of Richard McCormick and the "mainline" Protestantism of Paul Ramsey.

Despite the diversity of disciplinary perspectives and world-view commitments that go into the bioethical melting pot, a distinct number of central issues, methods, and principles have emerged in bioethical discussion. Arguments, case studies, and application of principles used in the study of bioethics call on a host of background concerns in ethical theory, in metaphysics, and in social and political philosophy. From these emerge the traditional discussion of rights, duties, and the proper role of law in governing society.

Nowhere in bioethics is understanding of the background more needed than in the treatment of abortion, perhaps the single topic that has most engaged the attention of bioethicists. In many scores of articles (more than 270 since 1970), books, and dissertations, abortion has attracted great theoretical interest. Why has abortion been such an absorbing topic? Perhaps it is because abortion raises deep questions about fundamental issues on which there is no clear consensus. What is personhood? What is required for a being to be considered a person with all the moral significance entailed by that status? How are the rights of the fetus to be balanced against those of a woman, for example, to control her own body in the intimate area of reproduction? What are our basic duties to one another? What should be the relation of moral right and wrong to the formal, secular control of the legal system?

The Nature of Ethical Reflection

Bioethics, as its name implies, is the study of ethics as it relates to living things as understood through the life sciences. Since so much of our ethical concern relates to biomedical treatment of human beings, bioethics is a major concern of the health professions. "Ethics" as used here does not refer merely to morality, to standards of right conduct; rather, ethics is the rational investigation of those standards. Ethical reflection often begins at the point at which our traditional understandings of those standards begin to fail us. This may be because we find ourselves faced with conflicting moral considerations, such as when the doctor's obligation to tell the truth conflicts with the responsibility to spare the patient possibly dangerous emotional stress. Then again, it may be because the concerns that call for decisions are new and untried, such as the treatment that we should accord to frozen human embryos. In the rapidly changing area of health care, such ethical puzzlement has become daily fare.

Since the days of Socrates, "ethics" has involved the application of clear, fair-minded, and hard thinking to questions of how we should live. It calls for reasoned solutions to moral questions that refer back to basic principles, rather than the application of merely subjective judgments that may not be supported by reason. It is no easy task to make sound moral decisions in the face of moral questions, in this case those about abortion, in such a way that we can commend our conclusions to the wider society.

We must first realize that moral judgment is really the end of a rational process that begins by applying (1) a very general ethical *theory* to a specific, concrete moral problem. Theories support (2) ethical *principles,* such as justice, respect for persons, and beneficience ("promote benefit/avoid harm"). These in turn generate (3) *rules,* which apply the principle to problem areas and arrive at (4) a *judgment.* While quite often we find that judgments or decisions are hastily made without due consideration of rules or principles, our objective is to establish principles and rules that can be widely accepted and lead to well-supported judgments. The structure of moral justification, then, moving from the general to specific, is (1) theory, (2) principle, (3) rule, (4) judgment.

Ethics presents us with a number of competing theories. Consequentialists contend that results are of crucial importance, specifically, benefits to human beings. Noteworthy in this group are utilitarians, who argue that the right thing to do is to promote the greatest amount of happiness for the greatest number of people affected by the action. Deontologists stress the importance of how we get those results, and in particular whether we follow or violate moral standards. Among this group, many biblical Christians believe that God's commands provide the standards for conduct. Within such diverse theories the same basic principles emerge—including, for example, autonomy, which directs us to respect the liberties of individuals. Rules drawn from this principle would itemize general ways that rights could be respected, supporting specific judgments in particular cases.

If the structure of theory-principle-rule-judgment is common to various ethical perspectives, why do we not all then agree on rules for moral decision making and arrive at the same judgments? Some barriers to this are lack of agreement on facts pertaining to the situation, lack of agreement on meaning of terms, disagreement as to which principles to apply, and, sometimes, finding that principles seem to conflict.

Ethical reflection requires understanding of relevant facts, although they alone cannot settle a moral issue decisively. When abortion is the issue, it is helpful to know when conception occurs, or when brain waves begin in the fetus, or how insemination occurred in the first place, but there will never be a fact in biology, law, or psychology that will solve the moral problems related to abortion. Once the relevant facts are available, terms must be clarified and understood. A good example is the term "conception." If it means the union of egg and sperm as against the time of implantion of embryo in the womb, these events are separated by a matter of days and would make the difference in deciding whether or not the IUD causes abortion. Clarity and precision in facts and terms is important.

With facts and terms in hand, we can identify general principles that apply to other areas beside the one under scrutiny. In questions relating to abortion, we appeal to such principles as respecting life and individual liberty. If there are principles that seem to come into conflict, we must weigh them against one another to determine which is most truly applicable. At this point, we are ready to make and to defend our judgments.

On our way to making moral decisions about abortion that we hope to be able to commend to the wider society, a review of the efforts of bioethicists will be of invaluable assistance. At the acknowledged and very significant risk of overgeneralizing and oversimplifying the complex and subtle positions that have been developed, we can consider that five major contemporary bioethical positions on abortion are arranged on a continuum from the most "liberal," or "pro-choice" (#1) to the most "conservative," or "pro-life" (#5). We will survey the two most extreme views first (#1 and #5) and then the positions that fall in between, identifying the differing concerns that divide bioethicists. We will then look more closely at the basic issues of contention, identify new trends, and suggest responses that will appeal to evangelical Christians.

Contemporary Bioethical Positions

#1: Extreme pro-choice. The most extreme pro-choice position has been taken by a number of philosophers including Michael Tooley (cf. Munson 1983, 61–76) and Mary Ann Warren (cf. Beauchamp & Walters 1982, 250–260). Agreeing with Thomas Szasz, who has referred to the fetus as a "piece of tissue," these philosophers firmly deny that moral wrong can be attached to abortion at any stage of pregnancy and for any reason. To have a right to life, a being must satisfy certain characteristics; lacking those, a being lacks the right to life and thus can be killed for any reason whatever. Consistently, many advocates of this view, including Tooley and Warren, must allow for the permissibility of killing newborn babies as well, although there will be fewer reasons to do so since they no longer need the body of a possibly unwilling party to survive.

#5: Extreme pro-life. At the other end of the continuum is the extreme pro-life position, officially endorsed by Roman Catholicism and adopted by some evangelicals. This view holds that the developing zygote-embryo-fetus, from its earliest moment of life, must be regarded as a person and, from the moral standpoint, the same as an adult person. Since it is wrong to kill an innocent human being and since abortion is the direct killing of the fetus, abortion is wrong. No consideration can justify abortion, not even the life of the mother (although this is modified slightly in practice), to say nothing of her health, emotional stability, or personal welfare; the welfare of the family unit; circumstances of conception due to rape or incest; or prospects of severe fetal abnormality. As a person, the developing offspring is entitled to exactly the same consideration as any innocent and helpless human being.

Advocates of this position allow for the destruction of the fetus only if this is the foreseen but *unintended* consequence of another procedure. According to the doctrine of double effect, it is permissible, for example, to remove a cancerous uterus even if the fetus will die as a result, but it is never permissible to intentionally destroy the fetus, even if both mother and child will otherwise die. Both are of equal value, and it would be as wrong and arbitrary to kill the fetus to save the mother as to kill her to save the fetus.

#2: Liberal-moderate. Most positions have attempted to moderate between the seeming disregard of the fetus in #1 and the perhaps equal disregard for the mother in #5. To moderates, both the fetus and the mother need to be considered. A liberal-moderate view has been developed in a famous paper by Judith Jarvis Thomson (Munson 1983, 76–86). Thomson argues that it does not follow that abortion is always wrong, even if the fetus is a person. Using a number of ingenious examples, Thomson attempts to show that there remains the substantial task of showing that abortion is wrong, even when granting the fetus a right to life. The fetus has a claim not to be aborted, but that claim is not absolute; it can be overridden for reasons of self-defense or to avoid serious harms to the mother. Abortion should be seen not as a violation of the fetus's right to life, but as the denial of resources that it needs to live, particularly the "use" of the mother's body. It often is held that *need* of a resource does not establish a *right* to it. The fetus has a right to that "resource" only when the mother has explicitly granted it. In many cases, however, while abortion is not a violation of right, Thomson sees it as nonetheless morally objectionable—as, for example, in the seventh month of pregnancy because continued pregnancy would interfere with a vacation. It is "morally indecent" to deny the fetus what it needs to live when that can be given without great sacrifice on the mother's part.

#3: **Conservative-moderate.** These views have been developed by Jane English and Daniel Callahan, and yet more conservatively by evangelical D. Gareth Jones. According to this position, we can confidently proclaim the fetus neither a person nor a nonperson; it is a *potential* person, a potential rapidly unfolding as pregnancy progresses. The moral status of the fetus increases as it develops. English will accept abortion in the early months of pregnancy simply for the interests of the pregnant woman or her family; but she allows it in the second trimester only when continued pregnancy threatens genuine physical, psychological, economic, or social harms to the woman. After this point, abortion is countenanced only to save the woman from serious injury and death, although Jones's theological commitments about human life as God's creation and gift enjoin him to take a stricter view and to regard with much more seriousness the killing of even the early fetus. At any stage of its existence a potential person is entitled to "care, dignity, and respect" (Jones 1985, 157).

#4: **Conservative positions.** A number of more conservative ethicists have advanced the view that the fetus has a *nearly* absolute right to life, which can be overridden only by such extreme considerations as the mother's own right to life, and even then only in certain extreme cases. John T. Noonan, Jr., argues that the "human being" is morally protected from conception onwards and may only be killed when absolutely necessary to preserve the life of the mother (Munson 1983, 57–61). Paul Ramsey ascribes the developing human full status at the blastocyst stage, not at conception (see chapter 10 for biological terms), and only allows killing the fetus when pregnancy endangers the mother's life and when both would die without the intervention. Other conservatives grudgingly expand this to permit abortions whenever the mother's life is in danger, or when she will suffer grave medical consequences from giving birth, or when the fetus is conceived due to rape or incest or is so congenitally impaired that its prospects for minimal human existence are extremely limited.

Controversial Bioethical Issues

From the extreme liberal through the moderate positions to the extreme conservative view, judgments vary greatly about the permissibility of abortion and of the reasons given for these judgments. How can bioethicists, beginning with equal intelligence and grasp of the facts, arrive at such widely varying moral positions on abortion? As our discussion has indicated, a small number of key issues exist on which they take widely divergent positions.

Status of the Fetus

Perhaps the most crucial issue concerns the status of the fetus. Although fetuses are human beings from the moment of conception, bioethicists have insisted that the question of the fetus's moral status is not settled by that biological fact. Many bioethicists have argued that personhood does not seem to be just a matter of being a member of *Homo sapiens*. There are "persons" who are not members of our species (e.g., God, angels, and conceivably alien beings), and there are human beings in whom personal existence has been extinguished or has never existed (e.g., the anencephalic baby or the brain-dead accident victim).

The fetus is in a peculiar position from the standpoint of ethical analysis, since it is at once like and unlike those adult persons who make up the moral community to whom we customarily ascribe rights and for whom we accept duties. Like "us," the fetus is a member of the human race, conceived of human parents, with human genetic information; unlike us, in terms of its *present* capacities, it apparently cannot reason, will, communicate, act, love, or worship. In assigning fetuses a place on the moral "map," should we count their biological humanity, their present capacities, or their prospects for future life?

What are the characteristics that make us persons, beings of moral value? Philosophers have suggested various lists of such characteristics, including intelligence, communicative ability, ability to envision the future, self-concept, and so on. Just as nonhumans without these characteristics (such as fish) are excluded from the category of persons and the moral requirements it demands, so it is argued that neither are human beings who lack these characteristics to be regarded as persons. Other ethicists dispute this inference, arguing that human beings are never to be excluded from the human community; to be a member of our species is to be regarded as a full-fledged person, with full moral status.

Philosophers who do accept the distinction between biological humanity and moral personhood differ as to what this distinction implies. The extreme liberal denies fetuses any claim to moral consideration, while moderates may establish a point at which the fetus passes over into personhood. Whenever the fetus reaches this point—conception, the blastocyst stage, implantation, development of brain activity, quickening, viability, birth, or even some time after birth—it has passed the "critical stage" recognized by the theory and now is entitled to be regarded as a person for moral purposes. From this point on, its interests are to be given equal considerations with those of any adult.

Other philosophers have argued that even if the fetus is not seen as a full-fledged person, the extreme liberal has erred in blithely assuming that "merely potential" persons may be killed innocently. For some, fetuses have at least the claim of nonhuman animals not to be killed without good reason, while others would invoke various moral factors besides a right to life as the basis on which fetuses are to be protected. As at least a potential person, the fetus has a status that is far from insignificant, carrying with it strong claims to protection as a being quickly advancing towards full personhood.

Rights

The language of rights is frequently invoked in the moral discussion of abortion. We are asked to consider the right to life of the fetus, either as a person or as a potential person, and then to weigh this against the right of the mother to live, to control her own body, and to manage her own existence. A moral right is a claim, supportable on sound ethical grounds, for a certain type of treatment. No one seriously questions that persons have a moral right not to be unjustly killed, and no one ought to deny that, like anyone else, women have rights over their bodies. The problem comes in determining what sorts of entities have rights and how rights are to be weighed against one another. The extreme conservative argues that the right of a fertilized human egg is equivalent to that of a normal adult, and that from the moral standpoint there is no difference between taking a morning after pill to induce menstruation when pregnancy is suspected and murdering a neighbor. Not surprisingly, holders of this view fear that permitting abortion inserts a wedge from which will follow such practices as infanticide for imperfect infants and mandatory euthanasia for the elderly infirm. The other extreme—that fetuses have no rights or only slight ones that pale in comparison to those of the mother—would maintain that abortion is morally without significance. Between these two positions, moderates believe that having the right to life provides limited protection, a consideration that must be weighed against others.

How are rights to be weighed? How is the right to liberty in expression, for example, to be weighed against the right of others to be spared offense? Or, closer to the topic, how is the right of the mother to control her own body to be balanced against the fetus's right to be allowed to follow normal development and be born alive? One way to weigh rights is by comparing the different right-holders' moral significance. From that orientation, the rights of a full-fledged person would outweigh those of a merely potential person, even when the less fundamental or even relatively trivial rights of a full person are weighed against the right to life of a potential person. Or, we might evaluate rights by how fundamental they are to the life they are invoked to serve and protect. Using that standard, the right to life would outweigh a right to be slim for a school reunion.

Quality-of-life discussions engage many in the moderate camps. While both extreme positions will find quality of life irrelevant, moderates must consider the sort of life a child will have. Conservatives rightly recoil at the tendency of some liberals to stress high quality as a condition for being allowed to live, yet there are other considerations that might legitimately be given place in our reflections. Severe retardation, gross physical abnormalities, and prospects for a short and painful existence may threaten the child with a lifetime of institutionalized care devoid of significant human interaction and impose staggering and expensive responsibilities upon the parent and society. Quality-of-life considerations can be used in different ways. Sometimes they are used to spare society the expense of caring for impaired children, while at other times to weigh the expected benefits of life against the emotional and relational costs to the family, and yet at other times to attempt to discern what is genuinely in the child's own interest. The task remains to show on ethical grounds the level of impairment that is incompatible with meaningful human life and whether making such decisions is compatible with humane ideals.

Legislating Morality

Other moral issues in the abortion debate include the question of legislating morality or religious perspectives. What limits ought to be imposed on law as a means of social control? As a highly contested issue on which there are profound disagreements within society, abortion is regarded by some as murder and by others as a fundamental right of the woman. In such a context, can laws reflecting the views of one group— for example, outlawing abortion—be convincingly justified? Should a compromise be sought, centering on whatever moral consensus might exist in society and perhaps outlawing at least "later" abortions for reasons not related to maternal or fetal medical welfare?

Recent Developments

New technology has brought with it new wrinkles in the abortion issue. The lowering of the age of viability owing to advances in neonatal intensive-care technology will have an impact on the legal and ethical discussions. Ultrasound technology now makes it possible to visualize the fetus in the uterus; no longer invisible to us, the fetus can be observed moving in the womb. Other techniques make it possible to identify certain genetic abnormalities in the fetus, some of which may be treatable—if not now, in the years to come. Intensive-care technology has begun to allow physicians to save one child while a child with an identical defect is allowed to die. This raises serious questions about the rational consistency between our present pro-choice policies and the physician's role.

Evangelical Perspectives

How do we as evangelical Christians relate to the bioethical debate about abortion? First of all, we ought to recognize the genuine contribution to understanding that has been made, even by those who hold views we find unacceptable. Bioethicists have done a great service to those who wish to understand such an issue as abortion. Regardless of their varied conclusions, they have grappled seriously, carefully, and honestly with the fundamental questions arising out of abortion, many of which are neglected by our rapid-fire media and "quick fix" culture. To what extent *is* it relevant that a fetus was conceived by rape? That it is developing with severe defects in the nervous system? That the mother is an unmarried young adolescent? Such questions must be faced, and bioethicists have done valuable work with which we must seriously grapple before we offer our own pronouncements.

Second, as a human cultural activity, bioethics shares inevitably in the defects traceable to human limitations of sin and finitude. Reviewing the dialogue in the light of Scripture, we are struck by the extent to which many positions are shaped by presuppositions and assumptions about the nature of human reality that are widely shared in our culture but are at odds with Scripture. In particular, the abortion question has largely proceeded on the assumption that human beings are to be understood as independent, isolated social atoms, rather than as beings created for community. The valuable and sound ethical concept of rights has been used so atomistically that it has led to reductionism: an action is judged unobjectionable as long as it violates no one's clear-cut claim to rights. Christians endorse human rights as a way of recognizing the unique value and significance of human beings created in God's image and set to perform his works in the world. However, the self-centered, careful delineation of "*my* rights" and the boldness with which we pursue our own interests to the maximum limit that rights allow is inimical to the spirit of mutual forbearance advocated in Scripture and modeled by Christ.

Another related distinctive of an evangelical Christian approach to the bioethical discussion of abortion is its insistence on the biblical ideal of community and on the normative nature of the family. We believe that bioethical decisions must not be made from the standpoint of isolated individualism, but must take account of our nature as beings created for community, particularly the family community. The family perspective reminds us to respect the God-created link between sexuality and procreative potential in the family context. We recognize sexuality as a gift from God for mutual delight and expression of love as well as for childbearing, and we regard children as a blessing that God may add to sexual intimacy. Others in this debate often treat sexuality and procreation as being linked only accidentally: free sexual expression is the norm, and conception is a sometimes unwelcome and almost incidental sequel. Unplanned pregnancy has even been called "a venereal disease."

Against this ghastly perversion, we insist that sexuality, family, community, and procreation are concepts naturally connected in God's created intention for humanity. We will also agree with Paul Ramsey in arguing against the view that abortion is a personal decision only of pregnant women themselves from which even husbands are excluded. A community rather than an atomistic model will alert us to the ways that the individual's decision to participate in illicit sexual intercourse is heavily influenced by the community. Without denying individual responsibility for actions, we must recognize the extent to which a sexually provocative and permissive society encourages extramarital sex and the pregnancies that will eventuate. Similarly, the community model allows us to see that our punitive, unloving, and moralistic treatment of those unwed mothers who arise from our midst makes abortion an almost compelling choice for them. A pro-life community will lament the sin, to be sure, but will then recognize that neither are the rest of us without sin and in the position to cast stones. We will then forgive, love, and restore "the least of these" in Christ's name and encourage them to either raise their children or give them to other loving families in the community.

Evangelical approaches are likely to be similar to those of others in some respects, while in others evangelicals and other Christians might be relatively alone. Like many in the society at large, we believe in respect for the rights of others, the invaluability of developing human life, the necessity of justice for the weak, and the importance of taking responsibility for one's actions. We will find ourselves in scarcer company when we emphasize the themes of self-sacrifice and suffering. It is not that as Christians we believe that we should seek opportunities to suffer or to sacrifice our interests to those of others, but we do believe that in doing such things we can realize values otherwise missed. It is difficult to discern in the contemporary bioethical debate a positive appreciation for the role of suffering in human life or of placing the welfare of others above ourselves. While this will not necessarily commit

8

What Does
the Church Say?
Morris A. Inch

Cardinal Casaroli, the Vatican's secretary of state, was interviewed on the "Today" program by Bryant Gumbel. The latter asked the prelate for his reaction to recent statements by American bishops soliciting "a new commitment to economic justice" (*Chicago Tribune* article, April 5, 1985). The cardinal responded in part, "I would respect their right as citizens of the United States, but naturally, they couldn't speak on behalf of their magisterium as bishops." Such an incident graphically illustrates the problem we have in getting any clear impression of what "the church" has to say with regard to specific social issues. The evangelical church, because of its many denominations and the accompanying diversity, has had a difficult time speaking in a unified voice on difficult social issues.

In this section, we want to take a look at how the church expresses its conviction with regard to social concerns. This will take a historical turn at the outset, followed by certain theoretical observations, before finishing off with some specific comments on the abortion issue—as a case in point. We will attempt to keep the discussion on track, rather than taking interesting but time-consuming detours into related matters.

A Historical Backdrop

Our entire discussion will key into Paul Ramsey's provocative work *Who Speaks for the Church?* (1967). Ramsey notes that his volume is in part a "critique of the 1966 Geneva Conference on Church and Society, and of the methods and goals of the World Council of Churches, the National Council of Churches, and their member denominations when they deal with urgent social and political questions" (Ramsey 1967, 11). He complains:

> It has been easier to arrive at specific recommendations and condemnations after inadequate deliberation than to penetrate to a deeper and deeper level the meaning of Christian responsibility—leaving to the conscience of individuals and groups of individuals both the task and the freedom to arrive at specific conclusions through untrammeled debate about particular social policies. Radical steps need to be taken in ecumenical ethics if ever we are to correct the pretense that we are makers of political policy and get on with our proper task of nourishing, judging, and repairing the moral and political *ethos* of our time [Ramsey 1967, 15].

Ramsey inquires, "Must those who undertake to speak for the church, or in the name of Christian truth, choose between abstract irrelevancies and policy-making exercises?" (Ramsey 1967, 29). Hopefully not. Ramsey proceeds to outline a provisional model for making specific political pronouncements—which allows for prudential options that do not lock the church into categorical dissent or support.

What *can* the church say? One can perhaps recite biblical principles, insofar as they can be distilled from the historical setting in which they occur. Wilhelm Visser't Hooft protests that "we have no right to give only counsels of perfection (principles) to statesmen and other leaders who are faced with the ambiguities of positions, and have so often to choose between various causes, each of which may have grave consequences" (Ramsey 1967, 26). If so, are we to advocate specific policy options—as if endowed with some special insight into the nature of things? Ramsey responds:

> No doubt political leaders need the strength and the correction that can only come from broad and sustained debate of political questions. But what if some part of this advice is believed to be specially authenticated because it comes from groups in our society that are supposed to be unusually sensitive to human need and can perhaps discern the *kairos* better? The magistrate is then apt to feel that many good people are crying "Peace! Peace!" in a world where there is no peace, and that we churchmen are simply not in the position to bear political responsibility for the consequences of the particular course proposed for choice if it should turn out to be disastrous [Ramsey 1967, 7].

There remains the option of trying to steer a course between the two extremes, which is where Ramsey directs our attention and we accept his invitation.

Theoretical Considerations

We need first of all to lay a solid foundation for social involvement. John Coleman writes, "The Hebraeo-Christian commitment to a radical monotheism ascribes ultimate sovereignty to God over all nations, times, and institutions. No society or institution of society escapes his scrutiny, judgment, active sustaining presence, and care" (Coleman 1982, 19). This suggests that there is a sacral dimension to the social order in all its dimensions. "Indeed, it (the Church) is called today to an especial effort to make this apparent since the systematic exclusion of religion from politics and economics in post-industrial societies and the concomitant taming of the religious by relegating it to the private sphere have eclipsed this truth both for non-believers and Christians alike" (Coleman 1982, 20). The effort must begin with the church if it is to have any impact on society as a whole.

We can now better appreciate Ramsey's criticism of a selective approach to social issues. It fails to drink deeply of the Christian heritage and ends up justifying some partisan perspective. It turns out to be a subtle form of idolatry, having compromised its radical monotheistic tradition.

The first task of the church is to prayerfully deliberate on its biblical tradition. It has to sensitize itself to the distinctive teaching of Holy Writ. It needs to fall into step with divine revelation, rather than marching to the cadence of the world. A failure at this juncture would abort the whole enterprise.

The former step does not excuse the church from gathering such information as may be available concerning the issue at hand. God does not reward ignorance. Moreover, it is as the church disciplines itself to the rigor of investigation that it develops a proper humility. It begins to sense the complexity of social issues and the inadequacy of resolving them with a few available prooftexts.

Thereupon, the various alternatives can be discussed against the background of biblical teaching. Ramsey observes:

> If the churches and churchmen as such are going to issue statements that make particular recommendations or indicate quite specifically the direction in which they believe public policy should go, this is perhaps a way of doing this with a greater degree of self-imposed responsibility and of inducing more responsible deliberations among ourselves and in the public domain [Ramsey 1967, 121].

The church must expect to do its homework if it is to obtain any credibility from its social involvement.

All that has gone before leads up to decision, whether understood in individual or corporate terms. The church cannot afford the luxury of being incapacitated by the complexity of the problem or by its own limited vision. The decision is often on the order of gaining some high ground, from which greater success can be achieved. The church's failure to commit itself to a course of action is to admit defeat.

Organization follows decision. This resembles the procedure a contractor goes through in a building project. One must assess the task, assemble the needed resources, and structure the enterprise. Many an excellent idea has been lost for lack of exacting implementation.

Finally, there must be action—and the church ought to take the offensive. Nothing that we have mentioned previously can be employed as a substitute. We are reminded of James's comment, ". . . Show me your faith apart from your works, and I by my works will show you my faith" (James 2:18). Faith needs to be fleshed out.

We might summarize by saying that the church has to work on two fronts: in drawing nourishment from its biblical tradition and in improving its working relationship with society. David Moberg (1962, 59) observes that "Every institution overlaps and must be integrated with every other institution of society to operate efficiently." Otherwise, it is irrelevant at best and counterproductive at worst.

The church has gone about its integration with society in various ways. John Coleman illustrates this fact with five strategies employed by the Roman Catholic Church. The Christendom model comes first: "A carry-over from the Middle Ages, the Christendom model was the operative self-understanding of the international Church from the Counter-Reformation until almost the turn of the century" (Coleman 1982, 136). Thereby, the Roman Church pursued a position of religious monopoly for itself and an inclusive pastoral strategy—over all those within its domain and from cradle to the grave.

Coleman admits that the Christendom model never met the needs of the Roman Church in the United States. The American situation was viewed as something of an exception to the Christendom rule. It was tolerated and sometimes admired, but never promoted as a paradigm for the church as a whole.

This peculiar bifurcation continued until about 1920, when the Roman Catholic Church was faced with an aggressive secular movement that threatened its future. The Roman Church responded with a parish action model. As lay initiative was encouraged, Catholicism for all practical purposes became increasingly decentralized. Coleman concludes that "there is an assumption in America that the parish is the 'real' Church.

Renewal movements of the laity are somehow not really Catholic until they feed into the revitalization of the parish" (Coleman 1982, 139).

Each subsequent development in some ways carried over vestiges from the past. But there was always something distinctive about the new order. A new social-action pattern (1939–1960) moved further away from the institutional church toward a para-church structure for social involvement. The rise of the Christian Democratic Party on the European continent was an example of this movement. American Catholicism took a more direct approach to the political process by working through the existing parties.

Coleman suggests that "At Vatican Council II a new Church-society model emerged which promised, at last, to bear an elective affinity to the strategic needs of the American Church. In this Vatican II model, which I will call a cultural-pastoral or voluntary association model, the Church sees itself as a voluntary association within a wider non-Catholic or not explicitly Catholic host society whose autonomous competencies the Church respects" (Coleman 1982, 142). The logic of such a view is that the church would assume a role commensurate to other voluntary associations in the United States.

The liberation model (1970 and thereafter) concludes Coleman's survey of social-action alternatives. We are primarily acquainted with this through the Latin American experience. Here there has been a history of the Catholic Church's alignment with the political and economic establishment. The liberation motif realigns the church with the oppressed in their struggle for a better way of life.

What has been reported is a matter of record. The church does assume various approaches to its social responsibility. The approach is created as a result of interaction between the social ideals of the church and pragmatic realities of the situation. Thus, while the Christendom option was still normative for the Roman Catholic Church, its American branch made such adjustments as seemed necessary or desirable. It was not until Vatican II that an ideology was developed to meet the peculiar conditions of Catholicism in its American setting.

We see in these five strategies a mixture of three ingredients: the institutional church, the para-church, and personal initiative. Paul Ramsey (1967) questions the prerogative of the church to speak with such concreteness as to perjure the conscience of its membership. Similarly, Cardinal Casaroli allows that the American prelates can speak out as concerned citizens, but not in their ecclesiastical office. What appears proper in one of these three connections might be judged as inappropriate in another.

John Bennett concludes "that a distinction must be made between the basic Christian convictions that bind a member to his church and the opinions of church bodies on particular issues" (Bennett 1966, 259). There must be a decline of specificity as one moves from personal initiative through para-church to institutional church. This is because, strictly speaking, not all personal convictions are Christian convictions. They are indeed convictions that Christians hold, but they often differ from one another and are not of the order "that bind a member to his church."

What, then, is the alternative that Ramsey proposes? Coleman summarizes it for us: "Instead of specific condemnations of political actions or highy concrete programs for a new social order, Ramsey pleaded for middle-axioms which would provide a 'shaping, discriminating and nourishing address to the environing culture'" (Coleman 1982, 26). He explains further, "These middle-axioms are to be more than vague ethical generalities but less than concrete directives for policy. Ramsey foresaw a set of action-oriented and decision-oriented principles which would set a tone to political discussion without infringing upon the rightful autonomy of the political sector or of individual Christian conscience." Ramsey argued that the institutional church cannot say what should or must be done, but what *may* be done.

We ought to note in passing that the church is able to address the ills of society more concretely than its solutions. It can decry an existing problem in no uncertain terms, as in violation of the Christian conscience. It is less certain of what social program may best alleviate that difficulty without replacing it with some worse situation.

This middle course of action is meant to protect the conscience of the Christian and non-Christian alike, as well as the legitimate role of the civil magistrate. These are all construed to be aspects of living in this world. And it was never intended that Christians should escape the world and the obligations that implies (1 Cor. 5:9–10).

The para-church provides a helpful halfway house between the institutional church and personal initiative. Coleman warns that "Action on behalf of justice by the *institutional* Church, because of the Church's competency and limitations already seen, will not be sufficient to fulfill the Gospel mandate for justice" (Coleman 1982, 31). He adds, "For the Church has never failed to engender in its midst voluntary associations of committed Christians and community groups who are moved to join directly the concrete struggle of people at the neighborhood, urban, regional, national, and international level." Such groups speak *to* the whole church of the concrete direction its faith is inclined to take. They also testify to society of the conviction of Christians and the risk they are willing to accept as an aspect of their discipleship (for it is well documented that those who take the part of the oppressed risk suffering with them).

Coleman notes further that the concreteness of these para-church groups "challenges other Christians who might use social justice principles as an ideological mask to protect them from a real conversion to justice or real involvement. For in the order of history and the fallen world, not all possible choices are really compatible" (Coleman 1982, 32). Thereby are hypocrisy and complacency stripped of the social respectability in which we predictably clothe them.

On the other hand, these groups cannot presume to represent the whole church. Their strength lies in their freedom to speak from a partisan perspective. Their characteristic vulnerability is to fall prey to a self-righteousness that can see no option but their own. Although they aspire to be the true church, the faithful remnant among a faithless multitude, they must resist this temptation for their own sake and that of the church at large.

The para-church group also provides needed support for individual Christians who are struggling to understand the implications of faith for social practice and those who need encouragement to stand by their convictions. It functions in a more concrete fashion than the institutional church is able to do. It has moved out of the sanctuary and into the community, where individual Christians must make some very difficult decisions.

Finally, there is always the possibility that what seems for the moment a partisan position may be adopted as the stance for the institutional church. I have in mind the repudiation of slavery as a plausible case in point. Slavery, though once tolerated, has become anathema to the church. It is difficult to imagine a set of circumstances that would reverse this conviction.

The individual is least inhibited in expressing his faith in a concrete fashion if he is a Christian and a member of the household of faith. Otherwise, he stands to be reproved and disciplined by the church. No Christian is an island unto himself.

The "great men" view of history seems rather dated, but we ought not to lose sight of the truth it contained. One person can turn things around by taking a courageous stand. It does not always happen, and it apparently does not usually happen, but it *can* happen. Thus, when the individual speaks for himself, he may be soliciting the support of countless others in a cause that will eventually succeed.

But it is not the "popularity" of the position he espouses that makes it valid. William Stringfellow (1977, 109) complains: "A most obstinate misconception associated with the gospel of Jesus Christ is that the gospel is welcome in this world." The Christian should be prepared to promote unpopular causes—not because they are unpopular but because of the probability that they may be so.

Everyone must assume his or her own calling and the responsibilities this implies. That calling is of so demanding a nature that it requires our full commitment and energy. It is as we take seriously our vocation that we bear witness to God's concern for society. Whatever we undertake on a corporate basis builds upon this fundamental understanding of the nature of discipleship. Here, as in no other context, must faith be fleshed out in its most concrete fashion.

What the church says, it says by way of the institutional church and the para-church and through personal initiative. At times this must seem like a babble of sound; at other times we hope it resembles the blend of voices in a concert choir. What it says will be more or less concrete in nature, depending on the issue and at what level the church is involved. Because it will have to give account for what it says to the Almighty, it had best fulfill its responsibility carefully. But after all has been said and done, the church must seek the forgiveness of God. It will have done what it ought not to have done and will also have left undone what was its obligation to do.

The Agonizing Issue

Abortion, perhaps more than any other practice, deserves to be labeled "the agonizing issue." God must certainly hold us guilty for the wanton taking of life. Much of the debate over abortion seems little more than an exercise in casuistry. What more can the church say?

Bruce Reed observes:

We are, more than ever, conscious that we cannot "read off" laws from the Bible, because our society is so different from the communities of the Old and New Testaments, is changing so rapidly and is so diverse. The complexity of life today makes it impossible to formulate universal principles or laws, but this apparent disadvantage has forced us to investigate our presuppositions for action in the world more thoroughly [Reed 1966, 106–107].

He adds that the sovereign God "is to be encountered existentially in the persons and processes of life situations, and he is working through them toward a just resolution of the moral issues" (Reed 1966, 107). It is as we discern what God is doing in the situation that we learn how we should respond.

Reed concludes that this

thesis implies that we believe (1) that God is the Living God; (2) that God is actively working out his purpose for mankind through every situation; (3)

that a just resolution of a moral issue is one way in which God works out his purpose; (4) that we must use all our resources to ascertain the reality of the situation, that is, its truth; (5) that we have the gift of the Holy Spirit to lead us into the truth; (6) that the result of this will be a call to obedience—in other words, that when we discern what God is doing, we are called to cooperate with him; (7) that God accepts us as we are, with our limitations and powers, and will not call us to do what is beyond us" [Reed 1966, 107].

There is much in Reed's commentary that reenforces our previous discussion. At issue is not whether we can identify biblical principles, but whether we can "read them off"—as if they needed no application or explanation. Reed correctly indicates that we cannot do so without doing injustice to the Scripture and our current situation.

What might be a principle that relates to the practice of abortion? Clifford Bajema suggests the prohibition against murder. He reasons that there are four ingredients involved in murder: a person is killed, the killing is intentional, an innocent person is the victim, and an unlawful or sinful motive is involved (Bajema 1977, 44). He adds that these elements are all present in abortion, except in the instance of "critical abortion"—where the fourth ingredient is absent. Bajema's qualification concerning critical abortion alerts us to the fact that we cannot simply read off biblical principles as if they had concrete application (especially for the non-Christian) to every situation.

Must the institutional church, then, be satisfied with repeating the general mandate against murder, leaving any more specific reference to abortion to para-church or personal initiative? Ramsey thinks not. He offers instead what we have identified as the "middle axiom," which does not tell us what should or must not be done but what may or may not be done with impunity.

Here we must create some examples of the middle axiom, as might relate specifically to the abortion practice. They are illustrative only, and subject to review:

1. If the Administration, in order to preserve the integrity of life, chooses to exclude abortion-on-demand, it will find a substantial body of Christian support.

2. If the Administration, in order to protect the welfare or self-determination of the mother, in such instances as when her life is endangered or the pregnancy has resulted from rape, shall choose to allow abortion, it will not be forsaken by a significant segment of Christian opinion.

3. If the Administration, in order to provide a preferred alternative to abortion, shall publicize and encourage the practice of adoption, it will find overwhelming support among Christians.

4. If the Administration, in order to curb the population explosion, shall advocate birth control by abortion, it will lack Christian support.

There are several things to note concerning these axioms. In each case, the prerogative of the civil magistrate is guaranteed, as is the conscience of the Christian and non-Christian alike. An appeal is made to the basis on which a given action may be taken, which acts to raise moral concerns and press for a comprehensive understanding of what more may be involved than is obvious on the surface. There is a general indication of what measure of support may be forthcoming from the Christian community and on what grounds that support would be warranted. In addition, the configuration of Christian conviction becomes more clearly expressed as we multiply the axioms, without succumbing to trivial considerations.

Has the church anything more to say on abortion? If the line of thinking to this point is correct, the answer is in the affirmative. The church is not locked up to what can be expressed upon behalf of the institution. It extends to the para-church and personal initiative. These, too, are means whereby the church expresses its convictions.

However, the testimony of the church also becomes more diversified as we move to the para-church and then to individuals. It is as if the church were looking at the issue first from one perspective and then another. It is concerned on one occasion for the unborn life the mother carries and in the next moment for the mother herself. Or it may weigh the effect of abortion on public morality in general.

Coleman suggests:

> It would seem that in the fullest sense the Church could not assume the concrete struggle of the people without becoming a partisan political actor in society or an alternative state. Were the institutional Church to do that, it would lose its credibility as an ethical authority and forego certain mediatory political roles it can play precisely because it eschews direct partisan choices [Coleman 1982, 31].

But what the church cannot do directly as an institution, it can do indirectly through the para-church and personal initiative.

We err if we suppose that this indirect means of assuming a partisan role *necessarily* compromises the church. It is rather as if the church were expressing its willingness to stand with the people in their legitimate concerns, and against the evil that plagues even the noblest of efforts. However, when it uncritically equates the crusades of men with the kingdom of God, compromise has indeed resulted.

Ramsey concludes with a note of warning to individual Christians:

> As a citizen one may lean to one extreme or the other in this range of options. As churchmen, however, our concern should be that the range of relevant principles be not narrowed, and that the conscience of the nation and of the statesman be not deprived of perspectives and wisdom that may be needed in the decisions magistrates have to make [Ramsey 1967, 157].

As churchmen, we must be concerned not simply for some pressing issue—as critical as that may be—but for the whole counsel of God.

Conclusions

We sum up. The church has a social responsibility beyond simply keeping its own house in order. It fulfills this obligation in a complex fashion: through the institutional church, the para-church, and personal initiative. It must take care in the process not to violate either the legitimate role of the civil administration or the conscience of its membership and/or that of others in the society. However, it must strive for the good of society, as it understands that "good" in the light of its biblical heritage.

We have seen how Ramsey limits the role of the institutional church to the range of the middle axiom, which tells us not what should or must be done, but what may be done. Middle axioms invite moral reflection and probe for a more comprehensive appreciation of the issues involved. They also suggest what sort of support for a given action might be forthcoming from the Christian community and on what grounds.

The church continues to speak on many issues through the para-church and individuals. Since these voices can be more specific and partisan in character, they will for that reason tend to conflict from time to time. This is as if to call attention to the various legitimate concerns involved in an issue. It also reminds us of the frailty of human crusades to express in any ultimate fashion the comprehensive will of God.

We have represented the abortion issue in context of the kind of pressing social concerns that face us today, and other contributors to this cooperative venture provide a more detailed investigation of the topic as such. The church ought not to hesitate in decrying the current situation, where life is so blatantly being extinguished, and it ought to press beyond protest to appropriate social action. (Several action-oriented measures are suggested elsewhere in this book.) It does so by employing to its full potential the complex character of its involvement with society, while in the process continuing to draw upon its biblical legacy for inspiration, instruction, and correction. The church's efforts will be as successful as its weakest link, whether that link is its tie into society or its grip on biblical truth.

References and Further Reading

Bajema, C. E. 1974 (1977). *Abortion and the meaning of personhood*. Grand Rapids: Baker.

Bennett, J., ed. 1966. *Christian social ethics in a changing world*. New York: Association.

————. 1964. Churchmanship and controversy. *Christianity and crisis* XXIV (December 28):258–259.

Coleman, J. 1982. *An American strategic theology*. New York: Paulist.

Moberg, D. 1962. *The church as a sacral institution*. Englewood Cliffs: Prentice-Hall.

Ramsey, P. 1967. *Who speaks for the church?* Nashville: Abingdon.

Reed, B. 1966. Biblical social ethics: An evangelical view. In *Christian social ethics in a changing world* (105–118), J. Bennett, ed. New York: Association.

Stringfellow, W. 1977. *Conscience and obedience*. Waco: Word.

9

Teaching Self-Worth
and the Sanctity of Life
James M. Lower

Many important issues of our present age have a common basis of ultimate consideration and determination—the nature of man. From differing perspectives, philosophy and psychology alike contemplate the age-old rhetorical question, "What is man?" Rollo May well summarized the importance of our assumptions concerning people's basic nature when he stated, "The critical battles between approaches to psychology . . . in our culture in the next decades, I propose, will be on the battleground of the image of man." (May 1967, 90)

The issue of the sacredness of life has currently reached an apex in the present debates concerning abortion. The concerns for the values of life appear also at the latter end of life cycle in the lesser-debated concept of euthanasia. These life issues and concerns are witnessed at various junctures of life.

As suicide among adolescents and even children is increasing at an alarming rate, the child has all-too-frequent encounters with these value-laden matters of life and death. Young people are developing a mind-set by the conversations and suggestions in the press, television, records and tapes of the latest hit songs, and the classroom. To the extent that the school reflects the prevailing culture or social milieu, these influences can be devastating to the proper development of the

139

moral persuasion nurtured by Christian values. Life-depreciating influences learned in the schools may arise pointedly from the curricular materials and practices (e.g., "values-clarification") that may subtly address issues related to the sanctity of life. But of even greater importance in their cumulative impact may be those moldings of minds that arise from the ongoing, everyday treatment of the human lives who comprise the school—the pupils.

Everyday treatment of pupils and the day-by-day examples of who the teacher himself or herself is as a person may be education's greatest impact. Apparently these are comcomitant phenomena both arising from a common source—perception of personality. Teachers' perceptions of the nature of man have a reciprocal effect on their own self-image and also on how they perceive and teach their pupils. President Hudson Armerding, in addressing the Wheaton College faculty in the fall of 1968, raised a very penetrating and arresting rhetorical question, "What is the residuum of one's college education?" He assayed to answer that question in terms of his own experience as a student at Wheaton, identifying certain professors who had taught him as an undergraduate. Although he confessed his almost total lack of remembrance of the materials that they had sought to instill in him, he declared with firmness that he could never forget them as the teachers—persons—that they were. He then supported that claim by naming certain individuals, some still present as faculty members, and citing their personal characteristics and the enduring impressions they had made.

The prevailing milieu of Western culture, heavily scented with "naturalistic determinism" and hedonistic pragmatism, constantly gives evidence that "man," the person, is often, as the poem states, "auctioned cheap to the thoughtless crowd, much like the old violin." Mass media, epitomized by television, supplies persistent "reinforcement" (a behavioral-psychology term) to the materialistic dialectic, and its motif of a non-sacredness of life (e.g., violence) seems to result in a kind of cumulative hypnosis by the use of persistent and protracted suggestibility. The most pervasive and effective impact of this hypnosis on our citizenry, especially young people, is *not* violence—which certainly takes a disturbing second place—but the strange-but-sure learned response of *not* responding.

Schools, then, as unwitting or intentional purveyors of the given culture, through the individual commitment of their teachers' philosophic assumptions relative to the nature of man, are in a position to either devaluate or recognize the true nature and worth of the students before them. Gordon Allport expressed this succinctly when he said, "Theories of learning (like much else in psychology) rest on the investigator's conception of the nature of man. In other words, every learning theorist is a philosopher, though he may not know it" (Allport 1961, 84).

The Teacher as Philosopher/Psychologist

Perhaps the most potent factor in determining how your various teachers have gone about the task of attempting to teach you has been the way in which you were perceived in their eyes. Whatever were those images that made up their perceived collage of you—their reactionary image of you—rested ultimately on what they believed about the nature of human beings. That belief, being a most important philosophic position, accounts largely for the differences among teachers as far as what is intended and attempted in the classroom and often the manner in which information and ideas are presented. Simply put, the teacher's concept of the pupil as a human being has a very basic and far-reaching effect on the learning experience.

Every psychological method has its source in some attendant philosophical position. Every teacher, whether he or she knows it or not, is a practicing philosopher as well as practicing psychologist. Every philosophy held in education has its attending psychology to put it into practice. The operative psychology is merely the wheelbarrow, the servant, or handmaiden of the given philosophical persuasion. The one presupposes the other. They operate reflectively. They are reciprocally reinforcing.

Admittedly, teachers are psychologists. Whether or not they may be aware of it, they are learning theorists in a practical sense (and so often "impractical"). They have formed and continue re-forming some basis of operation—a *modus operandi*—as an attempted answer to whatever consideration they have given to educational psychology's ultimate question, "How, then, shall I teach?" As one writer suggested, "A 'theory of learning' is a set of propositions about the fundamental nature and considerations of learning. . . . Every teacher has a theory of learning. It may be a carefully formulated theory taken 'in toto' from the teacher's professors of education, or it may be a completely unconscious theory pieced together from experience in and out of the classroom" (Hill 1971, 142–143). It should be understood that here we are using the word *theory* in a broader and looser sense than we may find in the more comprehensive and systematic treatment in print in textbooks devoted to the consideration of learning theories.

Gordon Allport expands on this thought: "Psychologists who investigate (and theorize about) 'learning' start with some preconceived view of the nature of human motivation" (Allport 1961, 84). Most thinking people would doubtless concur. Consider further that the nature of human motivation in turn rests on the view that the theorist (in this case, the teacher) holds of the general nature of mankind, of the particular group of students before him or her, and, finally, of each individual pupil.

Morris L. Bigge is to be commended for his recognition of the basic importance of a learning theorist's (and teacher's) conception of what he calls "humankind's moral and actional nature." He holds quite logically that the psychological approaches to teaching and consequent learning—the basis for transfer, emphases in teaching, and so on—flow as natural consequences of the conception one holds of man's *moral* and *actional* nature (Bigge 1981, 10–11).

There are real differences in the various theoretical approaches to teaching. Differing views as to how people learn, beliefs about transfer of learned materials, and the resultant differing teaching methods continue to prevail. For example, what happens when pupils are taught by a teacher who follows the usual and most prevalent teaching methods, which rest on a simple "behavioristic" schema? Is human learning simply equatable to that of pigeons and rats—merely a predictable set of responses to a given stimulus and conditioned by receiving a form of "reinforcement" for proper responses? How can the pupil under this form of teaching possibly form a complete view of the sanctity of life?

How different is the educational experience when the teacher is convinced that there are cognitive processes engaged in human learning—that pupils, because of their very *human* nature, are able to make transpositions of generalized insights! Such a teacher is concerned for each student's continuity of life and the ability to restructure his or her motivational forces through experience and insight. This teacher will seek to promote insightful learning, will deal with experience, will seek to integrate content within an appropriate context—thereby assisting students to restructure their lives, broaden their perceptions and thus their understandings. Pupils under such teaching will gain not only a better understanding of the world, but of themselves and others. Differing theories of learning and their corresponding teaching approaches all ultimately rest on how the teacher perceives his or her students—who and what they are as human beings. Teachers' views of the sacredness (or non-sacredness) of life affect in pervasive measure their pupils' total educational experiences.

The Teacher's Effect on Students' Self-Image

The writer for the past eighteen years has been assigning sophomore and junior students at Wheaton College to a practicum experience—to work as unpaid teacher-aides in connection with their course in educational psychology. This is an attempt to relate the course materials to real-life situations, to teach content within a proper context. Some sixty to seventy students are so assigned each fall and spring semester. A notable number of these college students seem appalled at the coarse treatment that they witness pupils receiving in various ways and manners from certain teachers. These unfortunate pupils are not merely treated as "second-class citizens," but as something *less* than human, in sharp contrast to the college students' view of these young people as beings of worth. The teacher-aides usually feel constrained to include such demeaning incidents in their final oral reporting of their experiences. It is not uncommon for them to have difficulties when voicing these incidents, which so crushed their own inner sensitivities that they were at least empathetic, if not sympathetic, with the given pupil. For such reasons it has been found advisable to alert students in advance that for some of them such unseemly experiences might occur.

Teachers will teach what they believe, just as they will live what they believe. Students will detect these beliefs, especially what a teacher believes about them as human beings, by the way they are treated. Take, for example, a case related by a student from Nebraska, now doing advanced graduate work in education, who when she was a senior student some ten years ago, told of an incident she observed in a one-room school years before. Apparently the teacher in question, even if she did not actually "hate kids," must have held a low estimate of humankind, as judged by her treatment of the pupils. She spent most of her time sitting at her desk, grading workbooks and whatever else she saw fit to do, maintaining by strong reprimand that she was not to be disturbed by anyone coming to her desk. But, in spite of the don't-bother-me law enacted by this teacher, there was one little girl, Mary, who was either forgetful, a slow learner, or just plain willful enough to risk the venom of the teacher's wrath. In fact she was so persistent in this infraction that the teacher, tiring of her own verbal reprimands, resorted to the purchase of a pressurized can of Raid. After that, whenever little Mary approached the teacher at her desk, she would get her skirts sprayed with the insecticide, along with the reprimand, "You're a *pest*. Be gone!" Certainly this is a prime example of the in-shop saying, which I laughed to hear in my first year of teaching: "She could do a better job of teaching if the kids stayed at home."

It may come as a source of both encouragement and challenge for a teacher to simply recognize that "you can't fool the kids and the dogs." Sidney Harris in his editorial, "What Makes a *Good* Teacher *Good*," discusses the challenges of giving teachers promotions and pay raises based on their merit as a teacher rather than their length of service and admits that it is fraught with difficulties. But he concludes rather pointedly, ". . . ultimately only the pupils know who the *good* teachers are, and they cannot be fooled" (Harris 1967).

It is cause for hope and a boon to one's spirit to note, in students' journals of their practicum experiences as teacher-aides, evidences of proper sensitivities felt and shown toward pupils as being "image bearers of God." I noted the following from Jill K's journal, dated October 24, 1984 (Kroese 1984):

> I have worked with Penny for over a year now, and I wanted to note what happened today because it really affected me. Pen had "a no good, horrible very bad" day. She cried so hard out of frustration, misunderstanding, and disappointment. How very crucial compassion is. We, as so-called "educational achievers," cannot begin to know how difficult having a learning disability would be. Penny feels so alienated and humiliated from a few of her teachers, and that really tugs at my heart. I found this a few years ago; I wish every teacher out there would memorize it.
>
> > ". . . I have come to a frightening conclusion!
> > *I* am the decisive element in the classroom.
> > It is MY personal approach that creates the climate.
> > It is MY daily mood that makes the weather.
> > As a teacher, I possess tremendous POWER—
> > To make a child's life miserable or joyous!
> > I can humiliate or humor; hurt or heal.
> > In ALL situations it is MY response that decides
> > Whether a crisis will be escalated or de-escalated,
> > And a child 'humanized' or 'dehumanized'!"
>
> . . . I praise God for Penny's life.

Of all the comments and notes received by teachers from appreciative students, the ones most cherished are those that make some elaboration on one's *modus operandi:* "I felt that you cared; were concerned about me; knew me as a unique person." Such comments are of great worth to a purposeful teacher but of even greater benefit to the student who is able to say them, who has recognized that this teacher seemed to know him or her as a unique person. In other words, such a teacher affirmed the student's individuality.

Studies have shown that a teacher's unconditional affirmation of students as individuals is the most potent factor in enhancing their self-image or helping them develop a more positive self-concept. Studies conducted at Wheaton College in 1974 and replicated in 1977 gave convincing evidence that academically capable students have been influenced by their teachers toward a more positive self-concept and that a major way this was accomplished was by the teacher's affirmation of them as unique persons, not merely as students who were highly competent (Pryce & Lower 1974; Lower 1977). Both the pilot study in 1974 and the 1977 replication showed 93 percent of the students indicating that they had such teachers. (The 7 percent who could *not* identify such teachers in their experiences were all male students.) The most frequent response—which was given by 73 percent of these students when asked, "What sort of things *specifically* did those teachers do which resulted in helping you form a more positive self-image?"—was "acceptance as an individual person" ("knowing me in my uniqueness"). Other responses in order of frequency were: "active interest in the student" (54 percent); "reinforcement for performance" (47 percent); "encouragement, academically and otherwise" (37 percent). Related comments were "being given responsibility," "constructive criticism," "insight into my potential," "challenged to think," "were respected," "friendly."

Other studies have significantly demonstrated that teachers can effectively influence their students in developing a more positive self-image. By utilizing the principles of reinforcement and modeling, students in these studies developed significant gains in their concept of themselves (Flowers 1973; Parker 1974). It should also be noted that other studies emphasize (and we believe, correctly) that the teacher's role in shaping the self-concept of a child has not been sufficiently recognized. These contend that the general goal of education should be the encouragement of the child's dependence upon his or her efforts, decisions, and self-control (Mattocks & Jew 1974).

The Christian Teacher's Estimate of Human Worth

For Christian educators, there are certainly great claims and mandates set forth in the principles of Scripture. The worth of each individual is to be recognized, and every effort must be made to bring the student to his or her greatest potential as a *person,* first of all, and then as a student and citizen. This challenge is not to be left to school guidance workers alone, who (if they have been influenced by their course work at all) are also to act upon these principles. A biblical principle that emphasizes the worth of the individual might be applied to teaching by framing it in New Testament language: "What shall it profit the teacher, if the student gain the whole world of academic achievement and lose the vision of seeing himself as a more worthy person?" It is the privilege and duty of the teacher to increase each student's self-perception as a worthy person. The simplest and most effective way to achieve this is for the teacher to affirm the student's individuality, or uniqueness, in as many ways as possible.

For a teacher to succeed in helping students perceive themselves as worthy persons and better able to fulfill their ordained purposes in this world—ultimately "to glorify God and enjoy him forever"—the teacher must have a proper view of the nature of man. He or she must hold fundamentally and thoroughly to the principle of the sacredness of life. Teachers' presuppositions will show in how they teach, especially in how they treat and affect their students. The world-view of a teacher will project outward, reflecting his or her own self-perception, which usually bears a strong resemblance to one's perception of others. A teacher's approach has the potential to either help or hinder students in perceiving themselves as image-bearers of God.

Teachers and curricula both act from certain presuppositions when attempting to achieve their stated objectives. For example, Wheaton College, in formulating a statement of "Liberal Arts Objectives for General Education," noted as *Presuppositions* (Wheaton 1976, B):

> The proposed objectives presuppose a Biblical view of God and man. Since we are educating persons into a world created by God, we need to adopt a model which addresses itself to the issues of God, persons and the world. . . .
>
> Our starting point is the Biblical conception of persons created in God's image, fallen and yet redeemed in Jesus Christ so as to act responsibly and creatively in this world out of devotion to God. . . .

The writer can testify that it has been a privilege and joy to teach under this particular mandate. However, one does not need to be a faculty member of a Christian college or school in order to treat one's students in such proper manner. One's total approach to teaching simply begins and continues on from one's basic beliefs about God, the universe, and humanity. *Who*—or, in a real sense, *what*—is the pupil who now stands or is seated before the teacher? How is the student perceived by that teacher? *That* is the question! All of a teacher's teaching and treatment of the pupil flows from that. It is the treatment received by the pupil in the total day-by-day formal and informal contacts with the teacher that becomes the most effective dimension of the learning experience. How the pupil is treated is the clearest reflection and revealer of the teacher's perception of the pupil, which determines the teacher's attitude, purposes, goals, methods, and sense of commitment in all of his or her relationships with that pupil.

For educators to perceive their teaching as being something of a sacred commitment and/or calling, they must be firmly persuaded deep within their soul, mind, and conscience that all of life is sacred. A teacher's own life is sacred because he or she is a unique person, an image-bearer of God, and is also able to perceive others being framed in that same sacred image. The perceptive triad is completed when it reflects and reveres from every angle the sacredness of life as an integral part of one's view of God, self, and others. Indeed, "to the pure all things are pure . . ." (Titus 1:15).

All human life is sacred—babies, including the unborn; children; youth; adults; and the aged. The sanctity of life perhaps witnesses its greatest importance during the teachable and impressionable stages of life. It is then that the foundation of this precept is laid, and it is the parent and the teacher who are entrusted with the God-given responsibility for guiding young people's perceptions of their own nature and consequently the nature of others. The educator's total demeanor and treatment of pupils will reflect how that teacher views his or her very existence in the universe. This will in turn add to the daily input of concepts and ideas that will influence each pupil's self-image and world-view.

It should now be clear that our concerns for the sacredness of life are not only for the unborn (issue: abortion) and the aged (issue: euthanasia), but for the total input of ideas and attitudes that mold in the young a proper set of values and beliefs for each new generation. If we sometimes wonder why the majority of present-day Americans, including some Christians, are *not* against abortion, it may well be that their general view of humanity ("What is man?")—and their more specific attitude toward the unborn—has been misshaped by educators who did not hold an appropriately high view of the worth of the individual and treated their students accordingly.

The same might be said of parents, who play the primary and earliest role in formulating a child's self-concept and his or her view of others and the world as God's creation. It is here that all who are entrusted with education most need to heed this warning: "Awake, and strengthen what remains and is on the point of death, for I [Christ] have not found your works perfect in the sight of my God" (Rev. 3:2).

References and Further Reading

Allport, G. W. 1961. *Patterns and growth in personality.* New York: Holt, Rinehart & Winston.

Bigge, M. L. 1982. *Learning theories for teachers,* 4th ed. New York: Harper & Row.

Flowers, J. V. 1973. Modification of low self confidence in elementary school children by reinforcement and modeling. *Dissertation Abstracts International* 33 (8-B):3935.

Harris, S. 1967. What makes a good teacher good? ("Strictly Speaking"). *Chicago Daily News.*

Hill, W. E. 1971. Does learning theory apply to education? In *Classroom psychology,* W. C. Morse & G. M. Wingo, eds. New York: Scott Foresman.

Kroese, J. 1984. Teacher aide journal. Unpublished student paper, Wheaton College.

Lower, J. M. 1977. A replication of the Nancy Pryce 1974 study. Unpublished paper (N-300). Wheaton College.

Mattocks, A., & Jew, C. 1974. The teacher's role in the development of a healthy self-concept in pupils. *Education* 94:200–204.

May, R. 1967. *Psychology and the human dilemma.* New York: Van Nostrand Reinhold.

Parker, H. C. 1974. Contingency management and concomitant changes in elementary school students' self-concepts. *Psychology in the schools* 11:70–79.

Pryce, N., & Lower, J. M. 1974. The teacher's role in developing students' self-concepts by unconditional affirmation of them as individuals. An on-campus study (N-114). Wheaton College.

Wheaton College. 1976. Liberal arts objectives for general education. *Faculty Bulletin,* Wheaton College.

PART THREE

Facts, Figures, and Practical Concerns

10

A Biologist's Concern for Mother and Child

Dorothy F. Chappell

Do not offer the parts of your body to sin, as instruments of wickedness, but rather offer yourselves to God, as those who have been brought from death to life; and offer the parts of your body to him as instruments of righteousness.

Romans 6:13, NIV

This chapter is an appeal to you, the reader, to comprehend the beauty of natural processes in conception, human prenatal development, and birth, when they occur within the realm of God's blessings. It is also an appeal for you to contemplate the brokenness and destruction that occurs when the normal developmental processes of humans are disrupted.

Mr. Curtis J. Young, Executive Director of the Christian Action Council, is especially appreciated for his suggestions, encouragement, and provision of some materials for this project. Thanks go to Mrs. Sara Miles and Dr. John Sechrist in the Biology Department of Wheaton College and Dr. Gerrit Van Dyke in the biology department of Trinity Christian College, Palos Heights, Ill., and Laura Van Dyke (speech pathologist), for their reading of this manuscript and helpful suggestions. Mrs. Lorraine Whaley is especially appreciated for her diligence and patience in the typing and retyping of the drafts for this chapter. Mr. Dave Mortimer, intern with CAC and Kathy Woodliff, friend, are gratefully acknowledged for their suggestions. Ms. Jody Fulks, a medical illustrator in Columbus, Ohio, is greatly appreciated for taking time out of a busy schedule and rendering the drawings for this chapter.

The way in which our Lord Jesus Christ chose to enter the world reminds us of the potent expression of natural law within a spiritual world. His Father sent him through the processes of physical development by which we have also entered this world. Christ entered the world without sin, and he entered the world to conquer its sin. He went so far as to die for all the sins of the world, including those sins that can lead to the formation of human life outside the realm of Christian guidelines and the sins of destroying or maiming that life while it is developing within the mother.

There are times when the natural processes of human prenatal development and growth are interrupted and terminated. Sometimes this occurs for reasons and through methods not entirely understood by man (miscarriage), and sometimes this occurs through the conscious efforts of humans (abortion). The termination of a human life by another human is a violent and tragic act. It is often done for selfish reasons and to cover up other sins in an individual's life.

The abortion of a developing human is a violent and generally terminal act for the young human. It is also a destructive act of violence against the woman who is carrying that human being, since it leads to disruption of normal physiological processes. Abortion frequently leads to injury of the mother's reproductive organs in such a way as to leave permanent damage and/or prevent future effective conception and prenatal development within her body (Calvert n.d., 7).

Discussion in this chapter will focus on abortion from the perspective of the biological sciences. It will serve as a framework for understanding the physiology of human reproduction and fetal development—with the hope that knowledge about these God-ordained processes will underscore the need to halt the violence implicit in abortion-on-demand.

Genetic Complements

Living things are endowed with genetic material that makes each organism unique and distinct within the kingdoms of living things and within its own species. Man is no exception to this biological principle and has a splendid developmental sequence allowed for by the genes that direct the human developmental processes. The biological individual is ultimately a product of the expression of his or her genetic composition and the effects of environment upon the genes housed in that individual. The environment generally enhances or inhibits particular gene expressions. For example, a stunted child who has experienced maximum nutritional stress may have the genetic potential to be a full-grown and normally functional individual, but the environmental stress of a limited diet prevents optimal expression of his or her genes.

As we consider the genetic makeup of a human being, we need to examine both the origin of the genetic complements and the circumstances under which a full complement of genes for a human is realized. There are various hazards in arriving at the accomplishment of fertilization, which establishes the complement of genes for a human being.

Genes are found in the body (somatic) cells and sex (germ) cells of humans and function in two major capacities: they dictate the development and perpetuation of somatic cells; and, in germ cells, are the bridge between generations. We will examine both of those physiological processes in humans.

Gamete Formation

Let us look first at the formation of germ cells, the link between generations. Sexual reproduction in humans involves the formation of specialized cells called *gametes*, which contain one-half the genetic information needed to form the full complement of genes to fashion a human being. Gametes are formed in specialized organs called *gonads—ovaries*, which produce *oocytes* (precursors to eggs); and *testes*, which produce *spermatozoa*.

Humans, like many other organisms, have hereditary units that can be organized into discrete structures called *chromosomes*. Somatic cells of "normal" humans have the potential for the organization of genetic material into forty-six chromosomes (one member of each pair). Sex cells have genetic information for twenty-three chromosomes. A *zygote* (egg plus sperm) contains genetic information to form forty-six chromosomes (two members of each pair), twenty-three chromosomes having been contributed by each parent.

The formation of sex cells involves a nuclear division, *meiosis* (*oogenesis* in females and *spermatogenesis* in males) in which the chromosome number (genetic material) is reduced by one-half. When the union of dissimilar (male and female) gametes takes place, the normal complement of genetic material is reestablished. A critical feature of gamete production is that the appropriate amount of genetic information enters each gamete. If a gamete has the incorrect amount of genetic material and unites with a gamete of the opposite sex, particular types of abnormalities can occur, including the well-known Down's Syndrome.

Gametes are formed in the primary reproductive organs and are located away from the sites at which fertilization occurs. Fertilization in humans occurs within the oviduct of the female body. Oocytes are produced within ovaries through oogenesis and have the capability to develop into viable eggs. The fertilized egg has the potential to go through a series of changes, developing from a relatively nondescript homogeneous cell into a complex multicellular embryo. There is substantial evidence that the development of an early embryo is controlled primarily by the egg cell, which not only carries developmental sequences of genetic information but also supplies nutrients for the early embryo (Hopper & Hart 1985, 30). An egg has genes located within its nucleus. This nucleus, plus many other structures and chemicals within its cytoplasm, allows the egg to function as a unit that has the potential to be transformed into a complex human. The establishment of a human being, however, does not occur until the egg and the male gamete (sperm) have accomplished an effective union.

During the third month of fetal development of human females, the primary oocytes begin to develop. At birth, a female has approximately two million primary oocytes. These oocytes remain in this immature stage until particular times of hormonal influence (ovulation) when a primary oocyte becomes a secondary oocyte and is released from the ovary. Of the approximate two million primary oocytes present at birth, only about three to four hundred ever reach functional maturity (Curtis & Barnes 1985, 484). The nucleus of a human female oocyte is not completely ready for union with a male gamete until after fertilization. An oocyte in the ovary is released from a specialized structure called a *follicle* (oocyte with specialized cells needed for food and hormone production during oocyte maintenance in the ovary). The oocyte is carried from the ovary into an oviduct, or *Fallopian tube*. Specialized structures and muscular movement help move the oocyte through the Fallopian tube. The life expectancy of an unfertilized egg is approximately forty-eight to seventy-two hours. In order for fertilization to occur, however, sperm must make contact with the oocyte within the first thirty-six hours of its release from the follicle (Curtis & Barnes 1985, 485). Since it takes approximately three days for the Fallopian tube to guide the oocyte to the uterus, sperm must make contact with the oocyte in the oviduct (K. D. Johnson et al. 1984, 420). (See figure 1, The Human Female Reproductive Organs.)

Male gametes are produced in testes through a process called spermatogenesis. Unlike oogenesis in females, which is not a continuous process, spermatogenesis is relatively continuous in human males. Each spermatozoan (which contains one-half the genetic complement of its parent) is especially equipped for motility. The male gametes are delivered to the female genitalia through sexual intercourse, whereafter they move through the uterus and into the Fallopian tubes of the female.

As many as 400 million sperm cells can be released into the female vagina at ejaculation. Like the female oocytes, spermatozoa are not

Figure 1. The Human Female Reproductive Organs

Oocytes are released from specialized structures called follicles in the ovary. The oocyte is carried into the Fallopian tube, where it meets male gametes, called sperm. When oocyte and sperm unite, the genetic complement for a human being is established. The young embryo moves down the Fallopian tube into the uterus and is implanted in the inner lining of the uterus. The uterus is the womb in which the young fetus develops.

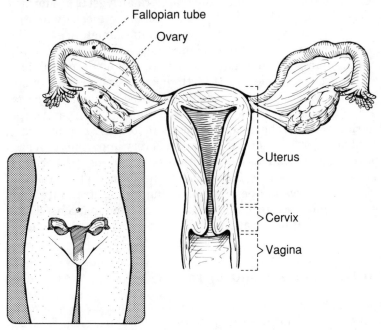

capable of fertilization at ejaculation but go through a process called *capacitation* in the female reproductive tract, which prepares them for fertilization (part of the coating of the head of a sperm is removed during capacitation). Only 300,000 to 400,000 of these sperm survive the journey into the oviducts. The sperm cells have a life expectancy of only about forty-eight hours after they reach the oviducts, where they swim against the specialized structures that enable the oocyte to move down the oviduct (K. D. Johnson et al. 1984, 420).

Conception

In order for fertilization to occur, numerous sperm must make contact with the oocyte, since apparently the presence of large numbers of sperm causes the chemical reactions necessary for only one sperm cell to penetrate an oocyte. When egg and sperm membranes make contact, an *acrosome* reaction occurs. (The acrosome—most anterior part of the sperm—releases enzymes that penetrate the exterior covering of the oocyte [Langman 1979, 23].) The membranes of the oocyte and sperm fuse, and an immediate mixing of their cell contents occurs. The oocyte nucleus then goes through the final stages of maturation and the genetic material of the oocyte and sperm unite. Fertilization of aging eggs and sperm sometimes occurs in humans, and abnormal zygotes are formed. This accounts for approximately 20 percent of spontaneously aborted pregnancies ("miscarriages"). There is an optimum gamete age for effective union in fertilization. Some evidence suggests that couples who practice natural family planning (rhythm method of birth control) have children with greater incidences of birth defects because the gametes may be "too old" when fertilization does occur (See *Population reports*).

The recombination of genes at fertilization (union of each parent's genetic material) restores the genetic capacity to forty-six chromosomes, the expected number for a normal human. It is very important that each gamete have the correct amount of genetic material to ensure the proper genetic potential of the new individual to be formed. The union of genetic material allows the new human being to have traits from his or her parents and ancestors, although in new combinations. These new genetic combinations make each human individual biologically unique.

Prenatal Development and Birth

After fertilization of the egg occurs in the oviduct, the first few cell divisions occur as it continues its journey to the uterus. The first cell division occurs approximately thirty-six hours after fertilization, and the second division at about sixty hours (Curtis & Barnes 1985, 488). As subsequent divisions occur, the cells become arranged in such a way as to form a hollow ball of cells, or *blastula,* which marks the polarization and differentiation of the cells. Part of the cells in the blastula will give rise to the embryo and part will form the membranes that will surround it. If an IUD (intrauterine device) has been inserted within the uterus, it will destroy the embryo in this stage of development, i.e., before the embryo is successfully implanted within the lining of the uterus. Occasionally an IUD will also destroy an implanted embryo. (See below, "Abortions in the First Trimester.)"

At the time of ovulation, the uterus is lined with cells rich in nourishment. After the embryo makes contact with this uterine lining *(endometrium),* it is subsequently surrounded by blood vessels from the uterus (Rugh & Shettles 1971, 25–26). Simultaneously, the outer membrane *(chorion)* surrounding the embryo is making projections that penetrate the nutrient-rich layers of the uterus. This is the site of the *placenta*. Both the mother and embryo contribute to the formation of the placenta, a highly vascular body of tissues through which occurs the exchange of oxygen and nutrients from the mother with wastes from the embryo. Through the umbilical-cord connection, the placenta is the lifeline of the developing embryo—a source of sustenance and method of waste elimination.

During the first month of development, the human embryo grows to about five millimeters (one-fifth inch) in length and has begun to differentiate the precursors for the central nervous system, a tiny pulsating heart, the precursors for muscles, bones, and associated tissues, and, remarkably, the beginning of the tissue for germ cell formation for the next generation.

At the end of the second month, the embryo has grown to four centimeters and weighs approximately one gram. Although the embryo is small, it is easily distinguished as a human (Kitzinger 1982, 63). Already beginning to form are such identifiable features as a head, obvious extremities in intricate detail, and internal body organs. From this time on, the embryo is generally referred to as a *fetus* (Curtis & Barnes 1985, 491).

During the first two months, the young embryo is differentiating the major body extremities and principal organs and generally laying the foundation for the physical body characteristics to be carried throughout life. If a major deformity occurs during this period of formation and differentiation, the abnormality will be perpetuated and magnified as the organs and other body features continue to grow. It is especially important for mothers to exercise great care not to expose themselves to certain viruses (such as *rubella*), chemicals (even simple across-the-counter drugs), and such environmental stimuli as radiation or sound shock during this early developmental time. However, exposure to these and other agents during *any* stage of prenatal life can pose a threat to the normal development of the embryo.

Toward the end of the first trimester of pregnancy (third month), the mother usually becomes aware of some fetal movements. The fetus is then at least nine centimeters long and weighs about twelve to fifteen grams. The fetus can then make different facial expressions; external genitalia become obvious; finger and toe prints are established; and all of the internal organ systems are distinguishable.

A mother becomes aware of extensive fetal movement during the fourth month, and the skeleton of the fetus is apparent. The placenta continues to develop into a massive structure and will occupy about half the uterus during the fifth month. The heart of the fetus is beating about 150 times per minute, and the respiratory system is specializing for its elaborate functions outside the mother's body. At the end of the second trimester (sixth month), the fetus can usually survive outside a mother's body, but generally only with extensive respiratory assistance. The fetus is usually 30 to 36 centimeters long and weighs about 680 grams at this time (Curtis & Barnes 1985, 493). If born prematurely during the sixth month, the young individual is no longer considered a fetus but a premature infant (C. Young 1984, 79).

Pregnant women should be especially careful to eat well-balanced meals during the third trimester (final three months of pregnancy). The fetus doubles in size during this time, and the biochemical and physiological processes in the fetus begin resembling those of an infant after birth. Accordingly, the fetus is highly susceptible to addictions or detrimental effects of particular drugs if the mother is using these substances.

The fetus is dependent on its mother's body for supplies of antibodies while living in the womb. The human placenta is the principal site of exchange between mother and fetus and has not been subject to extensive immunological study. The studies conducted, however, demonstrate that the placenta can evade host (mother)-immunological responses. There is much research today on the operational interface in maternofetal immunological interactions in the placenta (P. M. Johnson et al. 1980, 29). It usually takes one to two months after birth for the baby to manufacture antibodies in significant quantities to function effectively in immunological capacities.

Gestation (the time of carrying young in the uterus from conception to birth) is approximately thirty-eight weeks in humans. Many factors contribute to triggering the birth of the baby. Among these factors are fetal size, state of the nervous tissue, and hormonal influences. The uterus becomes greatly distended during pregnancy as the weight and size of the fetus increase. When the uterus reaches a particular size, it is ready to respond to the nervous and hormonal stimuli that initiate uterine contractions. It is interesting to note that human twins reach the critical surface area/volume ratio within the uterus before either twin is as large as a single fetus. As a result of the uterus reaching its "carrying capacity," twins and other multiple fetuses are generally born prematurely.

The mother's hormonal level, which has been greatly altered throughout her pregnancy, is an important factor in the labor contractions of the uterus. Among those hormones are *progesterone,* which reduces contractions of the uterus during pregnancy and is less abundant toward the end of pregnancy, and *estrogen,* which is directly involved in the contraction process. Both of these hormones prepare the uterus for stimulation by other hormones, including *oxytocin* and *relaxin.* If the levels of estrogen and progesterone are appropriate, and if

Figure 2. The Expulsion Stage of Delivery

The cervix of the uterus is greatly distended and the baby's head appears through the cervical opening. This stage can last up to one hour.

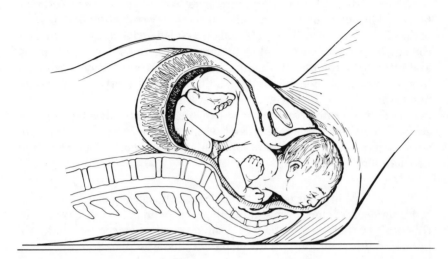

the uterus is properly distended, oxytocin speeds labor. Relaxin is a hormone manufactured only during pregnancy. It relaxes pubic ligaments and softens the cervix, thus facilitating passage of the baby through the birth canal. *Prostaglandins* are important in causing uterine contractions and work effectively with oxytocin at the normal birth time. Naturally-occurring prostaglandins occur in women in smaller quantities compared to the larger doses sometimes given to induce abortions. They are frequently used for second-trimester abortions because of their ability to induce labor (Strand 1983, 208). (Oxytocin is not generally administered with prostaglandins in abortion attempts.)

The hormones mentioned above are important in the initiation of uterine contractions. During *labor*, the cervix is stretched and the baby is pushed through the birth canal. Normal labor occurs in three stages. The first stage involves dilation of the cervix and can last up to sixteen hours. During this period, uterine contractions occur at about fifteen-to-twenty–minute intervals and are relatively mild. At the end of the dilation stage, they may be as frequent as one or two minutes apart. The cervix has begun to open during this stage and may reach ten centimeters in diameter. The *amniotic sac* surrounding the fetus usually releases its fluids during the first stage of labor.

The second stage involves expulsion of the baby into and through the birth canal and normally lasts up to one hour. The cervix is fully dilated in this stage and the head of the infant appears through the opening (see figure 2). The baby's head is normally in a downward position and helps in the dilation of the cervical opening.

The third stage, called the placental stage, occurs after the baby has been forced through the vagina during delivery. The placenta, uterine fluid, and blood are normally expelled from the uterus within half an hour of the birth of the baby. The umbilical cord is tied and severed. The mother continues to experience weaker uterine contractions for a short time, and ultimately the uterus shrinks from its greatly distended size. The infant is no longer dependent upon a lifeline to the mother for nourishment, waste removal, and other life-sustaining processes once he or she is outside the protective enclosure in which prenatal development occurred. Now the normal infant can breathe and survive in other circumstances but is still dependent upon his or her mother for care and nourishment.

The discussion so far has centered around the normal course of events in human conception, prenatal development, and delivery. It is only in this century that we have had a reasonably sound concept of what happens in fetal inception and development. Today, our understanding of the process of development within the mother is well enough understood to allow for correction of defects in some fetuses (Ellias & Annas 1983, 809). For example, surgery on children who would have been hydrocephalics at birth has been done fetally, and brain damage with associated retardation has thus been reduced. (See below, "Advances and Implications of Fetal Studies.") It is indeed ironic that we have within our society the freedom, technology, and variety of moral values that allow some of us to dedicate immense amounts of time, prayer, skill, and other resources to the improvement and preservation of human life still inhabiting the mother's womb—while other segments of our society are making the same kinds of investments to destroy that intrauterine life. Some parents have claimed the right to destroy lives that doctors can treat, preserve, and save.

Natural and Unnatural Abortions

Miscarriages

Spontaneous abortions, or *miscarriages*, occur "naturally" in mothers when the uterus goes into labor too early in pregnancy. This is sometimes due to abnormalities of either the fetus or the placenta. Recent data suggest that 50 to 80 percent of all human conceptions are spontaneously aborted. Of these, many have unusual chromosome numbers or chromosome structural aberrations. *Trisomy* is the most prevalent chromosome anomaly in spontaneously aborted fetuses. Occasionally a human *conceptus* will contain as many as five times the normal amount of genetic material (five sets of chromosomes instead of two, as previously discussed). Many spontaneous abortions occur within the first month of pregnancy, in a stage so immature that the mother carrying the human embryo does not even know that she is pregnant (Wagner et al. 1980, 310).

Induced Abortions

Unnatural abortions are violent and abusive to the human body and are performed in such a way as to render the fetus dead on arrival from the mother's body. Since most such abortions are elective, doctors are challenged to be able to define for their patients the risks associated with the abortion procedures in order for them to give truly informed consent. "The two major risks of greatest concern are death [to the mother] and loss of future reproductive capability" (King et al. 1980, 530). Abortions are abusive to sexual organs, sexual functionings, and normal sexual relationships. Above all, they deny life to a newly created human.

Numerous techniques have been developed for the purpose of aborting human beings and adapted to kill the fetus at different stages of its development. These techniques are not only violent to the fetus but may also cause severe physical and physiological trauma to the mother, although some studies have shown that when the data on abortion procedures were adjusted to gestational age, teenagers generally had lower rates of morbidity and mortality from induced abortion than older women (Cates et al. 1983, 621). But overall: "Abortions performed late in pregnancy are associated with higher death and complication rates, are more expensive, and are emotionally more taxing for patients and staff than abortions performed early in pregnancy" (Burr & Schultz 1980, 44).

When a woman elects to have an abortion, the abortionist must first examine her to determine how far along the pregnancy has progressed, since the age of the fetus determines the technique to be used.

Abortions in the First Trimester. Intrauterine devices (IUD) or intrauterine contraceptive devices (IUCD) and progestagen-only pill (mini-pill) are means of interrupting pregnancies during the first few days after conception. IUDs can be made of plastic, polythene, and/or copper. Their primary effect is to prevent implantation of the days-old embryo. The IUD has been described as an "abortifacient" (Cameron 1986, 46).

(Copper-containing IUDs can also prevent sperm from reaching eggs prior to conception.) The mini-pill greatly affects the mucous lining of the cervix, making it hostile to sperm. If a sperm manages to move through this barrier and accomplishes fertilization of an egg in the Fallopian tube, the uterine lining does not provide a favorable environment for the newly conceived embryo (Cameron 1986, 46) if it has been influenced by the mini-pill. The dose of prostaglandin in the mini-pill is enough to prevent implantation of the embryo.

Techniques involving suction are generally employed when the embryo is less than three months old. The mother is given a local anesthetic in the cervix, and—if *suction curettage* is employed—the mouth of the womb is forced open and stretched by dilators wide enough to allow the suction tube to be inserted into the uterus. After the suction tube is inserted into the back part of the uterus, the machine is engaged. The force created by the suction is more than two dozen times greater than that of a normal household vacuum cleaner. After the amniotic membrane and its fluid are sucked out, portions of the embryo are extracted (C. Young 1984, 85). An attempt is then made to remove the placenta, which is embedded in the wall of the uterus. Abortionists refer to the young embryo as "tissue," and once the suction tube has been applied, a curet is inserted into the uterus to scrape the wall of the uterus and thereby remove any remaining tissue of the embryo (C. Young 1984, 85). Many dangerous complications can occur when using the suction-curettage method of abortion. If sterile instruments are not used for administering the anesthesia or curettage, numerous types of infections are possible. Permanent damage can be inflicted on the cervix because of the force used to enter the uterus, or perforation of the uterus may occur, in which case a permanent scar is left in the uterus and can lead to sterility (C. Young 1984, 87). It goes without saying that the mother experiences pain during an abortion and/or in the hours that follow completion of the process. There is evidence suggesting that the fetus, too, experiences pain in the process. (This will be discussed in more detail below.)

A related technique used to accomplish abortion in the first trimester is *dilatation and curettage* (D & C), in which suction is not initially applied, but rather the curet is inserted into the womb and moved around to scrape the womb in such a way as to break up the embryo. Suction is then used to remove the body parts and placenta (C. Young 1984, 88). The inherent dangers of this type of abortion resemble those of suction curettage.

Abortion After the First Trimester: Chemical Methods. When the fetus is over three months old, other abortion techniques are applied. These generally involve *instilling a lethal substance* into the amniotic sac. The desired result in such cases is to kill the fetus and have the mother deliver a dead baby. Numerous problems exist here, including the possible delivery of a live but severely damaged fetus. One of the common substances used in this type of abortion is a saline (salt) solution, which is injected directly into the amniotic sac and leads to hemorrhaging and burns on the baby's body. Complications such as pain to the fetus and mother, infections, and possible delivery through tears in the uterus can occur.

Prostaglandins are hormones mentioned earlier in this chapter as causing violent uterine muscle contractions. In certain doses they can cause the uterus to expel the fetus from the body of the mother. Prostaglandins are usually injected directly into the amniotic sac. This injection results in a very painful abortion for the mother, although it appears that less tissue damage is done to her directly, unless the fetus tears through the wall of the uterus. The incidence of aborted infants "exploding" through the uterine wall is higher with the use of prostaglandins than with saline solution (C. Young 1984, 91). In that case, a *hysterotomy* must be done: the surgeon enters the uterus through the abdominal wall and removes the fetus. Hysterotomies involve major surgery, and the umbilical cord is frequently tied so as to kill the infant if it is still alive.

Incomplete abortions frequently occur through the use of prostaglandins. Some studies have shown that over 3 percent of women treated with intravaginal forms of prostaglandins deliver a live fetus. This is considered a "complication" by the abortionists (Surrago & Robins 1982, 293). The side effects of using prostaglandins include cramping, nausea, diarrhea, vomiting, and circulatory and respiratory problems. Since prostaglandins can stimulate uterine contractions at any stage of fetal development, they were thought at one time to be a recommended chemical means of performing abortions. However, the side effects and continuous flow needed for their effectiveness, as well as the unpredictable time needed for fetal expulsion (from hours to days) and the possibility of partial placental expulsion, have caused many abortionists to reassess the use of prostaglandins. Recent research in this area suggests that the administration of two slightly different prostaglandins, one that acts upon the uterus and another that acts upon the ovaries, will effectively interrupt pregnancy without inducing the side effects produced by other prostaglandins (Wilks 1983, 1407–1408). Scientific statements about abortion pervade the literature, encouraging researchers to discover more efficient substances and methods to induce abortions. Such an example includes, "An important goal in the development of a non-surgical abortifacient for early gestation is that it be self-administered by the subjects, preferably at home" (Brenner et al. 1982, 274).

Abortions After the First Trimester: D & E. Another technique sometimes used for mid-trimester abortions is *dilatation and evacuation*
(D & E). The entry technique into the uterus resembles that of the first-
trimester abortion but involves the insertion into the uterus of a forceps,
which is then used to cut the fetus into pieces. Crushing the head of the
fetus is the most difficult procedure in this technique and has raised
many ethical questions among medical support staff in abortion clinics
and hospitals (Hern & Corrigan 1978, 4–5). Extensive damage to the
uterus and cervix can occur when a D & E is performed, especially
when an unskilled abortionist is carrying out the procedure (C. Young
1984, 96).

Research in Chemical Abortifacients

In recent years considerable scientific research has focused on developing "safe" chemicals for use as abortifacients. Pressures brought on
by undesirable side effects of birth-control pills and an expansion of
worldwide birth-control programs (both contraception *and* abortion)
have led to the development of alternatives to conventional population-
control mechanisms. Abortifacient chemicals, including prostaglandins
(see above, "Induced Abortions"), have been developed and widely marketed for second-trimester abortions. The Upjohn Company of Kal-
amazoo, Michigan, has marketed at least three prostaglandins and
supported research to develop an early-trimester abortifacient, a sup-
pository tipped with a prostaglandin (C. Young 1985).

Upjohn insists that its long-standing program to develop prostaglandins recently ended, but it has made its accumulated data and chemicals
available to researchers who are continuing such studies. Upjohn has
sponsored extensive research on luteolytic effects of prostaglandins (Patwardhan & Lanthier 1985, 92; Toppozada et al. 1981, 209) and has led
the way in supporting research aimed at perfecting an abortifacient that
can be self-administered at home (Bygdeman et al. 1983, 125). Anti-
progesterone chemicals are being developed that would induce menstruation in a pregnant woman and thereby expel a fertilized egg from
the wall of the uterus (Archibald 1986, 2A). Prostaglandin $^{PF}2a$, a drug
introduced by Upjohn, has been used to destroy the *corpus luteum* (follicle which has released its egg and produces hormones that prepare the
uterus lining for implantation) in the ovary after ovulation. Progesterone is produced in the corpus luteum until the eighth to tenth
week of pregnancy (and in the placenta after that time). If progesterone
synthesis is suppressed early in pregnancy, the lining of the uterus
(endometrium) will not develop sufficiently to retain the fertilized
ovum. In effect, the suppression of progesterone activity prevents or
ends a potential pregnancy.

The intent of the primary research has been fertility control in an abortifacient form (Toppozada et al. 1981, 209). Tests have not shown prostaglandin to be a self-sufficient abortifacient in the early trimester. Analogs of prostaglandins are being developed to use as anti-progesterone nonhormonal steroids. One synthetic steroid, RU 486, was developed in France by a team of researchers led by Dr. Etienne-Emile Baulieu of the National Institute for Medical Health and Research (INSERM). Dr. Baulieu has coined a new phrase to describe the effect of RU 486, using the terms "countergestation" or "contragestion" to describe its effect (C. Young 1986, 3). This chemical has properties of progesterone and glucocorticoid antagonists and acts at the progesterone receptor level (Kovacs et al. 1984, 400). It has proved 70 percent effective in interrupting pregnancies of less than eight weeks and 100 percent effective when used with prostaglandin (AP Wire 1984). Uterine contractions are not induced by RU 486, but if it is used with a prostaglandin, which does induce such contractions, the drug's effectiveness for inducing abortion is apparent. The supplier for this drug is Roussel UCLAF of Paris, France, and much of the research for its introduction into human females has been supported by the World Health Organization (Kovacs et al. 1984, 409). The net effect of using RU 486 is that the drug binds to progesterone acceptor sites in the uterus and a pregnancy cannot be maintained.

There has been a great deal of controversy surrounding the use of National Institutes of Health funds (Rojas et al. 1985, 153; Nadler et al. 1985, 176; Nieman et al. 1985, 279) to support research efforts to introduce RU 486 into human females as a fertility-control method. Macaque monkeys have been used for experimentation pertinent to the progesterone antagonist RU 486, including tests of an intravaginal tampon device for RU 486. The results of these tests demonstrate that RU 486, when employed with a prostaglandin, has a high efficacy through the eighth week of pregnancy and decreasing efficiency thereafter (Hodgen 1985, 266).

Another chemical anti-progesterone agent—Epostane, or WIN 32729—is being developed by Sterling Drug's Winthrop Division (Pattison et al. 1984, 875). It is taken orally and inhibits progesterone synthesis in the corpus luteum and placenta. It has been billed by the researchers as having unique potential as an abortifacient (Pattison et al. 1984, 880) and anti-fertility drug (Van der Spuy et al. 1983, 532). The development of Epostane and other abortifacient drugs, including Trilostane, which is deemed as unsuitable for early human abortion (Van der Spuy et al. 1983, 526) is not as far along as the testing of RU 486.

The popular media are closely covering the testing of RU 486, which is being tested by the Population Council with approval of the FDA. The side effects include uterine pain, fatigue, nausea, vomiting, and heavy bleeding. Clinical tests are being conducted to determine optimum dosage and other timing factors to give optimum compatibility of RU 486 with other drugs (Archibald 1986).

Effects of Abortion on Mother and Child

The Mother

The effects of abortions on women are varied and hard to characterize numerically. Nigel Cameron (1986, 56) points out that studies on abortion are mostly retrospective not prospective, that is, past hospital records and questionnaires to women who have had abortions are used for data gathering.

There can be immediate complications, which include bleeding and infections. Sometimes excessive bleeding occurs at the site where the afterbirth was situated, especially if the uterine wall is damaged. If there is a perforation of the uterus, injury can occur to other structures, such as the intestine (Cameron 1986, 57). One cause for uterine rupture has been the use of prostaglandin F_2^α with other oxytocic agents during second-trimester abortions. Malmstrom and Hemmingsson (1984, 272) warn that symptoms preceding a rupture may be masked by analgesics prescribed in the high doses used for second-trimester abortions. Cervical bleeding is common in abortions. This is especially true when laminaria tents (dried seaweed) are inserted into the cervix to initiate the dilation process. Any infection is generally traceable to placental fragments left in the uterus, since the placenta provides a rich culture site for bacteria responsible for various pelvic infections and symptoms.

The long-term biological effects of abortion include infertility and difficulties in successfully carrying out subsequent pregnancies (Cameron 1986, 58). If the short-term infections discussed above later result in tubal blockage, a viable egg cannot be transported to the uterus. The psychological effects of abortion on parents must be recognized as significant long-term complications of abortion. (This is dealt with in chapter 11.)

The Child: Fetal Pain

Fetal pain has been the subject of much discussion as the various issues surrounding abortion have emerged. President Reagan, in a speech on January 30, 1986, to the National Religious Broadcasters Convention in Washington, D.C., called for a constitutional ban on abortion and contended that aborted fetuses suffer "long and agonizing" pain (Clines 1984). Some members of the American College of Obstetricians and Gynecologists challenged the President's statement and disclaimed evidence that would substantiate pain as being perceived by a fetus. Dr. Ervin Nichols, spokesman for the group, allowed that there were "demonstrated neurological reflexes that take place" in some medical procedures, such as a fetus moving a limb in reaction to an examining physician's probe. However, he added, "We have no evidence whatsoever that this is in any way interpreted by the fetus as pain" (Clines 1984). In response to Nichols's statement, a group of physicians, including two past-presidents of A.C.O.G., Dr. Richard Schmidt and Dr. Fred Hofmeister, wrote President Reagan in support of his statement. They called attention to the humanity and sensitivity of the human unborn. That letter is reproduced by permission of the writers.

February 13, 1984

President Ronald Reagan
The White House
Washington, DC 20500

Mr. President:
     As physicians, we, the undersigned, are pleased to associate ourselves with you in drawing the attention of people across the nation to the humanity and sensitivity of the human unborn.
     That the unborn, the prematurely born, and the newborn of the human species is a highly complex, sentient, functioning, individual organism is established scientific fact. That the human unborn and newly born do respond to stimuli is also established beyond any reasonable doubt.
     The ability to feel pain and respond to it is clearly not a phenomenon that develops de novo at birth. Indeed, much of enlightened modern obstetrical practice and procedure seeks to minimize sensory deprivation of, and sensory insult to, the fetus during, at, and after birth.
     Over the last 18 years, real time ultrasonography, fetoscopy, study of the fetal E.K.G. (electrocardiogram) and fetal E.E.G. (electroencephalogram) have demonstrated the remarkable responsiveness of the human fetus to pain, touch, and sound. That the fetus responds to changes in light intensity within the womb to heat, to cold, and to taste (by altering the chemical nature of the fluid swallowed by the fetus) has been exquisitely documented in the pioneering work of the late Sir William Liley—the father of fetology.
     Observations of the fetal electrocardiogram and the increase in fetal movements in saline abortions indicate that the fetus experiences discomfort as it dies. Indeed, one doctor who, the *New York Times* wrote, "conscientiously performs" saline abortions stated, "When you inject the saline, you often see an increase in fetal movements, it's horrible."

We state categorically that no finding of modern fetology invalidates the remarkable conclusion drawn after a lifetime of research by the late Professor Arnold Gesell of Yale University. In "The Embryology of Behavior: The Beginnings of the Human Mind" (1945, Harper Bros.), Dr. Gesell wrote, "and so by the close of the first trimester the fetus is a sentient, moving being. We need not speculate as to the nature of his psychic attributes, but we may assert that the organization of his psychosomatic self is well under way."

Mr. President, in drawing attention to the capability of the human fetus to feel pain, you stand on firmly established ground.

Respectfully,

Dr. Richard T. F. Schmidt   **Dr. Fred Hofmeister**
Past President, A.C.O.G.   Past President, A.C.O.G.
Professor of Ob/Gyn   Professor of Ob/Gyn
University of Cincinnati   University of Wisconsin (Milwaukee)
Cincinnati, OH

                                     (More signatories on next page).

Other authors and researchers have discussed the fetal response to stimuli. Reinis and Goldman (1980, 232) say that human sensory nerves approach the skin of the fetus in the eighth week and are in contact with the skin in the ninth week. Lip tactile reflex responses can be seen after seven weeks, and by ten and a half weeks the palms of the hands respond to light stroking with a hair. At eleven weeks the face and all parts of the upper and lower extremities are sensitive to touch. Reinis and Goldman further indicate that by about fourteen weeks the entire body surface, except for the back and top of the head, is sensitive to pain.

Debate continues in the medical and scientific community over the issue of fetal pain. Anesthesiologist Vincent Collins, a professor at the University of Illinois Medical Center, says that nervous-system structures are in place six to eight weeks after conception and can respond to painful stimuli. He says that natural pain relief acceptors are functional by the twelfth week of gestation (in Russell 1984). In a conversation with me, Dr. Richard Schmidt indicated "that those who defend abortion often confuse or ignore the distinction between feeling pain and forming an idea of pain. Most of us have at some time or other experienced a sudden, severe pain, reacted vigorously to it by withdrawing, jumping or crying out—these reactions occurring a perceptible moment before our higher cortical centers have identified the specific nature or relative severity of the pain or even its exact location. Is it intense heat or cold, or cutting or crushing? Is it one toe or the entire foot? It is only this integrating function which is incompletely developed in the fetus at a stage when it can clearly be demonstrated to perceive ('feel') and react purposefully to a painful stimulus."

Research on fetal pain is difficult to carry out, and legislation has been introduced into Congress that would require physicians to notify patients considering abortion that a fetus can suffer pain. The question of pain is perhaps best addressed by the physicians who signed the above letter, in which they clearly state that part of their "enlightened modern obstetrical practice and procedure seeks to minimize sensory deprivation of, and sensory insult to, the fetus during, at, and after birth." The "averted gaze" discussed by Joseph Sobran reminds us that private property, the work ethic, and sanctity of life have been forced to yield to the liberal imperative of relieving pain and misery of many kinds. Sobran says "most of them are far more bearable than what an aborted child, scalded, dismembered, or simply expelled from the womb before its time, might be suffering" (Sobran 1984, 4).

Advances and Implications of Fetal Studies

We are living in a society that has developed extraordinary techniques for accumulating knowledge about prenatal life.

One such technique is *amniocentesis,* which provides a prenatal diagnosis of some genetic characteristics of a fetus. (See figure 3.) This information is obtained by extracting cells from the amniotic fluid surrounding the fetus. (These cells are usually sloughed-off epidermal cells of the skin or respiratory tract.) By studying these cells, one can determine whether a fetus will have the correct number of chromosomes and whether chromosomal structure is normal. Chemical analysis of the amniotic cells sometimes reveals fetal defects that will respond to treatment during pregnancy. In the case of abnormalities for which no such prenatal treatment is yet available, early diagnosis and counseling is helpful in preparing the parents for the adjustments they must make in caring for the child after birth. Parents sometimes use the results of this test to determine whether they will keep a fetus if an abnormality exists, or even if the baby is the "wrong" sex. A classic and unusual case involving the use of this technique is one in which a doctor detected twins in a mother, one of which had Down's Syndrome. He subsequently destroyed the Down's child in the mother's uterus and left the other twin to develop normally. Several months later the mother delivered the normal child and the dead Down's infant (Kerenyi & Chitkara 1981, 1525).

Another technical advance used in diagnosing fetal problems is *ultrasound,* in which high-frequency sound waves are beamed at the fetus from the outside and reflected to a recording instrument. This tech-

Figure 3.   Amniocentesis

A syringe is injected into the abdominal wall of the mother and into the uterus. Epidermal cells from the respiratory tract and skin are sloughed off and are suspended in the amniotic fluid. Some of these cells can be extracted with a syringe. The cells are then cultured and chromosome counts for the fetus are performed.

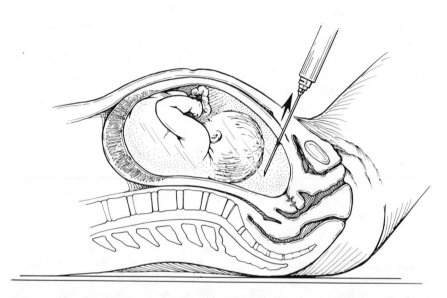

nology gives detailed pictures of a fetus without exposing it to the potential danger of x-rays. *Fetoscopy* is a technique by which a fetus can be examined with the use of a thin tube of flexible glass fibers inserted through a needle into the uterus. This allows technicians to take small pieces of skin and/or blood samples directly from the fetus. (Both fetoscopy and amniocentesis are performed in conjunction with the pictorial image of the fetus obtained through the ultrasound technique.)

Development of new therapies to treat fetuses and the use of such technical advances as amniocentesis, ultrasound, and fetoscopy are allowing for early diagnoses of fetal problems. Fetal surgeries are now being performed in which bladder and brain shunts are surgically introduced. A pioneering operation on a blocked urinary tract was performed in San Francisco in 1985, whereby a team of surgeons removed a twenty-three-week-old fetus from his mother's womb and successfully operated to correct a blocked urinary tract. The surgeons returned the unborn baby to his mother's womb and stitched the uterus back together. The boy was delivered nine weeks later and today is a normal, healthy, child (Blakeslee 1986).

In addition to fetal surgery, medications are being given to fetuses who suffer from other maladies. Noteworthy are successful treatments of fetuses with digoxin, a form of digitalis (Dumesic et al. 1982, 1129), and biotin (a vitamin) to give them greater survival advantages and to prevent abnormalities that would occur if the respective conditions were left untreated.

Ultrasound has been used to determine the gestational age of fetuses, which has implications for the type of abortion performed. For instance, in the first trimester, most abortions are performed by suction curettage (D & C or D & E). Second-trimester abortions are frequently performed by using a type of prostaglandin (James et al. 1984, 65). Fetuses who have survived until the third trimester stand a better chance of being born, since elective abortion is illegal (considered "manslaughter") in most states after approximately twenty-four weeks of gestation. Abortions in the third trimester are still legal in the United States if performed to protect the life of the mother or if there is a likelihood that the fetus would be born with a major deformity that precludes life (James et al. 1984, 66).

Mothers are encouraged to have any medically recommended amniocentesis prior to the eighteenth week of pregnancy so that adequate time is given to perform the chromosome study (up to four weeks can be required to perform this test). The time factor is important for handling treatable fetal defects, for preparing the parents for the possibility of having a child born with congenital defects, and—as a final consideration—for opting for an abortion, which would still be "legal" at that stage of pregnancy. If an ultrasound diagnosis misdates gestational age, the error may prevent a physician from legally performing the abortion (James et al. 1984, 65).

As the technical advances used in diagnosing fetal age and well-being are improved, we will continue to see them used for God's glory as fetuses are treated surgically and medicinally. Such treatments are sometimes directly on the fetus in the womb. In other cases, the mother is given drugs to benefit the fetus, and occasionally delivery is induced early in order that a particular fetal condition can be treated postnatally. Amniocentesis, ultrasound, and fetoscopy technologies are also being used to provide information for the destruction of human fetal life. Ernie Young, Ph.D., chaplain of the Stanford University Medical Center, predicts that as more sophisticated imaging techniques are developed, physical evidence of the viability and human qualities of the fetus will be enhanced, and there will be a shift in the spectrum of opinion in favor of the fetus (E. Young 1984, 44). We are further aware of many types of fetal experimentation outside the mother's body made possible by techniques unknown to man until a decade ago. Many issues raised by the studies of fetal life deserve thought, discussion, and action by both Christians and the community at large.

Conclusions

God created a perfect world as a home for man. Man's fall into sin allows him to be openly involved in activities that do not honor his creator. Such activities are exemplified by his poor stewardship over some of creation and abuse of his own body in such ways as to diminish sexuality and the normal reproductive functions. Sexual misconduct leads to vitiating the human body and can lead to creation of a human being so unwanted that no one will defend even his/her most basic right, the right to life itself. Issues surrounding promiscuity and abortion depict a glimpse of the fallenness of man.

This chapter has centered on the normal course of events in human conception, development, birth, and the trauma that occurs when these natural processes are disrupted. Human sexual behavior and procreation are divinely prescribed as God-ordained processes within the context of his guidelines. The destruction of human life within a mother's womb is a violent and tragic event in the life of the mother and is a violation of the child's most basic right. Our society currently allows for that destruction of life just for the sake of convenience of the parents.

While we should condemn illicit sex relationships and the destruction of human life by abortion, we must show Christian love to the children who are conceived in sin and the mothers who have already used abortion as contraception. We must remember that for those who are repentant, the death and resurrection of Christ have covered this sin. We must be willing to share this good news with mothers who are still living with the trauma of having had an abortion and mates who have encouraged sexual partners to have abortions.

Abortion is the most frequently performed operation in America today and unique in that its goal is the destruction of a living, responsive human being. It is being used as a contraceptive method and involves a morality centered around the convenience of the mother. Taking responsible action on this issue involves making choices centered in the role of responsible sexual behavior in the context of God's ordained laws. If humans practice sex within God's ordained patterns, the wholesale abortion demand centered around unwed mothers, unwanted teenage pregnancies, and other situations that contribute to unwanted pregnancies, would not be as prevalent as it is in this decade. Faced with the current abortion demands, we still have responsibility to respect and follow God's desires, and part of that responsibility lies in providing good alternatives to women who are considering abortion.

It is a staggering fact that the creator of the universe entered our earthly realm through a virgin birth and ultimately destroyed man's estrangement from God. He chose to enter the world in a mother's womb and to undergo the developmental sequences through which humans go. The beauty and good in God's created natural order can give us great joy, and the reality of how God entered this world calls us to authentically relate to him and be responsible stewards to the creation of which we are a part.

References

AP Wire, Paris. 1984. New pill offers abortion alternative. *Holland Sentinel* December 8:C7

Archibald, G. 1986. New pill controversy unites pro-life units. *Washington Times* January 22:A2.

Blakeslee, S. 1986. Fetus returned to womb following surgery. *New York Times* October 7:C1.

Brenner, P. F.; Marrs, R. P.; Roy, S.; & Mishell, D. P. 1982. Termination of early gestation with 9-deoxo-16, 16-dimethyl-9 methylene prostaglandine E_2. *Contraception* 26(3):261–277.

Bygdeman, M.; Christensen N. J.; Green, K.; Zheng, S.; & Lundstrom, V. 1983. Termination of early pregnancy. *Acta. Obstet. Gynecol. Scand. Suppl.* 113:125–129.

Burr, W. & Schultz, K. 1980. Delayed abortion in an area of easy accessibility *Journal of the American Medical Association* 244(1):44–48.

Calvert, D. n.d. *Repeat abortion: Its reproductive risks.* Duke University Medical School (Christian Action Council publication).

Cameron, N. M. de S. 1986. *Abortion: The crisis in morals and medicine.* England: Intervarsity Press.

Cates, W., Jr.; Schulz, K. F.; & Grimes, D. 1983. The risks associated with teenage abortion. *New England Journal of Medicine* 11:621–624.

Clines, F. 1984. Reagan tells broadcasters aborted fetuses suffer pain. *New York Times* January 31.

Curtis, H., & Barnes, N. S. 1985. *Invitation to biology.* New York: Worth Publishers.

Dumesic, D. A.; Silverman, N. H.; Tobias, S.; & Golbus, M. S. 1982. Transplacental cardioversion of fetal supraventricular tachycardia with procainamide. *New England Journal of Medicine* 307(18):1128–1130.

Ellias, S., & Annas, G. J. 1983. Perspectives on fetal surgery. *American Journal of Obstetrics and Gynecology* 145(7):809.

Hern, W. M., & Corrigan, B. 1978. What about us? Staff reactions to the D and E procedure. Paper presented at the annual meeting of the Association of Planned Parenthood Physicians, San Diego.

Hodgen, G. D. 1985. Pregnancy prevention by intravaginal delivery of a progesterone antagonist: RU 486 tampon for menstrual induction and absorption. *Fertility and Sterility* 44(2):263–267.

Hopper, A. F., & Hart, N. H. 1985. *Foundations of animal development.* New York: Oxford Univ. Press.

James, A. E.; Fleischer, A. C.; Sanders, R. C.; Bundy, A. L.; & Boehm, F. H. 1984. Ultrasound bears burden of fetal viability standard. *Diagnostic Imaging* 6(9):64–66.

Johnson, K. D.; Rayle, D. L.; & Wedberg, H. L. 1984. *Biology.* California: Benjamin/Cummings.

Johnson, P. M.; Brown, P. J.; & Faulk, W. P. 1980. Immunological aspects of the human placenta. *Oxford Rev. Report. Biol.* 2:1–40.

Kerenyi, T. D., & Chitkara, U. 1981. Selective birth in twin pregnancy with discordancy for Down's Syndrome. *New England Journal of Medicine* 304(25):1525–27.

King, T. M.; Atienza, M. F.; & Burkman, R. T. 1980. The incidence of abdominal surgical procedures in a population undergoing abortion. *American Journal of Obstetrics and Gynecology* 137:530–533.

Kitzinger, S. 1982. *The complete book of pregnancy and childbirth.* New York: Knopf.

Kovacs, L. S. M.; Resch, B. A.; Ugocsai, G.; Swahn, M. L.; Bygdeman, M.; & Rowe, P. J. 1984. Termination of very early pregnancy by RU 486—an antiprogestational compound. *Contraception* 29(5):399–410.

Langman, J. 1979. *Medical embryology.* Baltimore: Williams & Wilkins.

Malstrom, H., & Hemmingsson, E. 1984. Uterine rupture as a complication of second-trimester abortion when using prostaglandin F_2^α together with other oxytocic agents. *Acta. Obstet. Gynecol. Scand.* 63:271–272.

Nadler, R. D.; Roth-Meyer, C.; & Baulieu, E. 1985. Behavioral and endocrine consequences of long-term antiprogesterone (RU 486) administration to cynomolgus monkeys: Preliminary results. In *The antiprogestin steroid RU 486 and human fertility control.* New York: Plenum Press.

Nieman, L. K.; Healy, D. L.; Spits, I. M.; Merrian, G. R.; Bardin, C. W.; Loriaux, D. L.; & Chrousos, G. P. 1985. Use of single doses of the antiprogesterone steroid RU 486 for induction of menstruation in normal women. In *The antiprogestin steroid RU 486 and human fertility control.* New York: Plenum Press.

Pattison, N. S.; Webster, M. A.; Phipps, S. L.; Anderson, A. B. M.; & Gillmer, M. D. G. 1984. Inhibition of B-hydroxysteroid dehydrogenase (3B-HSD) activity in first- and second-trimester human pregnancy and the luteal phase using Epostane. *Fertility and Sterility* 42(6):875–881.

Patwardhan, V. V., & Lanthier, L. 1985. Luteal phase variations in endogenous concentrations of prostaglandins PGE and PGF and in the capacity for their in vitro formation in the human corpus luteum. *Prostaglandins* 30(1):91–98.

Population reports: Population information program: Periodic Abstinence. 1981. Baltimore: Johns Hopkins Univ. (Series I, No. 3).

Reinis, S. & Goldman, J. M. 1980. *The development of the brain: Biological and functional perspectives.* Springfield, Illinois: Charles C. Thomas.

Rojas, F. J.; O'Connor, J. L.; & Asch, R. H. 1985. Studies on the antireproductive mechanisms of action of RU 486. In *The antiprogestin steroid RU 486 and human fertility control.* New York: Plenum Press.

Rugh, R., & Shettles, L. B. 1971. *From conception to birth.* New York: Harper & Row.

Russell, C. 1984. Physician group supports president on fetus pain. *The Washington Post* February 14:A6.

Sobran, J. 1984. The averted gaze: Liberalism and fetal pain. *The Human Life Review* (pamphlet).

Strand, F. L. 1983. *Physiology.* New York: Macmillan.

Surrago, E. J., & Robbins, J. 1982. Midtrimester pregnancy termination by intravaginal administration of prostaglandin E_2. *Contraception* 26(3):285–294.

Toppozada, M.; El-Sokkary, H.; El-Abd, M.; El-Fazary, A.; & El-Rahmen, H. A. 1981. Induction of human luteolysis by high dose infusions of 15-methyl PGF_2^α. *Prostaglandins and Medicine* 6:203–211.

Van der Spuy, Z. M.; Jones, D. L.; Wright, C. S.; Piura, B.; Paintin, D. B.; James, V. H. T.; & Jacobs, H. S. 1983. Inhibition of 3-Beta-hydroxy steroid dehydrogenase activity in first trimester human pregnancy with trilostane and WIN 32729. *Clinical Endocrinology* 19:521–532.

Wagner, R. P.; Judd, B. H.; Sanders, B. G.; & Richardson R. H. 1980. *Introduction to modern genetics.* New York: Wiley.

Wilks, J. W. 1983. Pregnancy interception with a combination of prostaglandins: Studies in monkeys. *Science* 221:1407–8.

Young, C. 1984. *The least of these.* Chicago: Moody Press.

———. 1985. What Upjohn leaves unsaid. Virginia: Christian Action Council.

———. 1986. Controversy over new abortion pill. *Action Line* X(2):1–4.

Young, E. W. D. 1984. Improved imaging techniques may nudge abortion debate to the right. *Diagnostic Imaging* 6(9):44–45.

Further Reading

Bennegard, B.; Dennefors, B.; & Hamberger, L. 1985. Interaction between catecholamines and Prostaglandin F_{2a} in human luteolysis. *Gynecology* 40(6): 364–365.

Calvert, D. *Premature births and low birth weight babies in pregnancies following an induced abortion.* Duke University Medical School (Christian Action Council Publication).

Chi, I. & P. H.; Miller, E. R.; Fortney, J.; & Bernard, R. P. 1977. A study of abortion in countries where abortions are legally restricted. *Journal of Reproductive Medicine* 18(1):15–26.

Committee on the Judiciary, United States Senate. 1981. *The human life bill—S.158.* Washington: U.S. Government Printing Office.

Grimes, D. A.; Schulz, K. F.; & Cates, W., Jr. 1984. Prophylactic antibiotics for curettage abortion. *American Journal of Obstetrics and Gynecology* 150(6):689–694.

Hilgers, T. W.; Horan, D. J.; & Mall, D. 1981. *New perspectives on human abortion.* Frederick, Maryland: University Publications of America.

Lejeune, J.; Matthews-Roth, M. M.; Gordon, H.; & Ratner, H. 1981. *The beginning of human life.* Testimony prepared for the Subcommittee on Separation of Powers of the United States Senate Committee on the Judiciary. Law and Medicine Series. Americans United for Life.

Macaulay, S. S. 1980. *Something beautiful from God.* Westchester, Illinois: Cornerstone Books.

Martin, C. R. M. 1985. *Endocrine physiology.* New York: Oxford Univ. Press.

Nathanson, B. N., & Ostling, R. N. 1979. *Aborting America.* New York: Pinnacle Books.

Neubardt, S. 1977. *Techniques of abortion.* Boston: Little, Brown

Robins, J., & Surrago, E. J. 1980. Alternatives in midtrimester abortion induction. *Obstetrics & Gynecology* 56(6):716–722.

Robinson, D. N. 1985. *On fetal pain.* Statement prepared for the Senate Judiciary Committee, Subcommittees on the Constitution, May 21.

Smedes, L. B. 1981. *Sex for Christians.* Grand Rapids: Eerdmans.

Wassarman, P. M. 1987. The biology and chemistry of fertilization. *Science* 235: 553–560.

Willke, Dr. and Mrs. J. C. 1979. *Handbook on abortion.* Cincinnati: Hayes Publishing.

11

Psychological Consequences of Abortion

James L. Rogers

What are the psychological effects of elective abortion? Do women who elect abortion over term pregnancy eliminate an immediate problem but increase the risk of future psychological consequences? Is it possible to eliminate a "product of conception" and not be haunted by the thought that a "human life" was taken? Even if the possibility that this is murder—as many contend abortion to be—does not overtly enter the thinking of those who elect abortion, will the thought reside at an unconscious level and ultimately surface in anxiety, depression, or even severe mental illness? It is imperative that these difficult questions be addressed. If elective abortion constitutes even a small risk to future mental health, such information should be readily available, much like the potential side effects that drug manufacturers are required to list on the packages of marketed medications. If a woman elects abortion, she should do so with full knowledge of the potential risks, both psychological and physical.

The need for accurate information is particularly critical in light of the growing frequency of elective abortions, since even a small percentage of negative emotional reactions would represent a large number of women. Henshaw, Forrest, and Blaine (1984) reported that one and a half million abortions were being performed in this country per year; of every twenty women of childbearing age, one obtains an abortion. An invasive medical practice so widespread must be scrutinized for risk, regardless of one's philosophical or religious viewpoint concerning the morality of the procedure.

A natural place to look for information about the psychological impact of abortion is the scientific literature, and there exist a number of scientific studies addressing this concern. Through computer searches of a number of national bibliographic data bases (Science Citation Indexes, Psychological Abstracts, Index Medicus, etc.), the author was able to locate over three hundred studies. Approximately a fourth of these studies were either clinical case studies that reviewed individual women who had experienced emotional difficulty after an abortion or scientific research that sought to better understand the psychological characteristics of women undergoing an abortion. However, among the conclusions reached in these studies, there were many inconsistencies. For example, Wallerstein, Kurtz, and Bar-Din (1972) found adverse reactions in 50 percent of the cases they studied, while Osofsky and Osofsky (1972) concluded in a study published the same year that there were few, if any, adverse psychological reactions.

Because there is not a clear convergence of outcome across studies, the procedures and design (i.e., the methodology) of each existing study should be examined carefully. An understanding of the limitations imposed by the various methodologies that have been used will make it clear that some studies are more trustworthy than others. The statistical basis for the various conclusions reached in the literature should also be examined. Since inferential errors of data interpretation can occur if certain statistical criteria are not met, it is important to examine each study to determine the likelihood of such an error.

A number of methodological and statistical considerations will be presented in the following sections. These considerations will serve to underscore certain problems existing in the literature and help clarify some general conclusions implied by the combined literature. Though these conclusions are subject to modification as better research becomes available, they nevertheless should provide some practical help for those who need current answers as well as direction for future research.

Methodological Considerations

Perhaps the most important ingredient in a research study is the appropriate use of a control group. Studies that employ control groups, also called "controlled studies," compare individuals who do not receive the treatment under investigation (i.e., the "control group") to individuals who do receive the treatment (i.e., the "treatment group"). Elective abortion is the "treatment" under investigation in the present instance. The control group would be comprised of women who have not had an abortion. The treatment group would be comprised of women who have. Women who are not pregnant could be used as a control group, but a more meaningful control group, and the one usually found in existing studies, would be a group of women who have carried a pregnancy to term. It should be noted that some studies do not use a control group ("uncontrolled studies") and therefore are of minimal use in acquiring reliable knowledge about the psychological impact of abortion. The element of comparison between women who have had an abortion and women who have not had an abortion is simply absent in such studies. Controlled studies will receive primary attention in this chapter.

Ideally, the control group and treatment group in a given study should be identical in all respects *except* for the difference in treatment status. The optimal situation in studies that examine the psychological impact of abortion would be for women who have an abortion (the treatment group) to be identical to women who carry their pregnancy to term (the control group) on such background variables as socioeconomic status, religion, age, and marital status. If such background variables are not the same for both groups, the difference in one or more background variables rather than the presence or absence of an abortion, might explain any difference in emotional stability. For example, if a control group primarily consists of women in their late twenties who are married, but the treatment group primarily consists of younger women who are single, then age and/or marital status, not necessarily the presence or absence of an abortion, might explain differences found in emotional status.

Threats to Validity

Background discrepancies between treatment and control groups (such as age and marital status in the example above) constitute one important type of threat to the validity of any scientific study. The term "threat to validity" is commonly used by scientists in referring to any reason other than the treatment status that might explain the outcome of a comparison between a control and treatment group. Virtually all of the controlled studies to date that examine the emotional aftermath of abortion are hindered by the presence of various threats to validity. Space limitations make it impossible to enumerate all the threats to validity found in the controlled studies. However, a description of several very important threats to validity commonly found in the existing research will illustrate why the methodology employed in a study is crucial to the integrity of the study's conclusion.

Sample Attrition

"Mortality" is a very common threat to validity in studies examining the psychological consequences of abortion. As used here, this term refers to the loss (for any reason) of subjects in the control and/or treatment groups. Sample attrition can be an especially serious threat to validity if subjects with unique background variables related to emotional status drop out of the treatment group but not out of the control group (or vice versa). This type of mortality, often termed "differential dropout," can lead to discrepancies between the control and treatment group on critical background variables, thus making comparisons of emotional status at the end of the study impossible to interpret.

The point that sample attrition (mortality in general and differential dropout in particular) is a serious problem in studies examining the psychological impact of abortion is underscored in certain findings reported by Adler (1976). She reviewed seventeen studies dealing in various degrees with the psychological impact of abortion and found that subject loss before a study was finalized ranged from 13 percent (Barnes et al. 1971) to 86 percent (Evans & Gusdon 1973). In her own study (1975), Adler followed up subjects who did not complete the study and found them more likely to be young, Catholic, and unmarried. Each of these characteristics has been associated with a greater likelihood of negative emotional response to abortion (Adler 1975; Payne et al. 1976; Osofsky & Osofsky 1972). Adler concluded that "mortality," or more specifically "differential dropout," may result in underestimating the incidence of adverse responses to abortion. The practical meaning of this finding to those considering an abortion, or those counseling such a person about abortion, is that the literature to date may well underestimate the number of women who experience adverse psychological reactions after an elective abortion.

Quality and Bias of Measuring Instruments

A second threat to the validity of many of the studies in question concerns the quality of the measuring instrument (questionnaires, rating scales, etc.) used to assess emotional outcome. An adequate outcome measure is said to be "reliable," in that the measuring instrument will yield the same outcome when different investigators use it to acquire information about the same subject; likewise, it will yield an identical result when the same investigator applies it at two different points in time to a subject whose status has not changed. If outcome measures are unreliable, it becomes very difficult to make comparisons between a control and treatment group. Although certain statistical precautions can be used to guard against false conclusions based on outcome measures that are unreliable, these safeguards also make it easier to overlook real differences between the groups. Researchers should always use outcome measures known to be reliable or run reliability checks on unfamiliar measuring instruments. For example, studies interested in depression as an outcome might use either the Center for Epidemiological Studies Depression Scale (Radloff 1977) or the Symptom Checklist (Derogatis 1977) because these two instruments are known to have adequate reliability. Unfortunately, results in the existing literature that address the psychological impact of abortion have usually been based on a variety of self-report questionnaires, interview schedules, rating scales, and clinical opinions, almost always of undetermined reliability. There is rarely an attempt to establish the reliability of these self-determined measuring instruments, even though several relatively simple procedures exist for doing so.

Not only do the measuring instruments *per se* need to be reliable, but the circumstances surrounding their use should be unbiased. This has often not been the case in existing studies. During the acquisition of outcome information, practices have been embraced whose overall impact is to lessen the confidence that can be placed in the reported results. For example, information concerning the level of emotional adjustment has been obtained from sources other than the subject in the study (Meyerowitz et al. 1971; Jacobs et al. 1974; Pare & Raven 1970; Lask 1974); follow-up assessment has been conducted in the recovery room immediately after the abortion (Bracken et al. 1974; Osofsky & Osofsky 1972; Mosely et al. 1981); patients have been interviewed at unsystematic follow-up intervals ranging from one to five years (Kretzschmar & Norris 1967) or several months to seven years (Meyerowitz et al. 1971); and patients were included who not only received an abortion but also were sterilized at the same time (Sclare & Geraghty, 1971), thus making it impossible to determine whether the emotional response being measured was due to the abortion or to the sterilization. When unreliable measures are used and/or the circumstances surrounding their use are biased, both false negatives (missing an actual symptom) and false positives (reporting a symptom that really does not exist) can occur with alarming frequency.

Generalizability of Results

A third threat to validity concerns whether the results of a given study can be generalized beyond its specific context to other populations, settings, and times. Unfortunately, the majority of existing studies use small, self-selected samples of women who had their abortion at one specific hospital. Such selection bias would likely limit the generalizability of any conclusions reached, even if the problem of differential dropout or unreliable measurement instruments did not exist. For example, Niswander and Patterson (1967) asked the attending physician to approve or disapprove the mailing of a questionnaire to each of the patients who could possibly serve in their study. In effect, this procedure eliminated those patients for whom it was thought that the recollection of the abortion experience would be too painful. This practice almost certainly led to an underestimation of the actual number of negative emotional responses. Abrams, DiBiase, and Sturgis (1979) sent questionnaires only to those patients they felt were likely to respond. This practice, too, could seriously alter the generalizability of results.

Generalizability of results would be greatly enhanced if subject selection was evenly divided across the various settings in which abortions are performed. Indeed, the distribution of such settings can be approximated. In 1982, 82 percent of abortions in America were performed in non-hospital facilities, 56 percent in abortion clinics, 21 percent in other clinics, and 5 percent in physicians' offices (Henshaw et al. 1984). Unfortunately, no study of which this author is aware has attempted to make the research sample utilized in the study representative of these known demographic characteristics. The distribution of settings for the research sample being used is often not even specified in the published report.

A second obstacle to generalizability centers around the wide variety of emotional experiences the existing studies have attempted to measure. In one respect, the search for abortion-related outcomes of many different kinds enhances generalizability. However, to the degree that confidence in a given finding is retarded because the result has not been independently replicated by another investigator, the generalizability of the study is also limited. For example, some studies have defined negative psychological reactions as the presence of depression, anxiety, or guilt. Other studies have used such criteria as psychiatric hospitalization or the use of anti-depressant or anti-psychotic medication. Furthermore, some studies have relied solely on the subjective experience of the woman as she reported it in a self-report questionnaire. Greater confidence could be placed in the literature if there were subgroups of studies that consistently measured the same outcome variable defined in the same way.

Finally, generalizability across time is a crucial issue. Approximately half of the controlled studies available were conducted from 1967 to 1973, a period when abortion laws were being legalized and therapeutic abortions were allowable only on medical and/or psychiatric grounds. The remaining studies were conducted in the mid to late 1970s under the principle of abortion-on-demand (some of these studies were not published until the early 1980s). It is highly questionable as to whether conclusions drawn from studies utilizing women granted abortions on therapeutic grounds only, as was the case until 1973 in the United States, are generalizable to the current social milieu characterized by abortion-on-demand. Women in the earlier studies were often required to convince a board of medical experts that an abortion was necessary to maintain good psychological health. It is easy to imagine how symptoms might have been exaggerated under such conditions. Furthermore, as no new studies have been conducted in the current decade, studies performed in the years immediately following the legalization of abortion-on-demand in the United States are of questionable generalizability.

The Search for Valid Findings

It now should be clear that the existing scientific literature dealing with the psychological consequences of abortion contains numerous severe methodological problems that threaten the validity of the reported findings. Are any of the existing studies methodologically sound, or at least sound enough to provide an initial estimate of the emotional impact of induced abortion? As Mintz (1983, 74) has stated, "literally no number of anecdotal reports, uncontrolled trials, or poorly designed experiments can outweigh one carefully planned and executed experiment, if it results in clear and divergent findings." On this same issue, Smith, Glass, and Miller (1980, 64) write: "the important question in surveying a body of literature is to determine whether the best designed studies yield evidence different from more poorly designed studies. If the answer is yes, then one is compelled to believe the best ones."

The author has found only one study that appears to be methodologically acceptable. David, Rasmussen, and Holst (1981) have conducted the only study that used a control group, made an attempt to equate the control group and treatment group on pre-pregnancy mental health, used an adequate sample size, *and* used an outcome measure with adequate validity and reliability. What were the results of this study? Utilizing the computer linkage of the Danish national case registry, this research group examined the comparative risk of admission to a psychiatric hospital within three months of an abortion or term delivery for all women under age fifty residing in Denmark. Data on admission to psychiatric hospitals were obtained on 71,378 women carrying pregnancies to term, 27,234 women terminating unwanted pregnancies, and on the total population of 1,169,819 women aged fifteen to forty-nine. In determining the hospitalization incidence rates, only first admissions to psychiatric hospitals were recorded. Also, women with a psychiatric hospital admission during the fifteen months *prior* to delivery or abortion were excluded, thus increasing the similarity between the control and treatment group on pre-pregnancy mental health.

Danish women between the ages of fifteen and forty-nine who fell into three categories are compared in figure 4. The categories are women who delivered, women who had an abortion, and the entire Danish population of women in the age range of concern. As can be seen in figure 4–(a), women who were post-abortion evidenced the highest rate of psychiatric hospitalization (18.4 per 10,000); women who delivered had the next highest rate (12.0 per 10,000); and all women in the total age range, regardless of pregnancy status, had the lowest (7.5 per 10,000). In figure 4–(b) these incidence rates are shown for five different age categories. The same overall direction found between women who delivered and women who aborted in the composite data shown in (a) was found in every age bracket, with the exception of women aged thirty-five through forty-nine. In this age category, women who delivered evidenced a higher rate of psychiatric hospitalization than women who aborted (22.2 per 10,000 versus 13.4 per 10,000), although the rates for both the delivery and abortion groups at this age were still considerably higher than for the entire population of Danish women aged thirty-five to forty-nine (8.4 per 10,000).

Another extremely important finding made by David et al. is presented in figure 4–(c). Women in the abortion and delivery conditions were compared within three marital subclassifications: women who were currently married; women who were never married; and women who were separated, divorced, or widowed. Although the difference between women who had aborted and those who had delivered was relatively small in the first two classifications, there was a dramatic difference in hospitalization rates among women who were separated, divorced, or widowed (63.8 per 10,000 for women who aborted versus 16.9 per 10,000 for those who delivered). Finally, figure 4–(d) compares the abortion and delivery conditions within groups of women categorized by number of prior children. Regardless of the number of prior children, women who aborted evidenced a higher rate of psychiatric hospitalization, but this was especially true for women who had no prior children (22.4 per 10,000 versus 13.8 per 10,000) and women who had one prior child (23.3 per 10,000 versus 9.7 per 10,000).

Several points should be made about this study. First, both women who delivered and women who aborted were at higher risk of psychiatric hospital admission than women in general. Second, women who aborted, with the exception of those of age thirty-five to forty-nine, were at higher risk than those who delivered. Third, women who were separated, divorced, or widowed exhibited a considerably higher rate of psy-

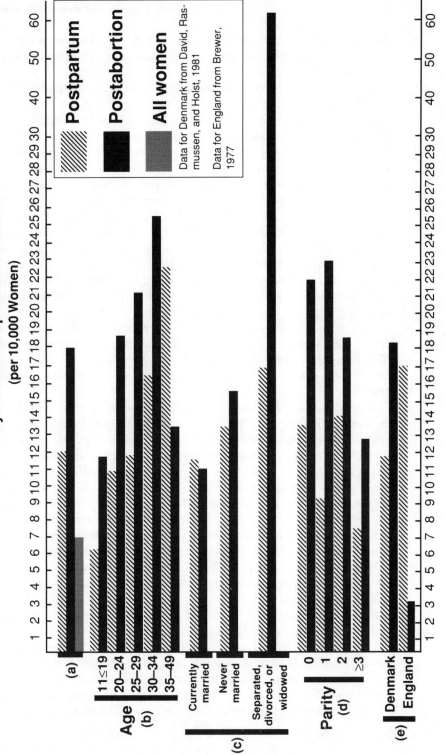

Figure 4. **Post-Abortion Psychiatric Hospitalization**

Psychiatric Hospitalization Rate
(per 10,000 Women)

Postpartum

Postabortion

All women

Data for Denmark from David, Rasmussen, and Holst, 1981

Data for England from Brewer, 1977

(a)

Age
(b)
11≤19
20–24
25–29
30–34
35–49

(c)
Currently married
Never married
Separated, divorced, or widowed

Parity
(d)
0
1
2
≥3

(e)
Denmark
England

chiatric hospitalization when abortion rather than delivery was elected. To a lesser extent, this was also true for women who had only one or no previous children.

It is important to note that David et al. used psychiatric admission as their outcome measure, a variable that is well defined and reliably measured. However, this variable fails to capture less traumatic (but very important) emotional episodes of depression, anxiety, and guilt. One could surmise that if abortion leads to a greater incidence of extreme psychiatric trauma requiring hospitalization, it would likely lead as well to an increased incidence of less-intense emotional trauma. This inference would appear reasonable to many individuals, but it is important to emphasize that it is not mandated by the data in this study. It is also important to realize that David et al. examined data for only the three months immediately following either abortion or delivery, thus excluding any later psychiatric hospitalizations that might have been precipitated by a woman's decision to abort or deliver. Finally, although women in the abortion and delivery groups had no known hospitalization for psychiatric reasons during the previous fifteen months, their status before that time was unknown. Therefore, differences in mental-health status between the abortion and delivery groups prior to this fifteen-month preliminary period cannot be ruled out. In short, this study is not perfect, but it is considerably better than any other existing study of which the author is aware.

A comparison of the Danish study by David et al. to a study done in England by Brewer (1977) will serve to highlight the discrepancies in methodological rigor existing in the literature. Brewer's study, published in the prestigious *British Medical Journal,* had the same objective as the David et al. study: to determine the incidence of psychiatric hospitalization that followed abortion and term delivery. However, Brewer's conclusions were much different. As shown in figure 4–(e), he found the post-abortion psychiatric hospitalization rate to be 3 per 10,000 while the post-delivery rate was 17 per 10,000. In his summary remarks, Brewer stated: ". . . childbirth is more hazardous in psychiatric terms than abortion . . ." (p. 477). Brewer's results are in the opposite direction from those reported in the David et al. study! Which study should be trusted?

In the author's opinion, Brewer's study is riddled with severe methodological pitfalls. First, Brewer sent questionnaires to psychiatrists residing in only one section of England. Not only do the responses lack generalizability beyond the local English area surveyed; but, more importantly, they depend on each psychiatrist's memory and/or ability (willingness?) to retrieve records. Patients were not questioned directly, nor were the medical records of all patients systematically examined.

Furthermore, a reliability coefficient (i.e., scientific index of reliability) was not reported for the questionnaire, and there is no reason to believe that one was computed at all. Also, there is no guarantee that the psychiatrists whom Brewer questioned were representative of all psychiatrists in the area or that these psychiatrists were otherwise unbiased. Sim and Neisser (1979, 3), in their published review of selected studies, claim that in Brewer's study, ". . . the psychiatrist with the greatest responsibility and experience in the area of the assessment and treatment of patients with instability associated with pregnancy did not participate." Finally, Brewer notes that the geographical practice areas of some of the psychiatrists in the study overlapped with another's. This overlap made it necessary for him to "estimate" the denominator he used to obtain the psychiatric hospitalization rates. Together, these practices sharply contrast with David, Rasmussen, and Holst's use of computer-held data for the entire population of Danish females in the specified age range. This computerized data base made it possible for the Danish researchers to match the post-abortion and post-delivery subjects according to incidence of psychiatric admission over the prior fifteen-month period, age, marital status, and number of previous children. No attempt was made by Brewer in his published report to calculate psychiatric hospitalization rates for specific subgroups of women (e.g., for separated, divorced, or widowed women; women with zero or one prior child; etc.) or to match the abortion and delivery groups on the prior incidence of psychiatric hospitalization.

Methodological considerations demand that the findings of David, Rasmussen, and Holst, not those of Brewer, be given priority. Although this brief paper will not permit a detailed comparison of the Danish study with other reports in the literature, it is the author's opinion that those studies, too, are inferior to the study reported by David's research group. *The best study to date indicates that women who undergo abortion are at greater psychiatric risk than women who deliver at term.*

Statistical Considerations

When a control and experimental group are compared, rarely will the two groups have exactly the same average (or percentage) value on the outcome measure of concern. This is true because the two groups contain different individuals and, by chance alone, the sample of individuals comprising one group may consist of subjects who on the average will score either higher or lower than those found in the opposite group. It is possible, on the other hand, that a unique difference between the experimental and control groups—such as the presence of either an abortion or term delivery—is responsible for any subsequent difference found on the outcome measure (e.g., depression, anxiety, psychiatric hospitalization, etc.). The researcher is invariably faced with the question of whether a difference between the control and experimental group on the outcome variable is due to chance or due to a difference between the groups on a specified characteristic.

To decide which is true, scientists normally conduct a "statistical-hypothesis test." This test is a mathematical procedure that, according to predefined rules, allows the researcher to decide whether a difference between the control and experimental group is due to nonspecific chance factors or due to the "treatment"—that is, due to abortion as contrasted to delivery. Even when a statistical-hypothesis test is conducted, there will always be some probability of reaching a false conclusion. Specifically, two types of errors are possible. The researcher might conclude that the two conditions are different due to the treatment, when chance is the real reason (i.e., commit what is termed a "Type I" error), or the researcher might conclude that the difference is due to nonspecific chance factors, when it actually has been caused by a specific characteristic that varies across the two groups (i.e., commit what is termed a "Type II" error).

For technical reasons beyond the scope of this paper, it is a rather simple matter to hold the probability of a Type I error to a minimum. Most existing studies run an acceptably small chance of a Type I error. However, if a study's sample size (i.e., the number of women who receive an abortion and the number who deliver) is not sufficiently large, it is not possible to reduce the probability of a Type II error. In the present case, a Type II error would mean the researcher had concluded that abortion and term women differ on an outcome variable due to nonspecific chance factors when, in fact, the difference was due to the pregnancy decision. Stated differently, a Type II error would lead to the erroneous conclusion that abortion was no different from delivery regarding the presence of subsequent emotional problems.

It is possible to compute an index, termed "power," that reflects the probability of *not* committing a Type II error. The value of power can range between zero and one, and the closer the power is to one, the less the chance of committing a Type II error. After making certain assumptions, the author has determined that eleven of the existing fourteen studies that compare an abortion group to a control group evidence statistical power of less than .27 (ten studies are less than .20). (The fourteen studies in question have been marked by an asterisk accompanying the references at the end of this chapter.) Thus, the majority of studies, when individually considered, have an 80 percent or higher chance of making a Type II error. It is emphasized that this conclusion is based on technical assumptions exceeding the scope of this paper. However, these assumptions were selected to produce the highest likely power for each study, and if a mistake has been made, it would probably be in the direction of overstating, not understating, the power values that exist for studies currently available.

Because the statistical power found in existing studies is generally low, little confidence can be placed in the frequent conclusion found among these studies stating that there is no difference in emotional risk between women who abort and women who deliver. The fact of the matter is that most existing studies run an unacceptably high risk of failing to detect an actual difference that might exist between an abortion and control group. It is important to note that the study by David et al. does not fall into this category. The statistical power estimated for this study is above .99.

One approach that lessens the problem of low statistical power entails pooling all available studies using a method called meta analysis (Rosenthal 1984). This method yields a single number that reflects the overall direction and magnitude of difference between all combined treatment and control groups. Intuitively, it makes sense to combine many small sample sizes into a larger sample, as this procedure should reduce the probability of a Type II error. This is the basic notion behind meta analysis.

When meta analysis was conducted on all studies located by the author that compare an abortion group to a control group, the result was that a small but statistically reliable difference emerged. The direction of the difference indicated that women who experienced abortion were at greater risk than women who delivered (Rogers et al. 1986). Not only was this true for studies that measured risk in terms of psychiatric hospitalization, but also for studies that focused primarily on less-severe emotional trauma such as depression, anxiety, and guilt. The meta analysis carried out by the author suggests that because many studies have sample sizes that are too small to statistically detect the negative impact that abortion seems to have, the authors of these studies have erroneously concluded that the degree of subsequent psychological trauma is no different between an abortion and term-delivery group. However, when studies are combined using meta analysis, the overall picture is that women who experience abortion are at greater risk.

Conclusions

The morality of abortion must be determined apart from any emotional consequence, positive or negative, that the involved adult individuals experience. Whether elective abortion is considered "right" or "wrong" will usually depend on the status that one grants the unborn. If the fetus is a human being, the fetus, like any other human being, has basic inalienable rights that must be protected. Although the emotional consequences for the adults involved are important and deserve attention, under no circumstances are these consequences *per se* pertinent to the termination of human life. It is important for the reader to understand that the present article addresses the issue of subsequent emotional risk to the woman having an abortion, but the presence or absence of additional emotional risk is irrelevant to the morality question. Women should be informed of any risk factor associated with abortion regardless of the morality of abortion.

The scientific literature addressing the question of psychological risk is riddled with methodological problems. Nevertheless, the information contained there, if scrutinized in the context of methodological considerations, does suggest that abortion is associated with a higher risk of subsequent emotional trauma than is delivery. There is a convergence to this conclusion when the literature is considered from two perspectives. First, the only study in the literature that manifests adequate methodology as well as adequate statistical power (David et al. 1981) indicates that women experience psychiatric hospitalization more frequently after an abortion than after term delivery, and this is particularly true of certain subgroups of women, such as those who are separated, divorced, or widowed. Second, when the methodological shortcomings of the existing studies are ignored and all studies are combined using meta analysis, the result is that there is a small but statistically reliable difference between an abortion group and a control group. Women who experience abortion evidence more trauma in terms of psychiatric hospitalization as well as such less traumatic emotional outcomes as depression.

Unfortunately, the current literature is too sparse and methodologically questionable to determine with any accuracy the *degree* of difference in emotional trauma experienced by women who abort and women who deliver. A single study was found that used acceptable methodology, but this study also used psychiatric hospitalization as the endpoint measure of risk. Almost everyone would agree that the emotional trauma likely to follow an abortion would usually not be severe enough to result in psychiatric hospitalization. Thus, the use of psychiatric hospitalization as an outcome measure bears the risk of missing a substantial number of negative reactions of an important but less severe nature. On the other hand, studies that measure such emotional trauma as depression tend to exhibit very low levels of statistical power and thus encounter a high probability of failing to detect this additional risk. Also, these studies have severe methodological difficulties, such as the loss through sample attrition of the very patients who are most likely to experience a negative emotional reaction. The type of methodological problems existing in these studies would in general serve to underestimate the presence of psychological risk.

It would be fair to say that to date the scientific literature suggests that women who experience an abortion are at greater risk of subsequent emotional trauma than women who deliver, and that this is especially true for women who are separated, divorced or widowed, and to a lesser degree also for women having zero or one prior child. At the moment, the *degree* of additional risk incurred by women who elect abortion cannot be accurately stated, particularly for emotional trauma involving depression, anxiety, and guilt.

As a concluding comment, the author would like to offer the following perspective to those involved in abortion-related decisions. Although abortion is legal, a very substantial number of intelligent and thoughtful individuals consider abortion to be murder. Individuals of this persuasion are found among top ranking political, medical, and religious leaders. It is probably not true that women who elect abortion will be able to totally dismiss the possibility that the abortion choice was a decision to commit murder. It makes sense that living with this possibility year after year, whether consciously or subconsciously, would have an emotional cost. It is certainly possible that the emotional impact of an abortion might not surface until years after it has taken place and therefore will evade detection by scientific studies, which generally extend over a relatively short period of time, not a lifetime. Also, psychological suppression of the abortion experience, if this occurs in at least some women, would make these individuals vulnerable to emotional reactions that seemingly would not be related to the abortion experience even though they really were. Considerations such as these, coupled with the scientific evidence discussed here, should be clearly understood and explained as necessary to those contemplating or advocating abortion.

References

Abrams, M.; DiBiase, V.; & Sturgis, S. 1979. Post-abortion attitudes and patterns of birth control. *Journal of Family Practice* 9:593–599.

Adler, N. E. 1975. Emotional responses of women following therapeutic abortion. *American Journal of Orthopsychiatry* 45:446–454.

———. 1976. Sample attrition in studies of psychosocial sequelae of abortion: How great a problem. *Journal of Applied Social Psychology* 6:240–259.

Barnes, A. B.; Cohen, E., Stoekle, J. D.; & McGuire, M. T. 1971. Therapeutic abortion: Medical and social sequelae. *Annals of Internal Medicine* 75: 881–886.

Bracken, M. B.; Hachamovitch, M.; & Grossman, G. 1974. The decision to abort and psychological sequelae. *Journal of Nervous & Mental Disease* 158: 154–162.

*Brewer, C. 1977. Incidence of post-abortion psychosis: A prospective study. *British Medical Journal* 1:476–477.

*David, H. P.; Rasmussen, N. K.; & Holst, E. 1981. Postpartum and postabortion psychotic reactions. *Family Planning Perspectives* 13:88–92.

Derogatis, L. R. 1977. *The SCL-90 Manual I: Scoring administration and procedures for the SCL-90.* Baltimore: Johns Hopkins School of Medicine, Clinical Psychometrics Unit.

Evans, D., & Gusdon, J. 1973. Post-abortion attitudes. *North Carolina Medical Journal* 34:271–273.

Henshaw, S. K.; Forrest, J. D.; & Blaine, E. 1984. Abortion services in the United States, 1981–1982. *Family Planning Perspectives* 16:119–127.

Jacobs, D.; Garcia, C. R.; Rickels, K; & Preucel, R. W. 1974. A prospective study on the psychological effects of therapeutic abortion. *Comprehensive Psychiatry* 15:423–434.

Kretzschmar, R. M., & Norris, A. S. 1967. Psychiatric implications of therapeutic abortion. *American Journal of Obstetrics & Gynecology* 98:368–373.

Lask, B. 1975. Short-term psychiatric sequelae to therapeutic termination of pregnancy. *British Journal of Psychiatry* 126:173–177.

*Meyerowitz, S.; Satloff, A.; & Ramano, J. 1971. Induced abortion for psychiatric indication. *American Journal of Psychiatry* 127:1153–1160.

Mintz, J. 1983. Integrating research evidence: A commentary on meta-analysis. *Journal of Consulting and Clinical Psychology* 51:71–75.

Mosely, D. T.; Follingstad, D. R.; Harley, H.; & Heckel, R. V. 1981. Psychological factors that predict reaction to abortion. *Journal of Clinical Psychology* 37:276–279.

*Niswander, K., & Patterson, R. 1967. Psychological reaction to therapeutic abortion: I. Subjective patient response. *Obstetrics and Gynecology* 29: 702–706.

Osofsky, D., & Osofsky, J. 1972. The psychological reaction of patients to legalized abortion. *American Journal of Orthopsychiatry* 42:48–60.

Pare, C. M., & Raven, H. 1970. Follow-up of patients referred for termination of pregnancy. *Lancet* 1:635–638.

Payne, E. C.; Kravitz, A. R.; Notman, M. T.; & Anderson, J. V. 1976. Outcome following therapeutic abortion. *Archives of General Psychiatry* 33:725–733.

Radloff, L. 1977. The CES-D scale: A self-report depression scale for research in the general population. *Journal of the Applied Psychological Measurement* 1:385–401.

Rogers, J. L.; Phifer, J. F.; & Nelson, J. A. 1986. *Psychological sequelae of abortion: A re-examination of published results.* Paper presented at annual meeting, American Psychological Association. Washington, D.C.

Rosenthal, R. 1984. *Meta-analytic procedures for social research.* Beverly Hills: Sage Publications.

*Sclare, A. B., & Geraghty, B. P. 1971. Therapeutic abortion: A follow-up study. *Scottish Medical Journal* 16:438–442.

Sim, M., and Neisser, R. 1979. Post-abortive psychoses: A report from two centers. In *The psychological aspects of abortion* (1–13). D. Mall & W. F. Watts, eds. Washington, D.C.: University Publications of America.

Smith, M.; Glass, G.; & Miller, T. 1980. *The benefits of psychotherapy.* Baltimore: Johns Hopkins Press.

Wallerstein, S.; Kurtz, P.; & Bar-Din, M. 1972. Psychological sequelae of therapeutic abortion in young unmarried women. *Archives of General Psychiatry* 27:828–832.

Further Reading

*Athansiou, R.; Oppel, W.; Michelson, L.; Unger, T.; & Yager, M. 1973. Psychiatric sequelae to term birth and induced early and late abortion: A longitudinal study. *Family Planning Perspectives* 5:227–231.

*Brody, H.; Meikle, S.; & Gerritse, R. 1971. Therapeutic abortion: A prospective study. I. *American Journal of Obstetrics and Gynecology* 109:347–353.

*Drower, S. J., & Nash, E. S. 1978. Therapeutic abortion on psychiatric grounds. *South African Medical Journal* 54:604–608.

*Greenglass, E. R. 1975. Therapeutic abortion and its psychological implications: The Canadian experience. *Canadian Medical Association Journal* 113:754–757.

*Hamill, E., & Ingram, I. M. 1974. Psychiatric and social factors in the abortion decision. *British Medical Journal* 1:229–232.

*Jansson, B. 1965. Mental disorders after abortion. *Acta Psychiatrica Scandinavica* 41:87–110.

*McCance, C.; Olley, P. C.; & Edward, V. 1973. Long term psychiatric follow-up. In *Experience with abortion* (245–300). G. Horobin, ed. Cambridge: Cambridge Univ. Press.

*Simon, N. M.; Rothman, D.; Goff, J. T.; & Senturia, A. G. 1969. Psychological factors related to spontaneous and therapeutic abortion. *American Journal of Obstetrics and Gynecology* 104:799–808.

*Todd, N. A. 1971. Psychiatric experience of the abortion act (1967). *British Journal of Psychiatry* 119:489–495.

12

Abortion and the Political Process

Lyman A. Kellstedt

For evangelicals, the abortion controversy has been the key public-policy issue of the past fifteen years. In fact, for some evangelicals, it seems to be the *only* issue. One Christian politician once remarked in an off-the-record session that when he answered questions before evangelical church groups, the first, and often the only, question was inevitably about abortion. He finally arrived at a point where he refused to answer questions on the topic until questions in other areas of controversy were raised. His point was that evangelicals need to be informed about other contemporary issues as well.

This writer agrees with the burden of the politician's argument, but it will not serve as the basis of this essay. Instead, the goal is to place the abortion controversy into an appropriate context that will, hopefully, enlighten evangelical thinking in this area. With this goal in mind, analysis is needed in five areas: (1) the Supreme Court; (2) the Congress; (3) state legislatures; (4) interest-group involvement; and (5) public opinion. We will first briefly examine each of these areas and then expand the arguments in the body of the paper.

Most evangelicals have not understood the role of the Supreme Court in American society, and, in particular, have not understood its abortion decisions beginning with *Roe* v. *Wade*. This has led to strong attacks on the present Court on the one hand and to exaggerated expectations of what might happen on the Court when changes in its personnel occur on the other. In addition, careful attention is needed as to *exactly* what the Court has decided, for proposed changes in laws dealing with abortion should be formulated with awareness of what the Court has decided. When it comes to the Congress, evangelicals have failed to understand the difficult and almost impossible task of obtaining a constitutional amendment, the only sure way to overturn *Roe* v. *Wade*. Evangelicals fail to recognize that compromise is at the heart of our political process, particularly in Congress, and that without some form of compromise, the votes are not present in the Congress of the mid 1980s for an anti-abortion amendment. At the state legislative level, evangelicals have at times failed to see the role played by the states in our federal system and at other times have failed to address this component of our system. When the votes are present at the state legislative level to bring about changes in abortion laws, bills have been passed with evangelical support that challenged the authority of the Supreme Court so directly that they were bound to lose in the courts (see the *Akron* case in 1983 and the *Thornburgh* decision in the 1986 Supreme Court term). Anti-abortion interest groups have only recently developed the sophistication needed to win the day in the political process. Previously, they majored in strong moral judgments, which may have contributed to building support *within* the evangelical community but did little to expand support beyond that community into other groups that are essential to legislative success. Finally, evangelicals have failed to grasp that there is a strong base of support for abortion in American society. This support goes well beyond radical feminists and is rooted in some strongly held American and democratic values: freedom of choice and right to privacy. In other words, the argument advanced here is that we as evangelicals have failed to change the abortion situation in this country—in part, because we have failed to understand the nature of American politics and, in particular, because of the difficulty in achieving fundamental change in the American system.

Before examining each of these areas in greater detail, it is important to develop an argument as to why an understanding of the political process is so important. It is through the political process that fundamental change in the area of abortion will come about. Failure to fully understand the nature of the American political process has impeded efforts to reduce, if not eliminate, the number of abortions in this country. The ultimate aim of evangelicals should be to eliminate abortion, but, in the short run, any reduction in abortions would be beneficial. Without a clear understanding of the political process, such reduction is unlikely, for the reductions will only occur as the result of compromises reached with other interest groups and other politicians, whose agendas are not identical with those of evangelicals. It is in the direction of understanding and then compromise that we evangelicals must turn. Our moral posturing on abortion has not reduced the number of abortions; in fact heightened evangelical activity in this area has occurred at a time when the number of abortions has increased. Instead, it is time to turn to political strategies that will reduce and eventually eliminate the plague of abortion from the land. Political strategies without political understanding, however, will lead to failure and frustration. The argument, then, is that if we wish to change the outcomes of the political process, we must enter the process itself and use it for ends that are more consistent with our values. To do so will be difficult and must be accompanied by understanding. But there is no other choice.

The Supreme Court

Few institutions are less understood than the Supreme Court. The "nine old men," now with one woman, operate in secret except when cases are argued before them and when they issue their opinions. Among opponents of abortion, there is strong antagonism to the Court and its seemingly undemocratic way of making decisions. This antagonism alternates with hope—hope that some of the old men (four are presently over seventy-five) will resign or even die, and that President Reagan will then appoint new justices who will oppose abortion and overturn *Roe* v. *Wade*. Is there basis for either the antagonism or the hope?

A brief review of Supreme Court history reveals that only on a few occasions has the Court been out of line with the values of the dominant groups in the society. The *Dred Scott* decision, which upheld slavery, was one such instance, and it was repudiated by the Civil War. In another example, the Court in the early 1930s tried to sweep away the New Deal reforms that were attempting to cope with the crisis caused by the Depression. They succeeded for a time, but eventually a few changes in Court personnel brought the institution back into line. Evangelicals must realize that abortion is not like the foregoing examples. The contending parties are too equal in power and influence. In *Roe* v. *Wade,* the Court had a choice that was bound to antagonize some but could also win praise from others. It is an oversimplification, of course, but if the society moved toward a strong anti-abortion stance, the Court would not be long in following.

On the other hand, it is naive to assume that a few replacements on the Court will lead to the repudiation of *Roe* v. *Wade*. The Court does not easily overturn past precedents, despite speculation in the media about the possibilities. In fact, it often goes out of the way to reaffirm earlier decisions. In the 1983 *Akron* abortion case, the Court loudly and clearly stated: "We reaffirm *Roe* v. *Wade*." Even new justices feel bound to decisions of their predecessors. Only if the evidence is overwhelming that the earlier decision was an improper reading of the Constitution or that the earlier choice led to some unintended consequences that had not been foreseen is the Court likely to reject the past.

Usually, when the Court charts a new and controversial course, it is because it arrives at a feeling that a grievous injustice is taking place and that the legislative branch is not dealing with the injustice despite numerous opportunities to do so. The cases involving the redistricting of legislatures may illustrate this best (*Baker* v. *Carr* [1962], *Wesberry* v. *Sanders* [1964], *Reynolds* v. *Sims* [1964]). Throughout American history, legislative bodies had been biased in their representation. Rural areas had many more representatives than the number of people living in their districts warranted. Although the fundamental democratic norm of equality was being systematically violated throughout the nation, the Court refused to force the hand of the legislature (*Colegrove* v. *Green* [1946]), giving it the opportunity to reform itself. When the legislatures refused to act on their own, the Court finally stepped in. Other examples include the extension of the protections of the Bill of Rights to the states within the past fifty years; in most instances the extension took place only when blatant inequality was being permitted in state courts. Thus, for example, when a Florida pauper was denied access to an attorney and went to prison in the vain effort to defend himself, the Court ruled that state courts had to provide for such attorneys as was required previously by the Constitution in federal courts (*Gideon* v. *Wainwright* [1962]). Only the failure of the states to act led to the intervention.

To summarize our argument so far: the Supreme Court is rarely out of touch with the dominant sources of opinion in the society; the Court tends to follow the decisions it has formulated in the past; it tends to defer to legislative bodies; and it charts new courses rarely, and normally only when a strong sense of injustice is perceived.

How does this argument apply to the abortion decisions beginning with *Roe* v. *Wade* in 1973? First of all, the opinion in *Roe* v. *Wade* was somewhat out of touch with certain sectors of mass public opinion, but without question the decision was more in line with the opinions of the leadership of the society. In a way *Roe* can be likened to the school-desegregation case in the 1950s (*Brown* v. *Board of Education*), in that segments of mass opinion were offended, while strong support was present as well. Clearly, the decision also provided affirmation for the women's movement just two years after a major breakthrough by the

Court for women's rights *(Reed* v. *Reed).* It was also just after the passage of the Equal Rights Amendment by the Congress.

The court in *Roe* v. *Wade* also acted consistently with a number of decisions affirming a constitutional right to privacy, beginning with a Connecticut birth-control case in 1965 *(Griswold* v. *Connecticut).* In this case, a Connecticut law prohibiting the sale of contraceptives was held to violate the privacy of individuals. Although the right to privacy is not explicitly mentioned in the Bill of Rights, the Court held it to be a logical extension of portions of the Bill of Rights. Questions were raised by some scholars about the reasoning in these privacy decisions, but they caused little stir in the mass public. What they provided for the Court was a legal rationale that they applied in *Roe;* the right to an abortion was deemed fundamental to the right to privacy. One may consider the application of the privacy decisions to abortion to be flawed, as does Justice White (and this writer), but from the perspective of the Court majority, the application was sound.

In *Roe* v. *Wade,* the Court chose not to defer to legislative bodies, in this case state legislatures. Congress had not passed laws regarding abortion, but many state and local legislative bodies had, particularly in states with large Roman Catholic populations. Why did the Court choose not to defer to legislative bodies in *Roe?* For the justices, a conflict was perceived between the emerging right to privacy and state laws that prohibited abortion. Given such a choice, the Court sided with the right to privacy.

Certainly, a new course was charted by the Court in its *Roe* decision. But from the Court's perspective, it was not a totally new course, in that it was linked to a chain of earlier privacy cases. But, in addition, the Court perceived injustice in abortion laws, which they felt contributed to a disrespect for law by the widespread practice of back-room, illegal abortions. And, finally, *Roe* v. *Wade* was seen by the justices as a key tool in advancing the cause of women's rights against injustices suffered in the past.

What are the major features of the decision in *Roe* v. *Wade?* One of the features that has made it so controversial is the trimester system of abortion rights. In the first trimester of pregnancy, or in the first three months, the rights of a woman to have an abortion relatively unfettered by State intrusion are paramount. In the second trimester, the rights of the State increase, while in the third period of the pregnancy the rights of the State to preserve the life of the unborn are strong. When can the State regulate the abortion procedure? And under what circumstances? According to *Roe:*

(a) For the stage prior to approximately the end of the first trimester, the abortion decision and its effectuation must be left to the medical judgment of the pregnant woman's attending physician. (b) For the stage subsequent to approximately the end of the first trimester, the State, in promoting its interest in the health of the mother, may, if it chooses, regulate the abortion procedure in ways that are reasonably related to maternal health. (c) For the stage subsequent to viability the State, in promoting its interest in the potentiality of human life, may, if it chooses, regulate, and even proscribe, abortion except where it is necessary, in appropriate medical judgment, for the preservation of the life or health of the mother.

Contained in the quotation above that defines and defends the trimester concept are a number of other important features of *Roe*. The role of the attending physician is given great weight. This suggests that the State will not be able to pass laws that do much to restrict the judgments of the medical profession as they advise pregnancy patients. The companion case to *Roe—Doe* v. *Bolton*—made it even more clear than in *Roe* that the State would not be able to circumscribe the behavior of doctors. This deference to the medical profession may be due in part to the fact that Justice Blackmun, the author of the opinion, had been the counsel for the world-famous Mayo Clinic in Rochester, Minnesota, before coming on the Supreme Court bench. Other abortion decisions that have followed *Roe* v. *Wade* have been very protective of the rights of attending physicians (see the *Akron* case in 1983 and the *Thornburgh* decision in 1986). Aside from this deference to the medical profession, states are given certain rights to regulate the abortion situation. Laws may be passed ". . . that are reasonably related to maternal health." Hence, laws will be allowed that insist that only qualified physicians perform abortions and in environments that are adequate to protect maternal health. Of course, such laws do little or nothing to protect the life of the unborn. Most important, from a pro-life perspective, is that *Roe* provides that subsequent to viability, or the point where the unborn child can survive outside the mother's womb, the State can regulate or even proscribe abortion except where the life or health of the mother is endangered. In fact, a careful reading of *Roe* v. *Wade* makes it clear that the majority is in no way making an argument that would encourage abortion. Numerous quotations can be mustered to support this point. For example, it is argued that the State has an ". . . important and legitimate interest in protecting the potentiality of human life." And, in another part of the decision: ". . . as long as at least potential life is involved, the State may assert interests beyond the protection of the pregnant woman alone." In decisions subsequent to *Roe,* the trimester division has been assailed, as has been the tendency on the part of judges that support abortion to have lost sight of their earlier nonadvocacy position regarding abortion.

Justice O'Connor has written a slashing attack on the trimester concept in *City of Akron* v. *Akron Center for Reproductive Health* (1983). She argued that the three-stage approach ". . . cannot be supported as a legitimate or useful framework for accommodating the woman's right and the State's interest" (p. 3 of her dissent). In fact, she went further and called it ". . . a completely unworkable method . . ." *(Idem.)*. First of all, it forces the State to continuously monitor contemporary medical and scientific literature to see if a state's regulations are consistent with current medical practice. Second, it forces courts to monitor the same literature in order to decide cases before them. As a result, both the State and the courts are put in an untenable position. O'Connor concludes:

> The *Roe* framework, then, is clearly on a collision course with itself. As the medical risks of various abortion procedures decrease, the point at which the State may regulate for reasons of maternal health is moved further forward to actual childbirth. As medical science becomes better able to provide for the separate existence of the fetus, the point of viability is moved further back toward conception [p. 7].

In addition, O'Connor argues that the *Roe* opinion had made clear that the State had an important interest in protecting the potentiality of human life, but that:

> . . . the point at which these interests become compelling does not depend on the trimester of pregnancy. Rather, these interests are present *throughout* pregnancy. . . . *potential* life is no less potential in the first weeks of pregnancy than it is at viability or afterward. At any stage in pregnancy, there is the *potential* for human life [pp. 8, 10].

O'Connor as well as Justices Burger and White, in *Akron* and in the 1986 case, *Thornburgh* v. *American College of Obstetricians and Gynecologists,* argue, in dissent, that majority justices have lost sight of the State interest in protecting the potentiality of human life that was affirmed in *Roe.* Why would the majority declare the "informed consent" provisions of the Pennsylvania law unconstitutional, White asks, if their goal is protecting the potentiality for human life and not maximizing the number of abortions? Accurate information regarding abortion and its alternatives is what the informed-consent provisions of the law were all about. Burger goes even further in his dissent. In commenting on the Court majority's invalidation of the informed-consent provisions, Burger argues:

> The Court's astounding rationale for this holding is that such information might have the effect of 'discouraging abortion, '. . . as though abortion is

something to be advocated and encouraged. This is at odds not only with *Roe* but with our subsequent abortion decisions as well. [Footnote, p. 2).

Burger seems to suggest that the majority has gone from a position of defending the possibility of abortion in *Roe* to an advocacy, or almost cheerleader's, position in the mid 1980s.

This review of arguments in the post-*Roe* period has emphasized attacks on the trimester concept in the original decision and how it does not stand up to developing medical technology. In addition, the review shows how the majority has gone from a position of permitting abortion to one of advocating it. The first of these points give anti-abortion advocates some hope, for it suggests that state laws that chip away at the trimester concept may hold up upon review by the Supreme Court. At the same time, if the majority of the Court has moved from granting the right to abortion to an advocacy position, it is not likely to look with patience on state legislative attempts to proscribe abortion under any circumstances.

No review of the decisions following *Roe* v. *Wade* would be complete without some discussion of provisions of state laws and local ordinances that the Supreme Court has upheld in the past decade. A state requirement that a woman would certify ". . . that her consent is informed and freely given and is not the result of coercion" was upheld (*Planned Parenthood of Central Missouri* v. *Danforth* [1976]). Such a law does not prohibit abortions but at least forces the mother to consider her decision and give informed consent to the procedure. Three decisions in 1977 dealt with abortions for the poor. First, the Court argued that states were not required to pay for nontherapeutic abortions for the poor *(Beal* v. *Doe);* second, the federal Constitution does not require that tax dollars be used to fund nontherapeutic abortions for the poor *(Maher* v. *Roe);* and third, public hospitals are not required to provide facilities for nontherapeutic abortions *(Poelker* v. *Doe).* Two companion cases in 1980 argued that the expenditure of tax dollars for "medically necessary" abortions for the poor was not required *(Harris* v. *McRae* and *Williams* v. *Zbaraz).* In the next year, the Court upheld a Utah law that required parental notice of an abortion by a minor who has not demonstrated her maturity or has not shown that an abortion without parental involvement would be in her best interests *(H. L.* v. *Matheson).* Finally, in 1983, the Court upheld provisions of a Missouri law that require a pathology report for each abortion performed after viability and mandate parental consent for minors in circumstances that would not prejudice the rights of the minor *(Planned Parenthood Association of Kansas City* v. *Ashcroft).* All of these decisions suggest that the Court is willing to accept "reasonable" restrictions on abortions, and open up the possibility that carefully drawn state laws and local ordinances that restrict and limit abortions may pass Supreme Court review.

Given the pattern of Court decisions since *Roe,* what is the appropriate stance to take by the evangelical as he or she contemplates the abortion issue? Reversing *Roe* v. *Wade* in one fell swoop, we have argued, is unlikely. Yet gradual reversal may be a possibility (cf. Cunningham 1985). Scientific and medical developments suggest that the viability concept that the Court developed in *Roe* may be vulnerable. Medical advances have moved viability from approximately the 28th to the 20th or 21st week of pregnancy. The possibility of test-tube babies and the development of artificial wombs may mean that the viability concept may have to be abandoned altogether by the court. Carefully drawn laws that take account of such developments may lead the Court to reassess its past decisions.

In addition, and in light of Court decisions, it is important to focus on what *Roe* v. *Wade* did and did not do. As constitutional scholar Laurence Tribe (1985) has noted, in *Roe* the government was barred only from prohibiting abortions under all circumstances except when the life of the mother was at stake, and from permitting abortions in unsafe circumstances. But in order to avoid placing a woman in a position to choose between an abortion and an unwanted pregnancy, Tribe suggests that there are a number of things that the State can do. It can provide better sex education and more widely available contraceptives; when unwanted pregnancy occurs, it can provide better prenatal care, better financial support for women with children, and expanded adoption opportunities; and finally, the government can provide much greater funding to advance the point of viability closer to the point of conception. None of these governmental actions would threaten the Court's findings in *Roe* v. *Wade* or later abortion decisions. And all of them would tend to lower the number of abortions being performed in the society.

This section of the essay has called for an understanding of the way that the Supreme Court makes its decisions. I have argued that the Court rarely is out of line with the attitudes of the dominant elites of the society, and—when it *is* out of line—it is not for long. The Court tends to follow precedent except in rare instances; when it charts a new course, it is as a result of perceived inequality and government inaction or intransigence. In its abortion decisions, this writer feels, the Court has taken a new direction, but the opinions are not in conflict with those of the dominant groups in the society. In the *Roe* decision itself, the trimester concept may be its weakest link, and state laws and local ordinances that are carefully drawn may be able to challenge the trimester concept successfully. But, at the same time, laws are called for that provide assistance to avoid pregnancy, during pregnancy, and after birth, along with increased government support for research dealing with moving back the point of viability. We should not expect that the Supreme Court will reject *Roe* v. *Wade* in its totality in the near future.

Congress

The only certain way for American public policy to reflect a pro-life position is for the United States Congress to pass a constitutional amendment banning abortions and for the state legislatures to ratify such an amendment. Unfortunately for pro-life advocates, this is a difficult procedure. Most important, it takes a two-thirds vote in both houses of Congress for passage. Next, three-quarters of the state legislatures must approve the amendment before it is ratified and becomes part of the Constitution. Considering the fact that there are only twenty-six amendments to the Constitution and that ten of them (the Bill of Rights) were ratified at one time in 1791, one can see that amending the Constitution is a rare occurrence and very difficult to achieve. This section will examine the impediments to achieving fundamental change in abortion policy in Congress.

The key to understanding the behavior of our legislators is to understand that above all else they are reelection seekers. In other words, if we wish to understand how members of Congress will behave, we should assume that their actions will be consistent with their desire to win reelection. In the abortion context, this means that if members assume that their attitudes and votes on abortion are critical to their reelection bids, they will vote accordingly. This analysis may sound crass, but it is based on the simple assumption that human beings will attempt to behave in accordance with their own self-interest and that reelection is in the best interests of members of Congress. If not reelected, a member cannot advance his or her long-term goals, such as a policy agenda or personal political ambitions. Obviously, the country is deeply divided on the abortion issue. To some degree, this frees a member to vote as he or she pleases when a bill dealing with abortion or a proposal for a constitutional amendment comes before Congress. The member knows that there will be some support for a pro-choice position if he or she takes that position in the Congress. At the same time, the legislator knows that a pro-abortion vote will make other members of the constituency unhappy. Since members work hard to avoid this unhappiness, hoping to offend no one, the most rational strategy for Congress in general is to try to avoid votes on the abortion issue. The small number of votes taken on the issue in recent years suggests that this avoidance strategy has been pursued.

There are institutional as well as political impediments that get in the way of achieving change in abortion policy on the congressional level. All proposals for constitutional amendments must find their way through committee hearings, committee votes, rules for debate on the floor of each house, and the two-thirds vote required for passage. To focus for a moment on just one of the potential roadblocks along the way to passage, we turn to an examination of the House Judiciary Committee, which must approve an abortion amendment before it can be sent to the floor for vote. The chairman of that committee is Democrat Peter Rodino of New Jersey. Although a Roman Catholic, he has opposed limiting abortions in previous votes on the issue. (cf. Barone & Ujifusa 1985, 861). Given Rodino's opposition, it will be extremely difficult for a pro-life amendment to emerge from his committee, since committee chairmen in Congress have considerable power. In addition, the language of the proposed amendment must be exactly the same in each house; otherwise, a conference committee, involving members from both houses, would have to iron out the differences in wording between the two proposals. If changes were made in the conference committee from the wording that had passed either or both houses, the proposed amendment would have to be returned for another two-thirds vote. The point of all this discussion is to suggest that an opponent of a constitutional amendment has numerous opportunities to derail a proposal. Given the normal propensity of members who wish to avoid votes on controversial issues, it is a wonder that Congress ever votes on anything of controversy. The above discussion is a very brief and superficial analysis of the institutional roadblocks available to the opponent of an abortion amendment and points to the difficulty faced by proponents of abortion reform. It also suggests a significant proposition about the Congress of the United States: major change is a very difficult thing to achieve. Proponents of change must be vigilant at every stage of the process in order to guide their proposals through the maze.

The two-thirds-vote plateau that must be surmounted for approval of any amendment presents political difficulties as well. The abortion controversy in the 1980s has generally become a partisan issue, with the Republican Party taking a much stronger anti-abortion stance than the Democrats. The problem here is that Democratic votes are crucial in attaining the two-thirds needed to pass a constitutional amendment. In the House of Representatives after the election of 1984, there were 255 Democrats and only 180 Republicans in the membership, while in the Senate there were 53 Republicans and 47 Democrats. Quite obviously, an abortion amendment will need the support of many Democrats if it is to pass in both houses. Too close an identification with the Republican Party is the kiss of death if the goal is passage. Is there evidence that the two parties are working together in the Congress to bring about a constitutional amendment to restrict abortion? Not that this writer is aware of!

Within the Democratic Party in Congress is one group of representatives that might be amenable to supporting the anti-abortion position: Roman Catholics, whose church hierarchy is adamantly opposed to abortion. In the fall of 1986, there were eighty-two Roman Catholic Democrats in the House of Representatives, a sizable number of potential supporters of an anti-abortion amendment. However, an examination of past voting records of these eighty-two members reveals that only thirty-eight took an anti-abortion position on votes on the issue in recent years. (Data on voting records were taken from *Almanac of American Politics, 1986.*) Thirty-two of these Roman Catholic Democrats voted in a pro-choice manner, including the aforementioned chairman of the House Judiciary Committee, two candidates for the U.S. Senate in 1986, as well as numerous members with many years of service in the House, and hence potential clout. (Twelve Democrats who are Roman Catholic were not recorded as voting on the abortion issue.) Obviously, in order to get the two-thirds vote needed in order to pass a constitutional amendment on abortion, many more House Democrats are going to have to either change their vote or be replaced in the chamber. Both will be difficult to achieve. But to return to the point where we began this discussion, if the abortion issue becomes more and more partisan in tone—with Republicans lining up as the anti-abortion party and Democrats supporting the pro-abortion position—any hope for change through the Congress is dead.

If the only sure way to get a change in abortion policy in the United States is by means of a constitutional amendment, what is the best manner in which to achieve such an amendment? First, we should note that too close an identification of the issue with the Republican Party is a great mistake, for there are now, and will continue to be, great numbers of Democrats in both houses of Congress who will be needed to achieve the necessary vote. Second, evangelicals and other pro-lifers may need to consider allowing abortions in the case of certain birth defects as one means of increasing support for an amendment and ensuring a better chance of passage. Third, opponents of abortion are going to need to study carefully the voting records of members of Congress and to provide organized support (money and manpower) for those who oppose abortion, regardless of party, and to work for the defeat of those members who take a pro-abortion stance. Many supporters of abortion will be difficult to dislodge, but it is the only sure way to achieve change. Only rarely do members change their voting patterns; hence a supporter of abortion at time one is likely to remain a supporter at time two.

Fourth, evangelicals must be prepared to side with anti-abortion supporters from other faith commitments in order to build a broad coalition
with a better chance of winning. Can the evangelical community and
their pro-life allies achieve the goal of a constitutional amendment banning most abortions in this country? The answer would seem to be in the
negative. However, a clear understanding of the pitfalls and possibilities
is the place to begin. There are examples in history, such as the anti-
slavery and prohibition movements, to show that it can be accomplished.
Finally, a fundamental assumption of this paper also provides hope in
this area. Remember that members of Congress are above all else reelection-seeking animals. If they perceive serious electoral threat from
the opponents of abortion, they can be expected to respond. But without
sensing such a threat, they will vote either in reponse to the pro-abortion forces or according to their own personal convictions.

State Legislatures

As we have seen, it is in the halls of state legislative bodies, and to a
lesser extent in city councils, that specific laws dealing with abortion
have their origin. Suggestions have been made in earlier portions of this
paper that state laws that directly challenge *Roe* v. *Wade* and the cases
that follow it are doomed to failure in the Supreme Court. However
shaky the constitutional ground, the Court seems committed to the
right to privacy and to the proposition that abortions are covered by that
right, at least during the early phases of pregnancy. We have nonetheless suggested that states may chip away at the trimester concept
adopted in *Roe,* both because it does not have unanimous support on the
Supreme Court itself and because it is under attack as a result of medical
and technological developments that move back the age of viability. In
addition, we have argued that there is much that can be done by state
legislatures to pass laws that would help to minimize unwanted pregnancy and to encourage bringing to term any unwanted pregnancies
that do occur. Finally, state legislative money can encourage research
into the possibilities of lowering the point of viability to conception.

Given the fact that this nation is composed of fifty states and thousands of units of local government, it is difficult to determine how effectively these legislative bodies are carrying out the objectives advanced
above. All concerned citizens must attempt to see for themselves. The
search should be governed by the assumption that state legislators and
city-council members are driven by the same reelection-seeking behavior that applies to Congress. State legislators and city council members are likely to be receptive to well-organized efforts to influence their
behavior. Like their counterparts in Washington, they aim to please the

electorate. In deciding what laws to pass in this emotion-charged issue of abortion, they are going to need the best advice that pro-life forces can muster. Laws that directly challenge *Roe* v. *Wade* are likely to be declared unconstitutional, no matter how well meaning the effort. State and local lawmakers are going to have to go beyond responding to emotional appeals and draw upon sophisticated legal advice that will produce legislation with a better chance to survive the legal challenges that will no doubt be forthcoming.

Interest Groups

Special-interest groups are organized or unorganized entities that share a common goal or interest. The American political process has thousands of interest groups pursuing varied aims and attempting to influence the results of legislative, executive, and even judicial decisions. Although a large number of groups have emerged in the arena of abortion since *Roe* v. *Wade,* this is not the place to attempt to catalog all the pro-life efforts. What we will attempt to do in this section is to place the anti-abortion effort into the historical context of the temperance movement and see what lessons that has for us today.

We argued in the introduction of this paper that the pro-life movement and its accompanying interest groups have been long on moral rhetoric and short on accomplishment. This, admittedly, is an oversimplification and at the same time a somewhat unfair charge. And, to some extent, the moral rhetoric is essential in order to mobilize groups and individuals to take action. Evangelicals and other opponents of abortion were taken by surprise by *Roe* v. *Wade.* It has taken time to build organizations to combat the evil of abortion from scratch, to develop the sophistication that such organizations as Americans United for Life are beginning to exhibit. Suffice it to say that moral rhetoric is not enough. The long-term goal is to rid the land of abortion, but the problem is to develop short-run strategies that move toward that end. What can be learned from the temperance movement that can help us to understand how the anti-abortion, or pro-life, movement can move toward the achievement of its aims?

The temperance movement had its beginnings in the early nineteenth century with calls for individual abstinence from the evils of drink. It culminated with the adoption of the Eighteenth Amendment prohibiting the manufacture, sale, and transportation of intoxicating liquors as well as the importation of same into the United States. The amendment was ratified by the states in 1919 and went into effect in 1920. (This account of the temperance movement is based on two fine monographs: Peter Odegard, *Pressure Politics,* 1928; and Joseph Gus-

field, *Symbolic Crusade,* 1963.) It took over a century to achieve prohibition from the beginning of the movement to the ratification of the
amendment. This suggests the difficulty of achieving fundamental constitutional change in this country, a point alluded to above. It also suggests the need to set short-term goals that advance one toward the
primary, long-term purpose that drives a movement. While never losing
sight of the goal of total prohibition, the temperance movement worked
toward the acceptance of local option laws and statewide prohibitions.

Crucial to the success of the temperance movement was the arrival on
the scene of the Anti Saloon League in 1895. This particular group
successfully mobilized the already existing opinion against the liquor
traffic that existed in this country and engineered the final assault that
led to the passage of the Eighteenth Amendment in 1917 and its ratification two years later. Note the symbolism in the name—Anti Saloon
League. Who could be in favor of the saloon? We see the same fight over
symbolism and semantics today. Anti-abortion forces constantly use the
language of "pro-life" and characterize their opponents as murderers.
Pro-abortion forces use the language of "pro-choice" and attack their
opponents as being opposed to freedom of choice and individualism. In
part, the battle is over whose symbols will most effectively influence
public opinion.

How did the Anti Saloon League prevail? It had to be something more
than its name. For one thing, the group cultivated with great sophistication its major base of support, the Protestant churches. By the turn of
the twentieth century, special Sunday offerings were taken throughout
the country to support the cause of prohibition. In some churches today,
both Protestant and Catholic, we see somewhat similar efforts on behalf
of the pro-life cause, but to a much more limited extent. Such efforts gave
the Anti Saloon League the financial muscle it needed to win the day,
while allowing them to solidify the support in the general public that
was already present. It is no doubt a more difficult task today to forge a
broad-based coalition of Roman Catholics and the many strands of evangelicals (fundamentalists, charismatics, Holiness churches, blacks, and
others) as well as other orthodox Christians (Lutherans, some Presbyterian groups, and so on) behind the cause of the anti-abortion, pro-
life movement. These groups are often more conscious of their differences with each other and may find it difficult to submerge these differences to unite in behalf of the pro-life cause, although some progress has
been made at the elite level.

The Anti Saloon League was successful because the leaders never lost
sight of their primary purpose. This allowed them to accept the support
of groups with which they had little in common except the common
desire to rid America of the evil of liquor. Although a small Prohibition

Party developed in this country, it never got very far, as happens to most third parties. The Anti Saloon League opposed this strategy, knowing that success depended on having the support of both major parties. All they asked from a public official was his stand on the liquor traffic. If he opposed it, he could count on the support of the Anti Saloon League. If he favored it, he could count on their enmity. Their support or opposition was not just verbal; they supplied money for their political friends and against their political enemies. In one year, the League helped defeat over sixty members of the Ohio state legislature by the old-fashioned, yet thoroughly American, way of working the precincts, going door to door for their candidates. Yes, the Anti Saloon League was a prototype of what is often referred to today (somewhat derisively) as a single-interest group. Sometimes, that is what it takes, given the forces that are arrayed against you.

How does the pro-life movement, with its multitude of interest groups, stack up in a comparison with the successes of the temperance movement and the Anti Saloon League? Unfortunately, not very well. As suggested previously, there is a tendency for today's anti-abortion movement to be too closely identified with the Republican Party. Certainly, the organizational muscle and financial strength exemplified by the Anti Saloon League are not present today. There is also the understandable tendency to include pro-life concerns in a package of issues that one is trying to market at the same time (pornography, drugs, crime, school prayer, school texts, Communism). Although there are many threats to cherished ways of life in this country, the question centers on how to best deal with these threats. The danger is that, as more items are added to your agenda, you lose potential supporters who may be with you on the abortion issue but are in opposition on something else. The Anti Saloon League saw this danger; the result is history.

In this section, we have given a brief description and analysis of the temperance movement in order to attempt to supply some insight for the pro-life movement today. It will be difficult for pro-life forces in the years to come to match the skill and resources displayed by the temperance movement and its leading interest group, the Anti Saloon League. One clear danger that seems at the forefront right now is that the pro-life movement is perilously close to being coopted by the Republican Party. Reaching out to pro-life Democrats is clearly in order in the immediate future.

Public Opinion

Earlier we argued that evangelicals have failed to grasp that there is a strong base of support for legalized abortion in society. In this section,

Table 1 **Percent Favoring Abortion Under Certain Conditions
(1972–1985)**

	Percent in Favor of Abortion			
	1972	1976	1980	1985
If the woman's own health is seriously endangered by the pregnancy	87	91	90	89
If she became pregnant as a result of rape	79	84	83	81
If there is a strong chance of serious defect in the baby	79	84	83	83
If the family has a very low income and cannot afford any more children	49	53	52	52
If she is unmarried and does not want to marry the man	44	50	48	48
If she is married and does not want any more children	40	46	47	45
If the woman wants it for any reason	+	38*	41	38

+ No data available.
*Not asked in 1976. Data are from 1977.
Data Sources: General Social Surveys, 1972–1986: Cumulative Codebook, pp. 227–229; General Social Surveys, 1972–1982: Cumulative Codebook, pp. 154–155.

we will examine the opinions of Americans on this issue and then explore some of the possible reasons for the state of opinion that we find. Finally, we will examine some of the implications of the findings for anti-abortion strategies.

In table 1, we examine data from a series of surveys conducted by the National Opinion Research Center at the University of Chicago. The figures cover the period from 1972 (just prior to the Supreme Court decision in *Roe* v. *Wade*) to 1985. A series of hypothetical possibilities were presented to survey respondents, who were asked whether they favored abortion if the life of the mother were endangered, in cases of rape and serious birth defects, in cases of families with low incomes, and finally "for any reason," the extreme pro-choice argument. Apparently, Americans strongly favor abortion in cases where the mother's health is in danger, where rape is involved, and where birth defects are a strong possibility. In these instances, the support for abortion was strong and steady throughout the time period studied. Proposals for changes in laws that do not permit abortions in such situations are going to meet strong resistance from the public at large. Particularly difficult to deal with are the findings showing strong public support for abortions when there is a possibility of birth defects. Although, for most evangelicals,

Table 2   **Anti-Abortion Attitudes by Religious Affiliation**
(White Americans Only 1972–1984)
Percent Against Abortion

Religious Group	1972	1976	1980	1984
Evangelical†	70	60	69	55
Other Protestants	50	48	27	34
Catholic	67	68	62	46
Jewish	19	11	21	13
No Religious Preference	25	24	25	15

*Abortion should either never be permitted or permitted only when the life of the mother is threatened.

†"Evangelicals" are members of the following denominational groups: Baptists, Southern Baptists, and members of small Holiness denominations (eg., Nazarenes), Pentecostal denominations (the biggest being the Assembly of God), and small fundamentalist sects and evangelical denominations that prior research has identified as probably evangelical (see Lyman A. Kellstedt, "Evangelicals and Political Realignment," Paper presented at the annual meeting of the American Political Science Association, Washington, D.C., August 28–31, 1986).

Data Source: Inter-University Consortium of Political and Social Research, The University of Michigan. Data analysis by author.

abortions under these circumstances are considered undesirable, proposals for a constitutional amendment to ban abortions that do not include these options are likely to be opposed by legislators in tune with public opinion on this emotional issue.

However, the data in table 1 show that the country is strongly divided in its opinions concerning the desirability of abortion in other circumstances. Americans are about evenly divided on support for abortion where family income is the problem, somewhat less supportive for reasons of "convenience," and even less in favor of an unlimited pro-choice position. Viewed from one perspective, these data show a great deal of opposition to "convenience" abortions. From another perspective, however, there appears to be at least 40 percent of the population that could be said to be hard-core pro-abortion. This suggests how difficult it will be to bring about fundamental changes in this area if this hard-core group is mobilized to defend unlimited pro-choice policy.

In addition, the University of Michigan, through its Center for Political Studies, has been examining the abortion issue for some time. In table 2, we examine the relationships between abortion attitudes and various religious groups. Note that support for the anti-abortion position (that it should be permitted only in cases when the life of the mother is threatened or not at all) has declined in the 1972–1984 time period for all the religious groups. What is ironic is that decline in support among

Table 3   **Changes in Anti-Abortion Attitudes
in White Evangelicals (1980–1984)**
Percent Against Abortion

Religious Group	1980	1984	Gain/Loss: 1980 to 1984
Denominational Evangelicals	69	55	– 14
Doctrinal Evangelicals in Evangelical Denominations	81	66	– 15
Doctrinal Evangelicals in Evangelical Denominations Who Regularly Attend Church	88	77	– 11
Doctrinal Evangelicals in Other Protestant Denominations Who Regularly Attend Church	80	73	– 7

evangelicals for the anti-abortion position was most precipitous during the four years from 1980 to 1984, the first presidential term of Ronald Reagan, an outspoken opponent of abortion. Of course, President Reagan has not made the issue a centerpiece of his legislative strategy, despite occasional public statements as to where he stands on the issue. Roman Catholic support also declined dramatically in the most recent time period, again despite Reagan support, but also during a period when the Catholic hierarchy in the United States became even more vocal and aggressive than before in their opposition to abortion. The data in table 2 not only chart the decline in support for the anti-abortion position, but also make it clear that only evangelicals and Catholics hover around majority support for an anti-abortion policy thrust. Without a more forthright stand against abortion from other religious groups or stronger opposition to abortion among Catholics and evangelicals, a change in current policy will be most difficult to achieve.

In table 3, we examine the data on religion and anti-abortion attitudes from a somewhat different perspective. Here we zero in on the years 1980 and 1984 and look at in-group differences among evangelicals. In table 2, evangelicalism was examined from a denominational perspective. In table 3, we look at doctrinal measures of evangelicalism as well as church attendance and denominational data. A "doctrinal evangelical" is one who has had a born-again experience and who believes in the inerrancy of the Bible. There is some overlap between doctrinal and denominational evangelicals (Baptists, Southern Baptists, as well as Holiness, Pentecostal, fundamentalist sects, and other small evangelical denominations). However, doctrinal evangelicals do come from other Protestant denominations, although in small numbers. The church-attendance variable is included in order to see if regular attenders have stronger anti-abortion attitudes than less-regular church-goers. This is what one would expect if the church is attempting to encourage anti-abortion attitudes among its members. The results demonstrate that doctrinal beliefs tend to strengthen anti-abortion attitudes more than does denominational affiliation. It is the combination of doctrine, denomination, and regular church attendance, however, that produces the strongest anti-abortion attitudes. These evangelicals are in the right place (the church) with the right set of doctrinal beliefs, and this combination seems to make them the most receptive to strong opposition to abortion. Yet, despite efforts to mobilize evangelicals to political action in the 1980–84 time period around such issues as abortion, the data in table 3 demonstrate a decline in anti-abortion feeling among evangelical groups.

From the perspective of political strategy, the data in table 3 suggest that the manpower for various types of political action (election campaigns to defeat pro-abortion candidates, protest rallies against abortion, letter-writing campaigns, visits to legislators, etc.) should come from the ranks of the regular church-going, doctrinally sound evangelicals. But can church-attending evangelicals be rallied to support collective political action? Can the individualist biases of contemporary evangelicalism be mobilized to collective action? These evangelicals will need to be educated to the nuances of politics, not simply to the more comfortable approaches of "right and wrong" so often raised in the past.

In other public-opinion data of this kind (but not presented here in tabular form), we find that there is a strong relationship between anti-abortion attitudes and low levels of political information. Moreover, given that highly informed individuals comprise the largest proportion of the politically activist segment of the society, the very forces that are most in favor of abortion have disproportionate power and influence on that issue. Only as the less-knowledgeable evangelicals become more politically sophisticated and more active is their declining power on this issue, as measured in the polling data presented earlier, likely to be reversed. Can it happen? Only if these evangelicals begin to feel that abortion is a fundamental threat to both the good society as they see it and to their everyday lives and then decide to use the political process to advance their aims. They are going to have to be mobilized by their pastors and by interest groups that already exist or are developed to achieve this end.

Another issue that these polling data raise, but do not answer, is why there is not greater opposition to abortion among Americans. Given the moral issues involved, it may seem incongruous to committed evangelicals that so many seem to favor the snuffing out of human life, or at least the potential for same. What is often missed by evangelicals is that the pro-choice forces have a powerful philosophical idea behind them—people should be able to freely make their own choices about matters that concern them as individuals. Freedom of choice, self-determination, and individual rights are powerful forces in American society, and they came of age in the abortion movement at a time when the women's movement was making great strides on its own to overcome past discriminations. Evangelicals often deny that sexual discrimination has had much of a history in the United States, but they ignore such Supreme Court decisions as (to name only two) the one that upheld an Illinois law making it unlawful for a woman to practice law (*Bradwell* v. *Illinois,* [1871]) or the decision that upheld a Florida law that made service on juries for women an option, which few chose, leaving rape cases to be tried by all-male juries (*Hoyt* v. *Florida,* [1961]). The women who fight so hard against such decisions, generally the feminists, inevitably see abortion in the context of women's rights. And they associate standard American values, including individual rights, with *Roe* v. *Wade.* They will be hard to beat. The public-opinion data indicate that the society is deeply divided on the abortion issue. This deep division, when coupled with the fact that the pro-abortion forces are well organized and have many allies in high political places, makes the task of the anti-abortion groups a very difficult one.

Conclusions

This paper has examined a number of areas of American politics that bear on the abortion controversy. We have argued that change in the anti-abortion stance of the Supreme Court is not likely to come about by a direct assault on *Roe* v. *Wade,* but it might be achieved by chipping away at the weak links of that decision, particularly its trimester concept. In addition, we have argued that a constitutional amendment, the only sure way to get around *Roe,* is unlikely to emerge from Congress in the foreseeable future. This is especially the case if a coalition that cuts across political parties cannot be forged. Even unanimity in one political party, when countered by strong opposition from the other party, cannot guarantee success of any pro-life thrust. Yet, Congress is responsive to the electorate, and if the climate of public opinion changes, we can expect Congress to change. But that is a very slim reed on which to hang pro-life hopes. In fact, the public-opinion data that we presented paint a very negative picture, with the country strongly divided between pro-life and pro-choice and with pro-choice positions gaining strength in the public at large since *Roe* v. *Wade,* even among evangelicals. In the short term, then, pro-life interest groups need to broaden their base, to move beyond a too-close alignment with the Republican Party, and to work within state legislatures to draw up legislation that will undermine some of the pillars of the *Roe* decision. In fact, to some degree that is what is already being done.

As an aside, the reader may find it unusual that in an essay of this sort the role of the President has not been given systematic attention. Is not the President, after all, the major actor in American politics? We have argued throughout this paper that the driving force in American politics is self-interest. First, on domestic issues in particular, the President has less of a role to play than is usually conceived, *unless* he is strongly supporting a position that is perceived by the Congress to be favored overwhelmingly by the electorate. Congress cannot ignore the President, but its members respond more directly to pressure from the voters. If the President and the electorate favor the same course of action, Congress will normally respond accordingly. But even a very popular President cannot have his way in the Congress if that body is divided and if members perceive strong divisions within the public. Such has apparently been the case with abortion. Second, in terms of the Supreme Court, there is little the President can do to affect its day-to-day decisions. When an opening on the Court occurs, he can attempt to place an anti-abortion advocate in its chambers. But even that is no guarantee of how that judge will vote over the years. Third, state legislatures are basically unresponsive to presidential directives unless his positions are shared by voters who pressure these legislative bodies for change. Finally, interest groups and the public at large may or may not be favorable to presidential initiatives. What we are saying here is that, in contrast to a foreign-policy initiative where the role of the President is crucial, in the abortion controversy the power of the President is limited. Only if he is prepared to make the issue a key policy initiative of his office during a year or term of Congress and succeeds in mobilizing public opinion behind his proposals is there a reasonable chance for success. For all his pro-life statements, President Reagan has been unwilling to go this far.

In conclusion, this paper has argued that fundamental change in the American political process is very difficult to achieve. Out groups in the society, such as blacks and women, have always known this to be the case. For much of American history, evangelicals were either in positions of power or were not having their ox gored by the decisions of the political system. *Roe* v. *Wade* changed all that, if the lesson had not been learned earlier. With patience and perseverance we must address the realities of the American political process and mobilize on all fronts to attempt to rid the land of the evil of abortion.

References and Further Reading

Abortion in America (a special issue). 1986. *Eternity* (January).

Akron v. Akron Center for Reproductive Health, 103 S. Ct. 2481. 1983.

Almanac of American Politics, 1986 (see Barone & Ujifusa).

American national election study, 1976: Pre and post election survey file. 1978. Ann Arbor: Inter-University Consortium for Political and Social Research.

American national election study, 1980: Pre and post election survey file. 1982. Ann Arbor: Inter-University Consortium for Political and Social Research.

American national election study, 1984: Pre and post election survey file. 1986. Ann Arbor: Inter-University Consortium for Political and Social Research.

Barone, M., & Ujifusa, G. 1985. *Almanac of American Politics, 1986.* Washington, D.C.: National Journal.

Cunningham, P. C. 1985. Reversing Roe v. Wade. *Christianity Today* September 20:20–22.

Davis, J. A., & Smith, T. W. 1986. *General social surveys: 1972–1986.* Chicago: National Opinion Research Center.

Griswold v. Connecticut, 381 U.S. 479. 1965.

Gusfield, J. 1963. *Symbolic crusade: Statute politics and the American temperance movement.* Urbana: Univ. of Illinois Press.

Odegard, P. 1928. *Pressure politics.* New York: Columbia Univ. Press.

Roe v. Wade, 410 U.S. 113. 1973.

Thornburgh v. American College of Obstetricians and Gynecologists, 106 S. Ct. 2169. 1986.

Tribe, L. 1985. The abortion funding conundrum: Inalienable rights, affirmative duties, and the dilemma of dependence. *Harvard Law Review* 99:330–343.

13

A Sociological Context for Abortion
The Problem of Teenage Pregnancy
Ivan J. Fahs

Most of us are familiar with the Joel Chandler Harris's "Uncle Remus" story featuring Brer Fox, who constructed a Tar-Baby from a mixture of tar and turpentine. Then, just as Brer Fox had hoped, along came his old adversary, Brer Rabbit. One thing led to another, and an angry Brer Rabbit struck Tar-Baby on the side of his head. As Uncle Remus describes it, "His fis' stuck, en he can't pull loose" (Harris 1921). Brer Rabbit lost the use of his feet and head in the same way and ended up in a sticky predicament, with Brer Fox laughing at him. Unfortunately for those who favor straightforward solutions to clear-cut problems, the abortion issue is not one and *only* one "sticky" issue. Rather, it has many parts and facets—and whoever tackles the problem may, like Brer Rabbit, end up immobilized.

Adam Clymer, in a *New York Times* article, noted that ". . . Americans do not see abortion in anything like the clear, black-and-white terms discerned by activists on the issue" (Clymer 1986). Similarly, in a thoughtful review of what Americans have thought to be acceptable conditions for a legal abortion, *Policy Review* surveyed the results of public opinion from 1972 until 1984. The author closed the article by noting, "When Gallup . . . asked Americans if they ever wonder whether their own position on abortion is the right one, 38 percent said yes" (Split verdict, 19). It seems to me that such a low affirmative percentage implies a rather high degree of uncertainty, and that abortion remains a complicated and ambiguous issue for many people.

In this chapter, the abortion problem is framed within three time intervals: *pre-pregnancy* (a phase before sexual contact); the nine-month *pregnancy* period; and *post-pregnancy* (the years involving care of a child from birth until maturity). The factors involved in deciding for or against an abortion during pregnancy are discussed elsewhere in this book, but I am especially interested in the pre-pregnancy and post-pregnancy periods, two integrally related time frames that are discussed infrequently. My bifocal consideration is deliberate. In my opinion, too much attention has been given to the pregnancy period and too little concern devoted to either the antecedents of an untimely pregnancy or its sequelae.

The Pre-Pregnancy Period: Adolescent Sexuality

Pregnancy among adolescents is one of the most pressing concerns in our society, and it obviously interrelates with and overlaps the entire problem of abortion. A recent issue of the *American Journal of Public Health* summarized the problem:

> Where does the United States now stand in the process of solving the problem of teenage pregnancy? The statistics have remained stable for a few years; five million sexually active teens and 1.15 million pregnancies (460,000 abortions, 153,000 estimated miscarriages, and 537,000 births of which 268,000 are to unmarried mothers). The outcomes with the most significant social consequences are the pregnancies that result in early out-of-wedlock births, occurring primarily among disadvantaged youngsters in inner cities or rural poverty areas. Most of these conceptions are unplanned yet, in the face of low school achievement and limited employment opportunities, these young pregnant women perceive little reason to terminate the pregnancy or to prevent the next one. Thus the problem of teenage parenthood can be viewed as a symptom of the lack of options available to poor youngsters who are disproportionately members of minority groups.
>
> If this analysis is valid, then the discussion of prevention must be broadened from concerns about access to reproductive health care to concerns about the total environment in which children live and are expected to develop into functioning adults. This is a comprehensive message that has been heard before, but it is as urgent as ever [Dryfoos 1985, 14].

In the decision to engage in sexual contact, two people are presumably consenting to the act. What is involved if those persons are adolescents or unmarried "yuppies"? On what basis do young people make the decision to relate intimately to one another? The onset of puberty, which can occur as early as ten years, marks the beginning of powerful physiological changes and their mental and emotional counterparts. During this time of "pre-pregnancy," adolescents are bombarded with not only their own physical urges but with highly suggestive media and advertising pressures to act upon those urges. As adults, and especially as Christians, we must examine the personal and social forces exerting influence on our next generation. What values are being presented in those formative years? What factors are bringing young people into sexual contact and potential parenthood, so that abortion might become an issue for them? Only in understanding the complex of internal and external influences that make up the total environment in which young people live can we begin to address the problem of sexual activity and pregnancy.

Of course, when a pregnancy occurs, we must also be concerned for the prenatal care of the growing fetus and the physical and psychological welfare of the mother. This area has been covered extensively in the media and elsewhere in this book. As will be discussed later in this chapter, society is relatively ill prepared for dealing with the period after childbirth, with helping a very young mother deal with the challenges involved with raising a child when she herself is immature and not equipped for the task.

The Role of Values in Decision Making

Sociologists are sometimes ridiculed for "elaborating the obvious," so forgive me if I state that it is necessary for a male and female to engage in sexual intercourse before a pregnancy can occur. To elaborate even further, this act involves the biological union of a male sperm and female ovum, resulting in a fertilized egg that is implanted in the woman's uterus for further growth. These physiological facts are irrevocable. A man and woman can never relive a specific act of intercourse with a more effective contraceptive, nor can they duplicate the act in a different time or setting or with "more appropriate" emotions and desires. Under certain biological circumstances, a pregnancy will occur.

Sexual intimacy obviously involves more than psysiology and textbook anatomy. As with other voluntary human activity, it reflects a set of values and a personal choice to act in accordance with or contrary to those values. In the case of young people, the value system may be relatively unformed and not sufficiently internalized to affect their decisions. Consequently, there will be little beyond their basic instincts to influence whether intercourse will be facilitated or inhibited. Of course, some might argue that even adults live without consciously stated personal values and that our society itself reflects weakened values. However, I seriously question this generalization. Values are imbedded to some degree in every person's makeup and are operative in the cultural context, even when they are not recognizable as such. "Valuelessness" itself is also a value. All humans act according to their internal urges and in response to stimuli from their cultural environment, both of which are modified by a set of values.

As personal values develop in an individual, they assume varying degrees of significance and become an integral part of who that person is. It goes without saying that the values inherent among such "antisocial" groups as organized crime, white supremacists, or Shiite terrorists are clearly different from those operative among the Sisters of Charity working with Mother Theresa of Calcutta, for example. There are many conflicting values at work in the subgroups of society. As these values compete and interact, the dominant principles emerge and influence how individuals will act.

The Evangelical Christian and Society's Value System

Here we come to an important entry point for the evangelical who is appropriately concerned about cultural values. The Christian, especially the evangelical Christian, acts upon and advocates Christian values and attempts to persuade others in the society to adopt proper values in their daily living. The man or woman who follows the teachings of Christ will assign worth to all persons and will lobby against the efforts of any individual or group that depreciates others. Since the integrity of every individual is a very precious Christian value, we are against any activity that lowers a person's worth—oppression of women, apartheid, child abuse, to mention but a few examples. Similarly, Christians will support activities that enhance people's worth—education, health care, artistic endeavors, and any other program that provides opportunity and enrichment. As Christians, we "lobby" for cultural aspects based on a high view of personhood. Frankly, we must sadly admit that we are not as skilled and successful in our efforts as we ought to be.

I, like many others, am not satisfied that Christian values have been sufficiently imbedded into the framework of our society. Why? Perhaps it is because we do not promote Christian principles by a process that itself reflects those values. I strenuously object to the recommendations of some Christian leaders that we adopt the tactics of political advocates, who often treat the "enemy" with verbal abuse, rhetorical trickery, harsh journalism, and half-truths, all of which are said to be necessary to achieve effective political action. But how can evangelicals promote Christ's love if they treat unlovingly those with whom they disagree? For example, where abortion is the issue, how can we rationally oppose violence against the fetus by supporting the bombing of abortion clinics? Christians who believe that all truth is God's truth cannot operate effectively if they dispense only the information supportive of "our" side. We cannot justify publishing accusations without scrupulously verifying their truth.

One of the "stickiest" challenges in many social problems is how to promulgate Christian values through a process that is itself permeated by those very values we want to promote. Let me risk sounding a bit like a preacher by calling upon my evangelical colleagues to cease with verbal diatribes, accusatory comments, and near-obscenities, and to advocate Christian values with gentleness, patience, and self-control in a culture looking for values that can make a positive difference. The prophet's role may sometimes be carried out in anger, but never with personal hatred. If we secretly admire Peter for his intemperance in cutting off Malchus's ear—and if we "excuse" our overzealous Christian brothers and sisters by saying they have the right motivation—we should remember that Jesus restored the ear to Malchus' head and in this way brought about healing and restoration. Indeed, the whole point of our Christian message is ultimate healing, reconciliation, and wholeness.

We need, I believe, an additional word about the values promoted by evangelicals and, in particular, an emphasis on salvation as a high priority item. The pluralistic features of modern evangelicalism make me cautious to speak for all of us, but I am certainly on firm ground when I state that encouraging everyone to accept the salvation that Christ offers is one of the most important activities we can carry out. To be sure, sometimes it appears to unbelievers that being "born again" is the only thing some evangelicals care about. In any event, we believe that people who have accepted Christ into their lives have thereby accepted a set of values that can make a significant difference in how they live—how they make moral decisions, how they exercise self-control, and how they define meaningful human interaction.

How adequately have Christians transmitted into society, and specifically into the lives of young people, their values of individual worth and whole-personhood—values supportive of life's sanctity and the importance of the family? We must consider whether these values have become so meaningful that our young people have become committed to them in their own lives. If these characteristics have not become imbedded in our culture, then evangelical Christians must bear at least some of the responsibility.

As Christians, we are often represented in the popular media as trying to impose religious dogma on society by force of law. Or, more crudely put, we are pictured as trying to jam Christian values down the throats of a resistant society. I am against such aggressive methods, since I believe that allegiance to the teachings of Jesus Christ should be a voluntary action. However, I do encourage my fellow Christians to articulate what those values are, realizing that Christian precepts will be mixing with contrary values in the culture. I have confidence that positive Christian principles can compete successfully among sets of alternative values if Christian standard bearers become more skilled in promoting their values. We must use our very lives as vehicles to witness to those eternal truths. One journalist was probably referring to some evangelicals when he wrote of "Bible-thumping rednecks" (Edwards 1986, 40). A bit pejorative, perhaps, but it is true that while leaning heavily on the trustworthiness of Scripture, we often fail to make a definite effort to imbed those teachings into our personal lives and social situations. Unless we fully exemplify proper values in our own lives, we cannot expect to have them make an impact in the culture.

Personal Choice

When we consider the lifestyles and values of young people during what I have called the pre-pregnancy period, we must take into account not only the values they have adopted but the related issue of personal choice—the freedom of individuals to make decisions affecting their actions. Vernie Dale, in a recent pro-life article noted:

> . . . the vast majority of pregnancies that ended in abortion were the result of some modicum of choice. Yet abortion advocates ignore the confusion, pain and despair that are often involved in this choice and zero in on the problem after pregnancy has already occurred. The underlying assumption is the woman does not have, and is not expected to have, any control over her own body until *after* a male partner is finished with it. Only then does she hear talk of "rights." No emphasis is placed on the *before,* or on developing her ability to assert herself before an unwanted pregnancy occurs [Dale 1986, 84–85].

Although Dale seems a bit hard on women, since the same point could be made about men, she is on the right track in referring to the "modicum of choice." A choice must be made rationally and responsibly and in a context of commitment and personal integrity. Dale adds, "Women need to be encouraged to summon up their own inner strengths, their own inner healing, to throw off the cloak of masochistic victimhood and develop their own power to choose" (Dale 1986, 85). I, of course, would adapt her challenge to men, too, and encourage us to throw off negative chauvinism and likewise develop our ability "to choose."

When one honestly assesses how effective the Christian church has been in facilitating the process of helping people freely choose the right values and imbedding those values into our society, especially into the lives of our young people, one admits to a dismal record. Indeed, Christians are losing the struggle. The values that seem to us so credible, sensible, feasible, and appropriate are perceived by some as negative, harsh, punitive, and loveless. Society's dominant and intensive commitment to narcissism has overwhelmed any contravening, wholesome Christian values. And we have conveniently blurred our failure to make a difference by saying, "That's the way the world is," implying that the task is so hopelessly tangled that we give up.

Joy Dryfoos made a strong plea, not for Christian values, but for something analogous—sociological structures that are strongly committed to the prevention of early childbearing. She wrote:

> Social institutions—the schools, the welfare system, labor unions— must be held accountable for the future lives of the children who need and want support and structure. At stake is the plight of millions of children growing up in America with little hope and limited opportunities. The environment that sows the seeds of early parenthood must be altered to include a vision of future opportunities that are realizable as part of the world of the teenager [Dryfoos 1985, 14].

At last, a correct perception of the context that presently encourages extensive sexual contact. It is clear to me that this must be changed so that it is anchored in positive, Christian values.

What am I trying to say? We have overcommitted our energies in the abortion problem to such questions as "When does life begin?" and have failed in the process of inculcating values that would serve as guides to behavior during the pre-pregnancy adolescent period. Christians have a major responsibility for transmitting the positive values of personal integrity, whole-personhood, family cohesion, and authentic love. If we do, we can make a difference against the negative values represented by narcissism, disrespect for personhood, macho-ism, violence, and immediate gratification.

The Post-Pregnancy Period: Helping the Parent

Post-pregnancy is a phase that somehow blends into the life cycle and, like pre-pregnancy, has been neglected. I think that post-pregnancy has been a very difficult phase for evangelicals to handle. On the one hand, the evangelical has been trying to teach commitment and a high view of personhood, warning against premarital sexual contact and praising the strengths of a patriarchal family structure. On the other hand, the evangelical must face the reality of an unmarried teenage mother who has rejected all those teachings and values and ends up with few resources to cope. Christ's teaching demands that we care for the fatherless, the weak, and the vulnerable. This means that as Christ's disciples we are to provide support and comfort, without demeaning the person who did not follow our recommendations.

I recognize the evangelical's poor record in facing the forces at work during post-pregnancy, but—for whatever it's worth—society in general does not cope effectively with the problems of single teenage parents. Pro-life writer Frank Zepezauer raised questions about the way many Americans go about raising children:

> We seem to hate the children we so generously "want." We consign many of them to nannies or to day care centers, hoping they'll find enough commitment to subordinate greed, incompetence and bureaucratic apathy. We hand them latch keys and feed their boundless curiosity with two hundred square inches of dancing electrons. We abandon them to the reciprocating confusions of their peer group and the isolating distortions of their fantasies. We bounce them between warring ex-spouses. We batter and abuse and sexually molest them. We alienate them from their grandparents. We cut them off from their family histories. We drag them into ad hoc alternative families with shifting memberships. We see a million of them a year running away from home, many thousands killing themselves, thousands more killing their spirits. Even when we work to strengthen our marriages and protect our families, we find whole sections of our cities out of bounds to families with children and tax laws that favor the dual-income aristocrats of Yuppieland [Zepezauer 1986, 60].

And feminist Barbara Ehrenreich sounded a similar pessimistic note in the way society relates to post-pregnancy issues:

> When society does step in to help out a poor woman attempting to raise children on her own, all that it customarily has to offer is some government-surplus cheese, a monthly allowance so small it would barely keep a yuppie male in running shoes, and the contemptuous epithet "welfare cheat." It would be far more reasonable to honor the survivors of pregnancy in childbirth with at least the same respect and special benefits that we give, without a second thought, to veterans of foreign wars [Ehrenreich 1986, 91].

In turning our attention to the abortion problem, I call upon my Christian brothers and sisters to align themselves with the agonies of single teenage parents who did not follow the recommended path. Their current situation is very difficult, making it likely that they are now searching to learn if and how Christ relates to them.

During the summers of 1985 and 1986, the Illinois Department of Child and Family Services conducted a program for teenage mothers. They brought the young mothers and their children to a camp setting in Wisconsin. While others cared for their infants, a professional staff taught these mothers principles of parenting, self-respect, nutrition, and similar topics. Evangelicals, many of whom are active in camping programs, might offer a modified program, drawing on the growing number of Christian single parents to serve as teaching staff. In this way, we turn ourselves to focus upon many of the unwanted pregnancies and become vehicles for the Holy Spirit to do his work among the fatherless, a group toward whom Jesus showed specific compassion.

The demographics of our cities show very large numbers of single parents with small children. They are usually poor and ethnically black or Hispanic. Perhaps the time has come for specific persons on the ministerial staff of each urban church to commit themselves to a neglected field "white unto harvest."

These thoughts are simple beginnings to what might develop into a much longer listing of creative ideas to assist with an important neglected part of the teenage pregnancy problem.

Conclusions

This paper calls for a wide-angle lens in focusing on the abortion issue. It recommends that evangelicals, in particular, look upon pregnancy as an issue inextricably woven into personal and social forces operative before the first trimester begins and long after the third ends. As faithful disciples, we are to advocate Christian values as skillfully and as effectively as we can, especially reaching out to the youth who need guiding values for their lives. Furthermore, if our advocated values are rejected, we are to align ourselves with the rootless—nonjudgmentally and with a spirit of Christian compassion.

References and Further Reading

Clymer, A. 1986. Abortion and ambivalence: One issue that seems to defy a yes or no. *New York Times* February 23:22E.

Dale, V. 1986. Abortion is immoral. In *Abortion: Opposing viewpoints* (83–87). St. Paul: Greenhaven Press.

Dryfoos, J. G. 1985. A time for new thinking about teenage pregnancy. *American Journal of Public Health* 75:13–14.

Edwards, J. 1986. The silent scream proves the fetus is human. In *Abortion: Opposing viewpoints* (38–41). St. Paul: Greenhaven Press.

Ehrenreich, B. 1986. Abortion is not immoral. In *Abortion: Opposing viewpoints* (88–91). St. Paul: Greenhaven Press.

Harris, J. C. 1921. Wonderful Tar-Baby story. In *Uncle Remus: His songs and his sayings*. New York: Meredith.

Split verdict: What Americans think about abortion. 1985. *Policy Review* 32 (Spring):18–19.

Zepezauer, F. S. 1986. Abortion should not be a woman's personal choice. In *Abortion: Opposing viewpoints* (57–61). St. Paul: Greenhaven Press.

14

Crisis-Pregnancy Ministry
Overcoming the Illusion of "Choice"
Diane S. and Jeffrey K. Greenberg

This essay is ultimately about real people trapped in the real world of unwanted pregnancies. What is written is not a portrayal of theoretical or abstract problems. Much has already been said about the taking of life that ends so many crisis pregnancies. We are well supported by a wealth of data from many sources, including the information contained elsewhere in this book, all of which validates our pro-life beliefs. Unfortunately, righteous opinions have not affected a change in abortion laws or practice. This is analogous to our compact car having the theoretical right-of-way at an intersection, but no actual advantage over the rapidly approaching runaway truck that in this case has no respect for our position. It has become obvious to many activists (cf. Young 1983; Whitehead 1985; Willke & Willke 1985) that practical service involvement must accompany efforts in pro-life education. The church speaks best and loudest when it expresses true sacrificial love. There are many avenues of pro-life involvement for those willing to work (see, for example, the list in chapter 6 of this volume). All this work is important but none more so than firsthand contact with those in crisis. And few things can be more detrimental than misconceptions about the circumstances of these women.

It might be asked what qualifications a homemaker and a geologist have for authoring the following article. We two, wife and husband, serve together as the parents of four children. All of these special people are adopted. Our younger two children, both daughters, were born with physical disorders—one with spina bifida and hydrocephalus and the other with a spinal-cord tumor. Other pertinent experience includes our direct participation in the work of crisis-pregnancy services and in educational aspects of the respect for life.

No Freedom in Choice

Advocates of the "freedom of choice" doctrine foster an illusion. By definition, "choice" assumes that there are at least two options that can be taken. Pro-choice ideology also demands that a pregnant woman always has the right to choose between abortion and its natural alternative, birth. The illusionary character of the freedom to choose in this context takes various forms. First of all, it can be well argued that this freedom as a right is entirely the 1973 fabrication of a biased Supreme Court (cf. McDowell 1984; Buckley 1985; Nakell 1985; Noonan 1985). As Joseph Sobran has observed (1984, 13–14), what the adamant "freedom" proponents really want is not expanded "choice" but abortion itself. By eliminating rhetoric, pro-choice correctly translates as pro-abortion. The ultimate clincher in the appraisal of "choice" is that the freedom in question does not even exist. Until about the last five years, attitudes that dominated our culture had often made birth appear as a very undesirable alternative to abortion, and in a growing number of actual crisis situations, birth was not seen as a credible option. How do we know this? In the second part of this paper, we will share the circumstances of women and girls representing literally thousands who describe their crisis pregnancies as a one-way street. Severe lifestyle difficulties are well illustrated by the women interviewed in Franke (1978). Social structures and personal relationships, including parents, sexual partners, co-workers, and friends, characteristically exert intense pressure on the pregnant woman to do the "easy" thing. When the world suddenly imposes a threatened loss of love and security, it *is* easier to rapidly end a new life than to oppose overwhelming coercion for many long months. Add to this the realization that birth means either parenthood or relinquishing through adoption the life chosen. Given all these circumstances, one can hardly castigate the poor souls who feel propelled into taking their own child's life.

The responsibility for stopping the monstrous tide of abortion-on-demand belongs to God's people. Through human efforts, we may be able to divert one attempted abortion, but what about the next time or times this woman is again pregnant as a result of her lifestyle? Only the gospel has the power to change the dreadful circumstances that trap women into crisis pregnancies. Volunteers who fully believe that abortion means death—and that the gospel means life—serve as the real instruments of healing. Conversely, individuals or groups, even professing evangelicals who are not convinced of abortion's evils or of the sovereign power of Christ to change lives, are themselves part of the problem.

Wolves in Sheep's Clothing

Again, we will assume that through this book or other available sources, the reader is aware of the multifaceted basis for a Christian's pro-life attitude. Any casual newspaper reader or television watcher is probably also familiar with the arguments defending current abortion practices. Included among abortion's defenders are some religious factions, most under the "liberal" umbrella of the Religious Coalition for Abortion Rights, or RCAR. Diversity within RCAR is united by a low view of Scripture and a corresponding rejection of biblical ethics. Certain synods, conferences, and congregations—but, more commonly individual clergy within the Lutheran Church in America, United Methodist Church, Presbyterian Church in America, United Church of Christ, Unitarian-Universalist Association, and some Jewish groups—adhere to RCAR's statement that

> Individuals have the right to make responsible personal decisions without unnecessary government interference. Freedom of choice—whether it involves completing or terminating a pregnancy—represents the functioning of that right. Implicit in "Freedom of Choice" is the belief that the dignity of women should not be abridged by having decisions that so affect their lives and futures made by others.

Our Right to Choose (Harrison 1983), an influential book on pro-abortion apologetics by a professor of "Christian ethics" at Union Theological Seminary, is a good example of a radical social agenda as opposed to any evangelical biblical viewpoint. The three key words in the title—"our," "right," and "choose"—are given the author's own meanings, in conflict with their biblical usage. In keeping with pro-abortion dogma, her use of "our" refers only to women. This in effect isolates the pregnant woman from the potential influence of others, including her husband, boyfriend, or family. The Bible clearly expresses that women and men were made to exist in vital relationship to each other. Adam was only complete with Eve, and we can assume that the reverse dependence was also true. The biblical "our" is forever threefold: woman, man, and God. The selfish "our" of abortion seems defiantly militant but in the real world actually reveals a terrible loneliness.

"Right" is indisputably demanding, as used by Harrison, but it is a word without biblical counterpart. God's grace alone allows great privileges, not rights, and included among them is the awesome necessity of choosing. It is ironic that both Professor Harrison and Moses call for the exercise of choice. Harrison represents the viewpoint of autonomy, where any personal choice, including abortion, can be "good." In the thirtieth chapter of Deuteronomy, Moses sets forth the options of our free will to choose—option A: sin, the broad path to destruction; or option B: obedience, the narrow way to life.

Evangelicals might expect a broad pro-choice philosophy from "liberals." It is more difficult to understand the recent (as of 1986) publication of articles and books by evangelicals who also defend the choice of abortion. In some of these cases there is expressed a sense of abhorrence of abortion that contradicts the overall conclusion that freedom of choice in this matter is somehow justified. Note that discussion in these new public statements focuses not just on the hard cases of threat to maternal life, rape, incest, or handicapped fetuses, but in effect also gives room for abortion-on-demand, that is, for *any* reason!

Certain evangelical authors who are sympathetic to the illusion of choice speak with the authority of experts in various disciplines. Gareth Jones, author of *Brave New People* (1985), has undergone much evangelical criticism for his equivocal position on abortion, especially relative to such cases of hardship as unborn children with genetic defects. Dr. Jones draws ethical judgments from his field of anatomy. Dr. Robert Wennberg of Westmont College sets out in a 1985 book, *Life in the Balance,* to "unemotionally" investigate the abortion issue from the point of view of a philosophy professor. After declaring abortion "morally objectionable," Wennberg justifies a woman's freedom to choose an abortion on the basis of philosophical arguments. Most notable among his conclusions are the last three of five on page 173:

> (3) there is an increase in the value of the fetus as it develops, and we should be willing to accept progressively heavier burdens to safeguard the fetus as it increases in value, (4) the woman has the right to decide which burdens she will or will not bear, and (5) though the woman may act wrongly by not bearing a particular burden, nevertheless criminal law ought not be allowed to make the decision for her.

Richard Bube, a respected evangelical spokesman, is an engineering professor at Stanford University. In the pages of the *Journal of the American Scientific Affiliation* (1984), Bube has given outspoken defense of Jones. Book reviews in the same publication (1986) also show Bube's admiration for Jones's and Wennberg's conclusions.

The above theoreticians are joined by Mark Olson, who is editor of *The Other Side,* a magazine emphasizing social justice from a left-wing evangelical perspective. In the October 1986 issue, Olson takes separate opportunities, in one commentary and two book reviews (including *Life in the Balance*), to express his opinion on the abortion issue. Although he is strongly anti-sexism, anti-militarism, anti-nuclear, anti-poverty, anti-capital punishment, anti-apartheid, and so on, Olson is certainly *not* anti-abortion. Olson admits that access to abortion is that one social issue where his opposition cannot be adequately justified. While we believe his attitude toward abortion is inconsistent with fellow Christians, it is certainly consistent with non-Christian and even anti-Christian agendas. Nowhere does Olson mention the relationship of abortion to human struggles. He, too, speaks with a perspective far removed from the real world. So that the readers can make their own appraisals, a sample of Olson's commentary (1986, 36) follows:

> . . . but unlike those who flatly condemn all abortions, I refuse to fathom the biological process that leads to such beauty. I refuse to untangle the mystery and declare with certainty that I know when and how independent life begins and where and when some all-important dividing line is crossed including hard and fast *distinctions between the world of humans, animals, and plants.* . . .
>
> I grimace at abortion. I'm pained by those who champion it. I cry out for those whose only choices seem bad. But to take a clear stand against it requires certain *inferences from Scripture and science that seem to lack any rational basis.* I don't know why God hasn't given us a clear yes or no on abortion, why God hasn't told us what to do in every difficult situation. But I know that when God has been this silent, when God has left us in such a quandry, I must be very careful about *imposing on others* my tenuous biblical inferences, however important they might *feel.*

Our italics in the above quotes indicate that the viewpoints of Olson et al. are remarkably different from those presented in the present book. Does the disparity simply reflect a healthy diversity among evangelicals? We think not. Without going into more detailed analysis, let it suffice for us to pose a few possible reasons why some outspoken evangelicals take these compromising positions:

1. To reiterate, a common denominator among Jones, Wennberg, Bube, and Olson is that they are outside the experience and looking in. Arguments based on real pregnancy crises are not made.

2. As exhibited particularly by Bube's and Olson's writings, there is a certain Falwell-phobia, that is, a reactionary swing away from the Christian right and its agenda(s) and toward a more "intellectual" or socially-in-vogue centrist-to-leftist philosophy.

3. Abortion lingers in some pronouncements as a last-resort measure in an attitude of Band-Aid defeatism. This is as if to say that although contraceptive practices *should* get this job done, abortion may be necessary to stem the threat of overpopulation and teen pregnancies. With that attitude, abortion also avoids the many unpleasantries involving severely handicapped newborns.

4. The described authorities stand at biblical odds with the consensus pro-life theology (again, well presented by Wheaton College faculty in this volume). Wennberg exemplifies those who do some exploring in Scripture, only to find it subordinate to purely human invention—in his case, hypothetical philosophy. The quote from Olson's article explicitly shows a double standard. God is said to be silent on abortion, but is he really so loud and clear on nuclear weapons, capital punishment, feminism, and so on, as Olson's advocacy implies? If Christians honestly seek a scriptural basis to defend unborn people from abortion, let them read the articles herein, especially those by Hoffmeier, Bullock, Gordon, and Lake. We strongly assert that in some cases it is an avoidance of biblical principles and a naivete toward crisis pregnancies that keep individual believers from opposing abortion. For more information on the above as well as additional cases of rhetoric by evangelicals, see Paul Fowler's book, *Abortion—Toward an Evangelical Consensus.*

The above discussion exposes certain errors that can keep the church and individual Christians from responsible service. The other half of our thesis is perhaps even more important. We want to encourage action against abortion through the very positive ministry to people involved in a crisis pregnancy.

Personal Background

I [Diane] can never write or talk about pro-life concerns without briefly telling how I came to be pro-life and why I am compelled to be *actively* pro-life today. At the time of the Supreme Court *Roe* v. *Wade* decision in 1973, I was in college. Abortion was a very controversial topic on college campuses at that time, as it remains today. Back then, I pretty much bought the "woman's choice" argument, even though I knew that I would never choose an abortion for myself. Perhaps some of you reading this also feel that way.

I remained passively pro-choice from 1973 until 1977. On a Friday morning in November 1977 (exactly nine years ago, as I write this) a social worker placed a four-and-a-half–pound, eight-week-old infant boy in my arms. He was the fruit of another woman's womb, the product, literally, of another woman's labor, but he became my firstborn son. As I parented that very precious child, I began to be haunted by the knowledge that his sixteen-year-old biological mother could have chosen abortion ("safe," "legal," "quick," "cheap," "easy"). Had she done so, I would not have Derek. It suddenly became inescapably clear that abortion did not merely terminate a pregnancy; it took the life of—killed—a child. In no other situation in this country do we allow individuals to *choose* to take another's life. At that point, I realized that I could no longer be pro-choice. So I became passively pro-life. That change was actually much less than it might seem, and it is probably the same point at which many of you are. I was convinced that abortion was fundamentally wrong, but I cared little and did even less about it.

It was not until 1983 that Jeff and I began to act on our pro-life convictions. We joined our area Right to Life group and began reading some of the books and seeing some of the films on the abortion issue. By this time, Jeff and I had three adopted children, one of whom was physically handicapped. We lived with daily reminders of how precious "unwanted" lives were. Then I became a counselor (this term is not used in a professional sense) with a twenty-four–hour crisis-pregnancy phone line. After a year of volunteering with the hot line, I accepted a job as the first director of a newly opening crisis-pregnancy center (CPC).

Why *Not* Abortion?

When a client at the CPC had a positive pregnancy test, one of the first things I would do after giving her the test result was to present her with her actual options. She could have an abortion, carry the baby to term and parent it (single or married), or carry the baby to term and place it for adoption. Barring a spontaneous miscarriage, one of those alternatives *would* occur within the next nine months. For many clients, this was the hardest part of the counseling session. They had to accept the reality of their situation and realized that all their choices were hard. Their best choice, not to get pregnant, had already been forfeited. The choices they were left with would all be difficult and unpleasant and would have long-lasting effects on their lives.

The single most common comment I heard from women intending to choose abortion as the way out of their crisis was "I have no choice." They did not want to have an abortion but truly saw it as the only possible solution to their problem. Many of the women were mainly concerned with not hurting others—their boyfriend or their parents. Others saw no way that raising a child would be possible financially or as a single parent. The CPC I worked at was located in a university town. Many clients cited interference with an education in which they and/or their boyfriend had already invested many years and many thousands of dollars as their reason for "having to have" an abortion. Still others had extremely difficult or tragic personal and family situations. Almost all the women I counseled saw abortion not as a "good" choice, but as their *only* choice. CPCs exist to provide women with another choice and with the courage to make it.

The circumstances pushing a client toward abortion were always truly difficult ones. I saw only one client in over two years of counseling who had a casual, even flippant, attitude toward her intended abortion. Her comment, which I will never forget, was: "It doesn't bother me about killing the baby, but will it hurt *me*?" If you are not already firmly pro-life, working in a CPC will do little toward convincing you. The more tragic cases sometimes challenged my own pro-life beliefs. It was very tempting to see abortion as a good solution.

Why *not* abortion? There is only one answer that will suffice. Not every act of sexual intercourse results in conception (just ask the thousands of barren couples, like ourselves). When God does permit the creation of a new life, desired or undesired, we must regard it as Sovereign God-created life, and therefore we cannot take that life. Any lesser reason for being against abortion will not stand. If you are against the 98 percent of abortions performed for reasons of "convenience" (cf. Cushner 1983) but think exceptions should be available for the "hard cases," you have drawn an arbitrary line and are saying, in effect, "God's providence is sufficient for these relatively easy circumstances, but not for these harder ones" (see Isa. 59:1).

There is a God-ordained sacred bond between a mother and a child, born or unborn. It is illustrated in Isaiah 49:14 when Israel has accused God of forsaking her. He answers by asking a rhetorical question in Isaiah 49:15a (NIV), "Can a mother forget the baby at her breast and fail to have compassion on the child of her womb?" (authors' translation). The tone is incredulous, and the expected answer is obviously an emphatic "No!" Yet, in today's society, women are continually being both implicitly and explicitly encouraged to "forget" and to fail to have "compassion" on the children of their wombs. That this time would come is foreseen by the rest of God's response to Israel in Isaiah 49:15b, 16.

Abortion violates this sacred bond. Thus, every abortion has at least two victims, and there are two lives at stake—the physical life of the baby and the spiritual and emotional life of the mother. Choices always bring along with them their consequences. As a pastor put it in a sermon long ago, "You can't go around sowing wild oats and then pray for crop failure." When a woman chooses abortion, she is also choosing the physical, emotional, and spiritual consequences that will inevitably follow. Most women have no understanding of these consequences at the time they decide to have an abortion. It is exactly because of this that the ministry of CPCs is so necessary.

The Structure and Services of Crisis-Pregnancy Centers

In order to make an impact in the area of abortion, Christians *must* become actively pro-life. This does not mean bombing abortion clinics or physically blocking their doors. Such tactics are more *anti*-abortion than they are *pro*-life. To be pro-life means to care as much for the woman in the midst of a crisis pregnancy as for the baby. Anything done for her directly impacts her unborn child as well. To be actively pro-life involves attempting to meet the needs of pregnant women. CPCs represent an active pro-life ministry of Christians who are reaching out with practical help to women with crisis pregnancies.

All services provided by a CPC are free and confidential. The CPC of which I was director was affiliated with Christian Action Council. As with most such centers, we were entirely funded by contributions raised locally. All of our counselors were Christians who volunteered their time after receiving about eighteen hours of training.

Each client seen at a CPC has her own unique circumstances, which pinpoint her needs and the type of help the CPC might be able to offer her. Some women simply need a free pregnancy test, but most women who come to the center also need counseling. For the most part, these clients are young, unmarried, and unexpectedly pregnant. Their greatest need is to come to terms with the reality of their pregnancy and to make a decision about their own and their baby's futures. This is literally a life-or-death decision. It is most certainly the biggest decision they have ever faced, and they are often isolated and ill-equipped for making it. These clients require complete and accurate information in order to make an informed decision, yet they usually have only one contact with the CPC.

Other services that most CPCs provide are referrals to doctors, lawyers (usually related to paternity suits or adoption), and social or welfare services. Some clients have emergency or long-term need for housing. This can be arranged by the CPC if the client is no longer a minor, and it is always in the home of a Christian family. Some women have needs that continue throughout their pregnancies—transportation to doctors' appointments, help with other small children, and/or ongoing emotional support and friendship. Many clients come back for maternity clothes, baby clothes, cribs, car seats, and so on.

Working at the CPC was somewhat like the four years I spent working on an ambulance—I never knew what kind of a problem might need handling. Some days I went home feeling wonderful, other days wretched. Always, as our statement of principle said, the CPC was "committed to presenting the gospel of our Lord to women with crisis pregnancies—both in word and in deed."

The best way to explain the various services of a CPC is to look at actual clients' stories. Look for the clients' needs, and then see how the CPC, as an outreach of the Christian community, can meet those needs. (With the exception of Hagar and Ishmael, all names have been changed. Some details may also have been slightly altered to further protect identities.)

Hagar. Conceived in a love triangle that would do any soap opera proud, the unborn Ishmael presented his mother with one of history's first recorded crisis pregnancies. God himself then did history's first crisis-pregnancy counseling. His response to Hagar should be a model for our own efforts.

Genesis 16 tells the story of Abram, Sarai and her Egyptian maidservant, Hagar. When Hagar conceived the child of Abram that Sarai could not, the two women no longer got along. The feelings of jealousy, anger, superiority, and possessiveness that must have been experienced are not detailed. They are not difficult to imagine, though, as similar situations still occur today. The effects of sin and of failing to trust God for Abram's promised descendant are also operating in this story. Genesis only tells us that once Hagar had conceived, she looked on Sarai with contempt. Sarai complained to Abram, who like many men even now, refused to get involved. He told Sarai to "do what is good in your sight." Verse 6 then tells us that Sarai "treated her harshly, and she fled from her presence" (NAS). Then Hagar, unmarried and pregnant, became a runaway slave, wandering around the land of Canaan. Not many situations, even today, could be more desperate.

God then directly intervened to meet Hagar's needs. We are told that "the angel of the LORD found her." Calling her by name, he asked her where she was going. Hagar had no answer except to say she was fleeing from Sarai. The Lord instructed Hagar to return to her mistress and submit to her. He then spoke to Hagar about her future and that of her baby, and she was assured that the Lord "has given heed to your affliction." The Lord was aware, of course, that Hagar was "with child." Indeed, he told her that she would bear a son, and even what he would be named. Then the Lord told Hagar what her still-unborn child would be like as a grown man and revealed some of his plan for Ishmael's life to her.

The Lord's handling of Hagar's crisis has many things in common with what a CPC can do to help a woman today. The fact that the Lord *found* Hagar and called her by name was indicative of his deep concern for her. Though most women come to a CPC on their own initiative, not the other way around, the deep and personal concern of the volunteers is one of the most important hallmarks of this ministry. It also distinctly sets CPCs apart from the abortion business. CPCs exist because people care; abortion centers exist to make money.

Since the fact of Hagar's pregnancy was already known to both God and Hagar, he did not need to offer her a free pregnancy test. He did, however, deal first with her most immediate need—a place to live while pregnant. He not only sent her home, which is often the best place for any pregnant woman to go, but he also gave her advice about her attitude, which would make the living arrangement work. Many of today's pregnant teens need just such advice, though perhaps phrased a little differently.

Besides solving the problem of Hagar's housing, which would also supply her other physical and material needs throughout her pregnancy, the Lord spoke to her at length about her baby. He demonstrated to Hagar that he knew about her pregnancy, that he cared, that there was a reason he had allowed this to happen to her. The most important thing that can be said to a woman with an unwanted pregnancy is that God cares and has a plan for her and her child. Even when the circumstances of a child's conception are outside of God's will, God has a plan and a purpose for the life of that child, and he stands ready to forgive and to supply all the needs of the mother. This truth can be conveyed to virtually every woman who comes to a CPC, even when presenting her with the gospel, in an evangelical sense, cannot.

I have shared the story of Hagar with many clients at the CPC. Almost invariably, they respond to it. They can identify with the feelings of jealousy and anger. Though not actually homeless, many women come to the CPC feeling very isolated by virtue of not having told anyone of their suspected pregnancy and are, in a real sense, "fleeing" from parents, boyfriend, or peers. They also expect to be "treated harshly." They usually already know about men who don't want to get involved. (During the time I worked at a CPC, I saw only two couples. In every other case, the woman came either alone or with a friend, but not the father of her child. We have much to teach young men about male responsibility!)

Now that we have seen how God responded to Hagar's crisis pregnancy, let us look at some more recent examples of women who came to a CPC looking for help.

Kelly. My first CPC session with a client happened even before construction of our office was complete. A friend who worked with her had heard an announcement about the CPC on a local Christian radio station. The friend reached me at my home. Kelly was already ten weeks' pregnant and considering abortion. She wanted someone to talk to. They lived about fifty miles away and both worked full-time, but Kelly's friend was willing to drive her over one evening after work. We arranged to meet in the kitchen of the professional building where our office was to be located. Since it would be at night, no one else would be using the kitchen. We met on Valentine's Day—a sad reminder that love is not all roses.

Kelly was twenty-five and unmarried. She had had a previous abortion and also had a four-year-old daughter. This was thus her third pregnancy, each with a different man. She had no real interest in this baby's father and was primarily concerned about her ability to raise two children alone. Though she knew it would be hard, she agreed she probably could handle it. Her own parents were in the area and she believed they would be supportive. Kelly very much loved her daughter. She had not liked having her previous abortion, but it had not really bothered her either. She was very unsure of what to do about her current pregnancy.

After gathering all this information, I was quite unsure of how to proceed. Because I had just finished counselor-training classes, I went "by the book." That included providing a client with information and pictures on fetal development. Once our office was open, we had a videotape for clients to watch, which would present this information. Because I could not set that up in the kitchen, I had brought along some pictures. I almost skipped them—surely a twenty-five-year-old woman in the middle of her third pregnancy knew how babies developed! That was the first of many wrong assumptions I made about people while working at the CPC. Kelly looked at the ten-week-old fetus with amazement. She was just at this point in her pregnancy, and her previous abortion had been at about that time also. Literally, one look convinced her, although not all cases were so easy. "I never knew it looked like that," she said. Kelly had been told at the abortion center that her baby was only a "blob of tissue."

Kelly decided against abortion immediately, but we talked some more about managing money, time, and other practical concerns with two children. As she was getting ready to leave, she said, "I still keep thinking that I could go to the abortion center and all these problems would be over within ten minutes." My heart skipped a beat, because that *did* seem to be true—even to me sometimes—and I was stuck for an answer. Then I found myself saying, "So would all the joys." Kelly's face lit up instantly; her whole manner changed. "Yes," she said softly, "that's true." I realized, too, that it was God's truth!

Nancy. Ten years before I met her, Nancy had been in an automobile accident and had sustained serious internal injuries. On the advice of a doctor, she had had an abortion the year before. Now she was pregnant again. The same doctor had again recommended abortion for health reasons. Thirty-five, unmarried, and a career woman, Nancy thought this might be her last chance for children. She wanted this baby. Could we help?

We referred Nancy to one of only three pro-life doctors (Family Practice or Ob/Gyn) in our area. Before the CPC opened, we had sent questionnaires to all area doctors who delivered babies. The questionnaire asked if they ever performed or referred for abortions, if they would accept referrals from the CPC, and if they would waive their usual fees for a client with financial problems. Many doctors responded, but only three were pro-life. They were a real blessing to us and to many of our clients.

Though Nancy was eventually referred again to a high-risk pregnancy clinic, the initial positive support she received from our doctor gave her the courage to carry her pregnancy to term. She experienced no problems and had a healthy baby girl. To borrow a cliché, mother and baby are doing fine.

The Korean couple. The thick accent made understanding the man on the phone very difficult. Finally I got the following information. He and his wife were international students who had recently arrived at the university in town. His wife, who spoke no English, was pregnant. They had no insurance, and because they were not citizens they could not qualify for medical assistance. They had decided on abortion as their only possible option. Their pastor suggested they call the center before going through with it. Once again, we referred them to a pro-life doctor, who charged them nothing for prenatal care or the delivery. The Catholic hospital arranged an extended-payment plan for the hospital costs.

An announcement telling of the birth of their son arrived at the CPC. His Korean first name was that of the couple's pastor. His middle name was American—that of his mother's doctor!

The Mexican family. A frantic call from a county social worker came in to the CPC one day. It was not unusual to receive referrals from social workers. Even though most of them did not agree with our stand on abortion, they knew we could help clients who "fell through the cracks" in the welfare system. This was one such case. The social worker had learned of an extended family of eleven Mexicans who had just arrived in town. They had found a two-bedroom, unfurnished apartment—their furniture consisted of just one table. The family included a fifteen-month-old and a two-month-old. They had arrived from Texas in the middle of winter with only the clothes they were wearing, and we had two feet of snow on the ground! The social worker had started their processing for welfare payments, food stamps, and other assistance, but it would take a few weeks. Could we help with their immediate needs?

This family just about cleaned us out. The CPC kept on hand used maternity and baby clothes and baby furniture, all of which had been donated. One trip to the center yielded two bulging bags of baby clothes (one for each child), one crib, one cradle, one changing table, two car seats, and a stroller. These were all routine items for us to distribute, but this family's needs were more than routine. And God had known they would be coming! Several weeks before, someone had delivered some used furniture for one of our counseling rooms, two chairs and a sofa. The furniture was not appropriate for our use, and we had stuck it in our basement storeroom, making a mental note to call Goodwill. It was still cluttering up the storeroom when the Mexican family moved to town. A second trip to the center with a borrowed pickup truck yielded at least the beginnings of their living room. While helping to haul the sofa up two flights of stairs from the basement, I wondered why it was so heavy. When the bottom fell out, we all discovered it was a sleeper sofa! They were so grateful to have it—and we were so grateful to get rid of it. God is good!

The above situation did not even involve the issue of abortion. The children were already born. However, to tell any woman not to have an abortion without being willing to help once the child is born, puts us on the receiving end of the warning in James 2:15–17.

Tammy. Many women try to deny the fact of their pregnancy for as long as possible. They put off having a pregnancy test, hoping their period will start "tomorrow." Tammy was the most profound case of such denial I have ever known. She called and made an appointment to come for a pregnancy test. But when she arrived, I hesitated; she was obviously pregnant! Filling out the client-information sheet with her, I found out she had not had a period for six months. I also found out she was a sixteen-year-old high-school sophomore. Her parents were divorced. She lived with her mother and her eighteen-year-old mentally retarded brother. She had been the victim of incest before her parents' divorce. Asked if she was sexually active, she said no, but added that she had been "sort of raped" by several boys at a Christmas party during which everyone was drinking heavily. When I asked if she had any other medical problems, she told me about severe backaches that she had been having for the past month. She denied any symptoms of pregnancy and said she had not felt any movement of the baby.

While Tammy's pregnancy test was running, we talked some more. She told me that everyone in school was talking about her being pregnant. She also described how she had to lie down on her bed and hold her breath every morning in order to get her jeans fastened (remember those backaches?). When I told her the results of her very positive pregnancy test, Tammy sighed, "I guess I'm the last to know."

Before Tammy left, I made an appointment for her with one of the pro-life doctors, talked about how to tell her mother, and gave her some information about adoption. I also gave her several pairs of maternity pants—and my home phone number. The following Saturday she called me at home to say that she had told her mother and things were going "all right." She wanted the phone number of the adoption agency. "You know," she said, in closing, "ever since you gave me those maternity pants, I've been feeling the baby move like crazy." In just two days, Tammy had already made much progress in coming to terms with her situation.

Annie. I never actually met Annie, but I talked with her on the phone. She was a thirty-one-year-old woman from a middle-class background. She called the CPC with the hope of finding an authority who could give a good reason to her "boyfriend" why she should not have another abortion. Annie had two living children in addition to four who had been killed in abortions. Annie had never been married, but Carl, her live-in partner, was the father of one of the living children and of all but one of those aborted. This time was different and Carl was furious. "I'm so tired of all this," Annie said. "I just know it's not right. Someone told me I might even have to have a hysterectomy. Is that true? I need to know. If I bring Carl, would you talk to him?" Annie and Carl had no way of getting to the center, so I volunteered Jeff to both drive them there and help with the counseling, especially with talking to Carl.

Jeff later told me what had happened when they arrived. They had not been there five minutes before Carl accused the center of "pushing Christian morality." He refused to discuss Annie's concerns; nor could he be encouraged to ask any questions about the center. He left the office cursing, without Annie. She did not apologize for Carl, but she immediately talked about her life with him. Words and emotion poured out of Annie for the next hour and a half. Carl had said he would listen to her only if someone credible (to him) could "prove" that another abortion would harm her. Carl, a graduate student, and his parents (both college faculty members) were together pressing Annie to go through with "the procedure." Of the only two other people she considered her friends, one felt she should do whatever she wanted, whereas the other said that

Annie would be "nuts" to keep another child. Real support to bear her child was lacking, but support was what she needed if her choice could be honored. Carl threatened to remove his financial support and his companionship. She admitted that there was no actual love between them. Annie repeatedly voiced her concern that Carl was showing the effects of a drug dependency, and she also suspected that he was sexually involved with others, including at least one man.

In the time spent with Annie, all that could be done was to listen and offer support. Before Annie left, she confided that nothing could change her mind in favor of experiencing another abortion. She really did not want to "kill my baby," but was afraid of losing Carl. The counselor and Jeff each gave Annie a hug; her eyes showed that she deeply appreciated the empathy expressed. Each of them also offered to bring her into their church families. She thanked them, but with regrets, because God "would not want" someone like her.

As in Annie's case, there is often the feeling that much we would like to share with a client goes unsaid. Much necessary healing is still left to be done after that first encounter. For Annie and many others, we persist in trying to offer anything we can to them whenever we can. Each encounter may be the last. We are left with joy in knowing that Annie's child was born. There is also a lingering pain because she continued to live where and how her troubles originated. In the following months, Annie was not willing to return to the center for support. Her life at home had become more difficult. Her relationship with Carl had further declined, but something kept her from accepting our friendship.

Annie's story is neither victory nor defeat for our crisis-pregnancy ministry. It does represent the almost captivating power of a destructive lifestyle. Perhaps we should take solace that our counsel at least gave Annie a *real* sense of freedom in making her choice.

Amy. Her circumstances were not the worst I ever encountered, but I remember Amy as the most difficult case of all. I am still sad when I think of her.

Amy was in her early twenties and living on her own. She had had a previous abortion and was planning to have another if her pregnancy test was positive. It was. She was about ten weeks pregnant. Information and pictures on fetal development left her no doubt that a baby's life was at stake. Amy's previous abortion had been decided by her parents when she was only fifteen. Now the decision was hers alone. These facts made justifying her decision to abort much more difficult. She left in tears, and her distress was even greater than when she came.

That was one of the days I left feeling wretched, and my distress was great also. I wondered how adding to Amy's guilt feelings could qualify as helping her. Were the accusations leveled at CPCs right, after all? Should we be doing this? What would Jesus have done?

On my way home in the car, I thought of many of the people whom Jesus had encountered: the Samaritan woman at the well, the woman caught in adultery, and those who had been healed, raised from the dead, had demons cast out. All seemed to have responded immediately to his words. But then I remembered the story of a man who chose not to accept Jesus' truth about his life. Each of the Synoptic Gospels tells the story of the rich young ruler (Matt. 19:16–22; Mark 10:17–22; Luke 18:18–23). The story ends: "he went away sorrowful. . . ." I have always thought of those words as one of the most poignant comments in Scripture. That day I had seen for myself the distress of someone who had also heard the truth but "went away sorrowful."

Jeff later observed that my hurt at witnessing this must be some of what our Lord constantly feels as he watches over us. Those wise words gave me insight into the mind and heart of God. Ezekiel 2:7 states, "And you shall speak my words to them, whether they hear or refuse to hear. . . ." That, then, is the answer to my question "Should we be doing this?" Yes! But the greatest assurance comes from Jesus' words to his disciples immediately following the rich young ruler's departure: "What is impossible with men is possible with God" (Luke 18:27; cf. Matt. 19:26; Mark 10:27).

Sally. Already knowing she was pregnant, Sally came to our center. She had come to town from another state to stay with friends during her pregnancy and had made a firm decision to place her baby for adoption. Sally had good understanding of all that would involve—she was adopted also. Basically all she needed was a referral to a doctor in the area and information about adoption.

Sally was in her mid-twenties. She had become a Christian in high school; no one else in her family was a believer. She was a college graduate and worked as a manager at a sporting goods store, where she came in contact with many young men. One of them was Brian, also in his mid-twenties and a college graduate, and a rising young professional. Brian was not a Christian. He and Sally had been dating for about a year before becoming sexually active. Sally knew it was wrong but finally gave in to pressure from Brian as well as her own deep attraction to him. She also knew that spending so much time with Brian and his friends had caused her to slip away from her own beliefs and Christian commitment.

When Sally became pregnant she was devastated, but there was little question about what she would do. Although Brian wanted her to have an abortion, he agreed to respect Sally's choice. It was clear, however, that Brian did not understand Sally's decision, and his lack of understanding was one of the reasons she decided to leave home during her pregnancy. When Sally relocated, she gave up her job, her friends, and her relationship with Brian. But she had really repented of her recent lifestyle and was determined to recommit her life to the Lord. She knew that moving in with Christian friends would give her the support she would need.

It was easy to refer Sally to a doctor. The adoption arrangements were more complex, as she had to choose between independent or agency adoption. She visited both a Christian lawyer and a Christian adoption agency. Finally she settled on an independent adoption in order to be able to choose the parents of her child. This is the main reason that the numbers of independent adoptions are greatly increasing compared to agency placements. However, as I watched Sally struggle to find the best possible couple for her baby, I realized for the first time the tremendously heavy burden of that responsibility. At the top of Sally's list of priorities was the requirement that the family be active and growing Christians. When the choice was finally made, God graciously gave many indications of its rightness. Sally met with the couple several times before her child's birth, and a bond quickly developed, born of common deep devotion to one small and as yet unborn baby. The importance of this affinity cannot be adequately explained to those who have never been closely involved with an adoption.

Sally had an uneventful pregnancy and delivery. Within just a few hours of birth, Baby Sam had been in the arms of both of his moms. I saw Sally and Sam later that same day; she was holding him when I entered her room. We had given much thought as to how much contact Sally should have with her baby in the hospital. Although she had decided that it should be limited, once Sam was born that plan was discarded. For the two days she had him, Sally spent as much time as possible with Sam. This did not reflect a change in her decision to relinquish him. Just the opposite—it was because she knew she had such a brief time in which to love him. As she told me later, such close contact made the feelings of loss much greater, but it also made her even more sure of her decision.

The night Sally left the hospital ranks as my most unforgettable experience in over two years of crisis-pregnancy counseling. Sally had decided to have a dedication service for Sam. It took place in her hospital room. Present were Sally, Sam, his adoptive parents, the couple Sally was staying with, and myself. Sally sat in a chair in the middle of us holding Sam and a box of Kleenex. For almost an hour, prayers and Scriptures were offered for Sally, for Sam, for his new parents, for how God had blessed *all* our lives through them. Sally's prayer expressing great joy to God for the miracle of Sam's life was the most moving part of the service. But all the prayers were heartfelt because we were all deeply touched by God's Spirit in that hospital room that night. The box of Kleenex had to be passed around often. At the end of the dedication service Sally walked over and gave her son to his new mother. Tears were streaming down her face, as would be expected, but Sally was *smiling*. I will never forget it.

Since Sam's birth, Sally has put her life back together with God's help. She has moved back to her home state but taken a new job. She had kept in close contact with Brian throughout her pregnancy and has shown him pictures of their son and tried to share her feelings about his birth. Brian does not really understand. He says Sally seems different somehow. She is. She has grown tremendously in her relationship to God, and the spiritual gap between her and Brian has widened accordingly. Neither one wishes to reestablish their relationship, although their bond to each other will always be strong. Sally is trusting God for a Christian man to marry and a baby to keep someday. She wants that very much.

In the meantime God has given Sally many opportunities to share her experience. She is now working as a counselor at a CPC where she can help women who are going through what she did. She has also spoken to youth groups and singles organizations, hoping to prevent some of those young women from having to suffer a similar experience. Her overwhelming theme is always God's faithfulness.

When Sally left my town, I gave her a small figure of Love-a-Lot Bear—the Care Bear with two hearts on his chest. That is what I will always remember most about Sally—that she loved a *lot*.

Beth and Steve. Next to Sally, the story that most moved me was that of Beth and Steve. Once again, the faithfulness of God was striking. The phone rang one Saturday just a few weeks after the center had opened. A young man asked if he and his girlfriend could come in immediately for a pregnancy test. I sighed and said yes. We were supposed to close in half an hour; a pregnancy test took ninety minutes. Counseling often took longer, and they were not even there yet. But the crying I could hear in the background made it impossible to say no.

When Beth and Steve arrived, I started her pregnancy test at once. As we talked, I was very impressed with how committed they were to each other and how forthright Steve was in accepting responsibility for their present situation. They had been dating for about a year and a half and had both graduated from high school the month before. Beth was working in a secretarial pool at an insurance company. Steve had not yet found a job. Neither had plans for college. They had only recently become sexually active, which Beth felt very guilty about. She came from a Christian family. Steve had been raised a Catholic, but about three months before, he had begun meeting with Beth's pastor in order to join her church. They planned to marry in about a year but were not officially engaged. Steve's family situation was not good (alcoholic parents), and they were not supportive of his relationship with Beth, who was especially afraid of Steve's mom.

Beth's family was an entirely different story. She had a close family and a good relationship with her parents, as did Steve. However, her father had been in the hospital for the past three months and was terminally ill. He had had cancer for five years. Beth lived at home and sort of held things together for her mother. She felt very strongly that she must continue doing so.

This couple had decided to have an abortion if Beth was pregnant, which she was. They cited several reasons for this: age, financial situation, the failure of most "shotgun" weddings, and fear of both of their mothers' reactions. It is difficult to say which they feared most, being rebuked by Steve's mother or disappointing and adding to the burdens of Beth's mother. They also greatly feared telling their pastor. They were totally miserable; Beth cried for most of the two hours she was at the center.

Before they left, they had changed their minds about having an abortion. Neither had ever wanted one but had felt they had to. Beth was especially vulnerable because of the stress of her father's illness. Steve felt more optimistic about their ability to manage. He admitted to looking forward to marriage and fatherhood. They decided to tell Beth's mom that night, as they were already planning to take her out for dinner. Steve volunteered to tell his parents alone and spare Beth their initial anger. They also decided to become engaged immediately and get married as soon as possible. The thought of a ring even cheered Beth up a little. We prayed together and hugged all around before they left. That was one of the days I went home feeling wonderful.

Beth and Steve's plans changed somewhat when Beth's father died only two weeks later. He had lapsed into a coma and never knew of his daughter's pregnancy. Beth and Steve delayed their wedding for about three months, and by that time Steve's parents had accepted their situation. Beth's mom had gotten over the initial grief of her husband's death and was able to enjoy the wedding preparations. Even more so, she looked forward to the birth of her first grandchild. After five years of coping with cancer and waiting for death, it was a joy to anticipate new life. Beth gave birth to an infant son, just as they wanted. He was promptly named Benjamin, after his grandfather. And Beth says, "He has made my mom smile again." Who else but a sovereign God could have designed such a plan to bring good from evil. He almost never got the chance.

Et alia. I could have told you of the mother and newborn baby who lived with us for two months because they had nowhere else to go, or the foster baby that we nurtured for ten days while his single mom (with two other children) struggled to keep from going under. I could have told you about getting lost in a low-income housing project after dark, looking for a client's apartment. Caring for three children under the age of four prevented her from coming to the center to talk about her current pregnancy. She was twenty. I might have mentioned the young woman whose pregnancy test was negative, but after talking to one of our single counselors for two hours, she bowed her head and sobbed, "I know I'm not living the way God wants me to." There was the distraught mother who called because she had just learned that her fifteen-year-old daughter was five months pregnant and scheduled to have a saline abortion the next day. I ended up at their home that evening and watched as mother, father, and daughter tried to heal some of the hurts in their relationship.

I could go on and on, but then I already have. I hope the stories I have detailed have given you an idea of the ministry of CPCs. There are many more stories, equally touching, from just our one center. Multiply that by hundreds of CPCs across the country to get an idea of the magnitude of lives being touched and helped.

Accepting the Challenge

Together let us change the world, at least one part of it. We end with this plea. We do not request that you send an emergency financial gift to stave off disaster. Neither do we include pictures of starving children or the butchered unborn, tactics that simply play upon emotions. The facts—the stories of victory and misery and deception—speak for themselves. However, let us not reject all emotions as irrelevant. These can be valid, distinctive expressions of our humanity. We can rightly cry out against abortion, just as Jesus wept over premature death. Even so, emotional reactions are not enough. Conviction, commitment and action must follow.

Although there are ever-present opportunities for each of us to take part in helping prevent abortions, the reasons for inaction are legion. In addition to our society's fictitious "freedom of choice," with its deluded religious and secular proponents, there are evangelical leaders who prefer some kind of gentle moral persuasion to any significant involvement. Evidence that our evangelical character can somehow passively rub off on others has yet to be discerned. Jesus' point was not made by *suggesting* that the money changers leave the temple!

From newspaper accounts and commentaries by Chuck Colson, we read that Mayor Edward Koch challenged each of the churches and synagogues of New York City to take in a couple of the homeless and thus compensate for government cuts in social programs. This chari-table action would effectively eliminate a problem of great human suf-fering. The response was perhaps predictable—there was outrage that the Mayor would dare to suggest such a thing. There were light and heating bills to consider. How about building security? A great oppor-tunity was missed, and an illusion was exposed. There was little in the way of good works to back up externals of religion.

What rich opportunities for action are there for the taking! If just a few families in each of our evangelical congregations would make their homes available to pregnant women in need; if one family per con-gregation could be encouraged and supported to adopt a handicapped or otherwise unwanted child; if each church could sponsor and send out just a couple of trained counselors to reach those in crisis; if only one person per church body would give some of his or her time and talents to the direction of a crisis-pregnancy ministry—we would begin to see a won-derful acceleration of the small changes already started in America. As God's people, we possess today the resources to change the world for many thousands of women and their unborn children.

This article is written especially for those who prefer a positive ap-proach and dislike the supposedly negative aspects of anti-abortion ac-tivism. Please accept our challenge to be positively *pro*-life. We hope that there is no room left for excuses.

References and Further Reading

Bube, R. H. 1984. An open letter to Inter-Varsity Press about *Brave new people*. *Journal of the American Scientific Affiliation* 36, 4:256.

———. 1986. Book reviews of *Brave new people* and *Life in the balance*. *Journal of the American Scientific Affiliation* 38, 2:142–145.

Buckley, J. L. 1985. Sound doctrine revisited. *The Human Life Review* 11, 3:80–91.

Cushner, I. M. 1983. *Testimony in constitutional amendments relating to abor-tion*. U.S. Senate Committee on the Judiciary, S.J. Res. 17–19, S.J. Res. 110, 97th Congress, First Session.

Fowler, P. B. 1987. *Abortion—Toward an evangelical consensus*. Portland: Multnomah Press.

Franke, L. B. 1978. *The ambivalence of abortion*. New York: Random House.

Harrison, B. W. 1983. *Our right to choose*. Boston: Beacon Press.

Jones, D. G. 1985. *Brave new people*. Grand Rapids: Eerdmans.

McDowell, G. L. 1984. Lincoln didn't defer to court on moral issue. *Wall Street Journal*, December 18.

Nakell, B. 1985. The right to life. *The Human Life Review* 11, 4:54–63.

Noonan, J. T. 1985. Knee-jerk spasms on Roe v. Wade. *Los Angeles Times,* August 8.

Olson, M. 1986. Just life: A cause for sadness. *The Other Side,* October:34, 36.

———. 1986. Book review of *Life in the Balance. The Other Side,* October:51.

Sobran, J. 1984. "Choice": The hidden agenda. *The Human Life Review* 10, 4:5–14.

Wennberg, R. N. 1985. *Life in the balance: Exploring the abortion controversy.* Grand Rapids: Eerdmans.

Whitehead, J. W. 1985. *Arresting abortion: Practical ways to save unborn children.* Westchester: Crossway Books.

Willke, J. C., Willke, B. 1985. *Abortion, questions and answers.* Cincinnati: Hayes Publishing.

Young, C. 1984. *The least of these.* Chicago: Moody Press.

15

After the Abortion
Herbert K. Jacobsen

What does a Christian—especially a pastor—say to someone who has had an abortion? How do you understand her? Does one say the same thing to everyone—or do the comments change according to individual circumstances and the reasons for the abortion?

At one time these questions were more academic than pastoral. No more. The chances that someone close to you will have an abortion are high, and the need to offer understanding and love is great.

One writer a few years ago claimed that abortion was "a profoundly pastoral issue" (Wallis 1980) because nearly 1.1 million abortions were being performed annually. Today, at an estimated 4,500 abortions daily (Griffith 1986, 15), there are nearly 40 percent more abortions in the United States than there were in 1980. Most of these women, we may hope, will have had some counseling or other significant guidance before actually aborting the pregnancy. The decision to continue with a pregnancy or to abort it is too important to be made without discussion. We should be grateful whenever individuals seek help in this matter, even if we disagree with the conclusion reached by some. The effort itself indicates that people generally realize that abortion is a serious matter about which a decision should not be made until fully informed as to its consequences and alternatives.

Yet, ironically, most available counseling is not directed to the 4,500 who have had abortions.[1] Rather, it focuses on the pregnant woman at the pre-abortion stage. The woman who has had an abortion and who suddenly feels a need to reconsider what she has done may find herself in a vacuum of counseling information. This essay will reflect upon the theological and ethical framework that would give perspective and guidance to assist the person who has had an abortion understand herself. Some of these perspectives have implications for other people as well. Hence, the intended audience is actually wider than those who have had an abortion.

It would be presumptuous to try to address every situation that might arise. Instead, I hope to indicate the principles that one would follow in a counseling situation. The reader is trusted to make appropriate application of the general comments to specific situations.

Theological Context

A Christian understanding for interpreting abortions needs to be placed in the context of various biblical doctrines. Among these we may include an explicit or implicit view of humankind in the image of God; marriage as a creation of God in which husband and wife are devoted to each other; and children as a gift from God and a joy to both parents. From this perspective, the Christian must argue that abortion is wrong.

The Christian must also include a profound appreciation for the effect that sin has had on the creation. Sin distorts our knowledge of God and casts us out of Eden. No longer can we claim that all husbands and wives are so devoted to each other that they become "one flesh." Nor can we claim that children are always perceived as gifts from God and treated with all the respect that such a trust suggests. We have even forgotten how to love ourselves.

Of course, the presence of sin in the world is not a justification to abandon the basic principle that abortion is wrong. Even with the difficulties mentioned above, there are some Christians who continue to insist that abortions never be performed. For others, the presence of sin means that sometimes an individual is placed in the tragic situation of needing to choose between two undesirable alternatives, such as the choice between the life of the mother or the fetus. For these people, at least, some abortions are considered justifiable.

In response to the dilemma resulting from a creation perspective versus a sin perspective, the Christian must also be reminded of the

---

[1]We may observe parenthetically that even less counsel seems to be directed toward the woman who has completed the unwanted pregnancy. She, too, or others in her family, might feel the need for counseling.

redemption perspective, which includes the doctrines of Christ and the church. Just as individuals within the family unit can forgive each other and learn to trust and make sacrifices on each other's behalf, forgiveness must be the overriding consideration in a counseling situation.

With this rough outline of the biblical orientation that should underlie most Christian counseling sessions, let us proceed to what might be expected in a session that involves a woman who has undergone an abortion.

Setting the Tone

The counseling session should first try to determine what has brought the woman to the point of wanting to discuss her abortion. Earlier assumptions about women who terminated a pregnancy often claimed that these women would suddenly be stricken with feelings of guilt and remorse. Some were, but others were not. Many have reacted simply by feeling unjustly ostracized from their communities. They experience pain and hurt because they cannot share their personal experience for fear of being misunderstood. They have no deep pangs of conscience. Between these two extremes one finds a wide range of possible reactions. Since, in an actual counseling situation, it is most important to respect the person who has come to discuss the abortion, one must be sensitive to her reasons for opening the conversation. Determining what motive brings the woman into the session will help set the tone and the agenda for the discussion.

There is no way to set the agenda beforehand. For some people, the motive might actually be to celebrate! Women have been "liberated." No longer are they chained to the values of a male-dominated culture, but they have achieved the freedom of self-determination. For women who come with this perspective, the rising rate of abortions is something to be applauded. Based on certain assumptions about polling instruments, one might claim that overall public support for abortion has been growing over the last decade.[2]

Others might experience extremely deep personal guilt, a remorse that prevents them from trusting other people or themselves. This feeling might be so deep that they feel not even a loving God could find something lovable in them. A few might even speculate that their experience and the fact of thousands of abortions daily means that a holocaust looms over the land.

---

[2]For an examination of the difficulties in polling to determine social attitudes and in reading the polls, the reader is referred to chapter 12 by Lyman Kellstedt. One will notice that the polls may also indicate that our society might be levelling off in abortions-on-demand.

Clearly, the Christian counselor does not respond to these two perspectives in the same way. Although each may have discovered some truth about herself and her faith, each may need further insight and understanding.

A Place to Start

Recognizing that abortion is not a one-dimensional issue is a good place to start a counseling session. At the very least, any statement about abortion may be discussed from each of the three doctrinal contexts mentioned above. Various ethical and scientific perspectives are also profitable, as this volume of essays has already indicated. In this essay we consider abortion from the perspective of social structures and values.

An abortion has a great deal to say about the values of our society. Every society establishes values for its citizens that mark success or failure in that society. Whenever we rate one value above another, we find ourselves promoting the acclaimed values by compromising lesser ones. Sometimes these values are of our own choosing and making, but other times they are imposed on us by the society.[3]

Some years ago, an inner-city pastor in New York discovered that even with Herculean effort, some of the men and women in his congregation who desired to provide for their families found themselves unable to do so because the system had shut them out. Over the years, there have been many witnesses, from automobile workers to farmers, who have found that personal effort by itself does not always produce gainful employment. We might also recall the story of one man who found it necessary to "provide" for his much-loved family by deserting them, because the welfare system would then make it possible for his family to survive. He was unable to find sufficient work to support them himself. In cases such as these, the structures and values of society significantly determine the way individuals function as responsible citizens. The "deserter" could make a plausible case that he was morally justified in his decision, given the social realities of his situation.

The city pastor mentioned above concluded that society had its values, good and bad, every bit as much as an individual might have his or hers. He also noted that at times the responsibility for the act of an

---

[3]Perhaps the first theologian to call our attention to the contemporary social dimension of the Christian faith is Walter Rauschenbush. Since Rauschenbush, others, such as Reinhold Niebuhr, have also given us brilliant insight into the influence of social structures.

individual might lie more with the social structures and values than with the individual.

Jesus' crucifixion poignantly illustrates this conclusion. The final authority for executing Jesus rested with Pilate, who had found Jesus innocent. In one of their conversations, Jesus explained to the procurator that the guilt of those who had delivered him to Pilate was actually greater than Pilate's (John 19:11). Since Pilate was obliged to keep the peace, those who presented Jesus to Pilate put Pilate in a cleverly devised moral dilemma. Whatever decision he made was likely to result in one injustice or another.

Later, when Jesus was on the cross, he looked toward those who had the immediate responsibility of killing him and prayed, "Father, forgive them; for they know not what they do" (Luke 23:34). Some interpret this statement as recognizing that *their* guilt was less than Pilate's. Indeed, one might make the double-edged claim that as soldiers they were "innocent" because they were ignorant, but that as members of a larger culture they bore some guilt.

This analogy illustrates that those immediately responsible for an act, say execution, may be less responsible morally for that act than someone else further removed from it. In fact, those further removed may believe they are acting to protect God's interests while committing an atrocity. In Jesus' case, this responsibility might have rested on the shoulders of the high priest, the mob demanding the release of Barabbas, or the passersby who did nothing more than jeer. The text only says that those who delivered Jesus to Pilate had a greater guilt. From a theological perspective, at least partial responsibility rests on all mankind.

If this point applies to an abortion, the pregnant woman might be more a victim of certain social values and structures than the perpetrator of an immoral act. If she feels solely responsible, she will need to realize that the moral responsibility is also borne by a larger body of people. If she feels little responsibility, she should realize that, except in cases such as rape or birth defects beyond her control, it is difficult not to imagine some compliance and responsibility on her part. Further, insofar as she contributes to the social milieu that encourages abortions, she is at least partially responsible for distorting the divine intentions for sexuality.

Obviously, this is not a call to justify abortions. This writer is neither invoking ignorance of what is taking place in an abortion as a justification, nor completely exonerating individuals in light of social structures. When individuals understand the biblical perspective on the family, even one abortion must be understood as a tragedy that compromises the creation ideal.

Implications for the Christian

What may we conclude from these observations about the societal context of an abortion? What message do they have for a Christian?

First, they call all of us to recognize that whenever a social value or structure is partially responsible for an abortion, then those who have supported that social system are also responsible. To the extent to which our values encourage the social context in which a woman finds abortion a responsible behavior, we are all partially responsible. We are no different in this regard from Caiaphas or Pilate, the crowd supporting Barabbas, or the passersby. If we are sensitive to this call, we will recognize that abortion is a shared guilt, acknowledge corporate responsibility, and seek ways to change certain social values and structures accordingly.

Many of these structures and values have already been identified in this book and elsewhere. In both the medical and legal professions, for example, decisions have been made that are partially responsible for the liberalization of abortion laws. Clearly, we should continue evaluation of the ethical dilemmas facing the medical and legal professions. In addition, we will need to understand the pressures that cause changes in the family structure. We must examine the contexts for significant sex education. And we will need to guard against the exploitation of sexual motifs in business, the media, and society in general. These destructive values and structures are already receiving considerable attention in the Christian community.

Some of the undesirable values, however, are more subtle and not so well recognized. One of the most important of these is the emphasis on autonomy. When an unmarried high-school female finds herself in a sexual encounter, it is partially as an expression of her "freedom" that the encounter takes place, not as a social act arranged by her family nor in the appropriate context of matrimony. Participation in the sexual affair asks only for a personal explanation—she wants it to happen. Likewise, a refusal requires a personal reason—she does *not* want it. Given the internalization of autonomy, the woman is not likely to convince even herself by the more traditional explanations of a refusal. "We are not married" or "My church and family would not approve" are no longer as convincing to individuals as they once may have been. Indeed, sometimes family and church disapproval may strengthen her belief that she is acting on her own decision. We must see autonomy and self-expression as a major social value that can have profound effects on a person's understanding of responsible moral behavior.

Where are the roots of this sometimes misused sense of autonomy? The idea of free self-expression is pervasive in our society and is in many quarters a sign of its strength. When teachers claim that education is a significant way for individuals to get ahead and to fulfill their destiny, they are supporting autonomy. When church leaders proclaim the Christian faith as a personal decision between the individual and God, they, too, support autonomy. This value exists in businesses that honor the entrepreneur and reward individuals with merit pay. It is the politics of one person/one vote. Autonomy, as a general social value, upholds the genius of our society and becomes most effective when individuals internalize it.

However, in regard to the value of autonomy, our task is a paradox. If we understand it correctly, we must uphold it to be true to our society. At the same time we must either discourage it or balance it against other values and social structures so that its internalization does not become the primary factor informing an individual dealing with a pregnancy or any other situation. For example, our society may need to develop structures to support education in such a way that the female student will be assured that her pregnancy will not prevent her self-fulfillment in other areas. Similarly, the church will need to see individuals in light of the corporate nature of the body of Christ. Changing undesirable social values, such as an overemphasis on autonomy, is not an easy task. For the Christian, this struggle amounts to a "wrestling with principalities and powers" (cf. Eph. 6:12). The dominance of these powers of "present darkness" has been broken, but their influence continues.

Our first conclusion calls us to be sensitive to all of society's structures and values and to do our part in promoting those that are worthwhile as well as changing those that are undesirable.

Second, our observations about social structures call us to encourage responsible personal behavior. Let us determine as best as we can what contributing factors led to the pregnancy for the woman we counsel. They may include a compromising situation, a beguiling friend, a vain hope on the woman's part, or any of a great variety of things. What can you do to avoid their influence again? Jesus' advice to the young woman caught in adultery is advice for all: "Go, and do not sin again" (John 8:11). We are not sure how Pilate would avoid confrontation with the rulers in future gatherings, but a desire for responsible administration would cause him to seek better relationships.

Third, our observations call for the Christian to deal with abortion in the context of grace. Because it is so easy to talk "clinically" of abortion and to sound self-righteous, no discussion of abortion should proceed far before it affirms the Lord's mercy. This is ". . . not a time for personal judgment and recrimination. It is a time for loving dialogue, understanding, and most of all for forgiveness" (Wallis 1980, 2). For the Christian, the ground of that love is in the Christ who loved us and gave himself for us. As much as a judgment might justifiably be rendered against someone who has had an abortion, and against a society as a whole, it simply cannot be done outside of the context of a God who forgives. This emphasis allows the counselor to treat with respect the woman who has come to discuss her abortion. It sets the tone for the relationship, but even more, it provides a basis for subsequent growth and fellowship. In Christ there is "no condemnation" (Rom. 8:1), and because of Christ, Christians are free to assume responsibility for their own actions and to serve their neighbors.

If these observations are correct, there are three specific comments to share with those who have had an abortion. First, from a Christian perspective, not only the high number of abortions performed daily, but even one, compromises the values in Scripture. As stated before, abortion is wrong. Second, because we do not live in an ideal world, the decision for an abortion generally results when a woman finds herself in a situation with a conflict of values, some of which are not of her own making. In these instances, the responsibility for the abortion is not simply to be borne by the woman who has had the abortion. Indeed, others may be more responsible than she. Finally and fortunately, the mercy of God allows the Christian to be a responsible citizen by offering an atonement for sin and by inviting all to new life in the kingdom of God.

References and Further Reading

Griffith, C. B. 1986. Just cause, just means. *Eternity* 377, 1 (January):15–18.

Wallis, J. 1980. Coming together on the sanctity of life. *Sojourners* 9, 11 (November):4